The International Library of Sociology

SOCIAL DEFENCE

Founded by KARL MANNHEIM

The International Library of Sociology

THE SOCIOLOGY OF LAW AND CRIMINOLOGY

In 15 Volumes

I	Comparative Criminology - Part One	*Mannheim*
II	Comparative Criminology - Part Two	*Mannheim*
III	Crime: An Analytical Appraisal	*López-Rey*
IV	The Criminal Area	*Morris*
V	Criminal Justice and Social Reconstruction	*Mannheim*
VI	The Education of Borstal Boys	*Stratta*
VII	The English Prison and Borstal Systems	*Fox*
VIII	The Explanation of Criminality	*Trasler*
IX	Group Problems in Crime and Punishment	*Mannheim*
X	The Institutions of Private Law	*Renner*
XI	Juvenile Delinquency in an English Middletown	*Mannheim*
XII	Legal Aid	*Egerton*
XIII	Pentonville	*Morris et al*
XIV	Social Defence	*Ancel*
XV	Young Men in Detention Centres	*Dunlop et al*

SOCIAL DEFENCE

A Modern Approach to Criminal Problems

by

MARC ANCEL

With a Foreword by

LEON RADZINOWICZ

Translated by

J. WILSON

ROUTLEDGE

First published in 1965 by
Routledge

Reprinted in 1998 by
Routledge
2 Park Square, Milton Park, Abingdon, Oxon, OX14 4RN

Transferred to Digital Printing 2007

British Library Cataloguing in Publication Data
A CIP catalogue record for this book
is available from the British Library

Social Defence
ISBN 0-415-17745-6
The Sociology of Law and Criminology: 15 Volumes
ISBN 0-415-17832-0
The International Library of Sociology: 274 Volumes
ISBN 0-415-17838-X

Publisher's Note
The publisher has gone to great lengths to ensure the quality of this reprint but points out that some imperfections in the original may be apparent

FOREWORD

by LEON RADZINOWICZ

Wolfson Professor of Criminology, University of Cambridge

MONSIEUR MARC ANCEL is perhaps unique in criminological circles. He combines a scientific and academic career with the duties of a Judge of the Supreme Court of France. He is editor in chief of the influential *Revue de Science Criminelle*, an inspiring force in the Institute of Comparative Law of the University of Paris, as well as a lecturer in the Criminological Institute, and rapporteur on a wide range of penal problems at many international gatherings.

The idea of a school of criminal law and criminology in the continental sense is alien to the lawyer in this country. But it is the first thing an Englishman interested in such matters encounters when he mixes with his European colleagues. 'England', remarked Sir Evelyn Ruggles-Brise, 'has not participated to any great extent in these controversies of the criminological schools, which have been so active and have excited so much interest on the Continent of Europe. . . . It may almost be said there is no school of criminology in England.'

Of such a school Monsieur Ancel is a member: he is indeed the leading exponent of the movement of 'social defence'. The very designation may well be puzzling to English readers and it is therefore particularly fortunate that we should have from him so eloquent, persuasive and vigorous a statement of his position.

The English may still feel that the continentals are too much under the spell of doctrinaire solutions and that what really matters most is the cumulative advance in practical improvements, cautiously pioneered over the years on an empirical basis. The continentals, on their side, may suggest that the English give too little thought to principles, and that they would have gone further, and produced a more coherent system, if they had known beforehand where they were going. Such differences of emphasis add to the fascination of a book like this.

I regard it as a privilege to introduce it to English-speaking readers.

LEON RADZINOWICZ

Institute of Criminology,
Cambridge,
June 1965.

CONTENTS

PREFACE

THE ORIGINAL EDITION of this book was published in Paris in 1954; a Spanish edition was published in Buenos Aires in 1961, with the title: *La nueva defensa social (un movimiento de politica criminal humanista)*, with a foreword by Professor Aftalion; and a Serbo-Croat edition in Belgrade in 1962, *Nova drustvena odbrana. Pokret humanisticke kriminalne politike*, with a foreword by Professor Srzentić. A second French edition was needed several years ago, but it was thought better to wait until the results of certain experiments carried out in various countries and international conferences should have shed new light on the problem, before publication. It is now possible to proceed with the revision of the 1954 edition, and this English edition is based on the second French edition, now in preparation.

It gives us great satisfaction to see this work made available to English-speaking criminalists and criminologists. We are therefore particularly indebted to all those who have helped to make the doctrines of Social Defence known in England. First our thanks are due to Mr John A. Mack, Director of the School of Social Study, University of Glasgow, who in April 1962 included a conference on Social Defence in the *Residential Course in Criminological Studies*, which he organized. We would like to thank also Professor Goodhart for accepting the text of this conference for publication in the *Law Quarterly Review*, October 1962. Our special thanks are due to Professor Radzinowicz, who was the real promoter of the English edition of this book, and who has thereby shown the ties which bring together Social Defence and Criminology. Our grateful thanks are owed too to Mr John Wilson, who has borne the heavy burden of translating the French text, to Miss Yvonne Marx, Assistant Director of the *Service de recherches juridiques comparatives* of the French *Centre national de la recherche scientifique*, who has kindly contributed to the text, and to Miss Denyse Chast, Assistant at the *Centre français de droit comparé*, who has helped in revising the manuscript. Finally, I thank Mr David Evans too for his help towards the publication in England of our book.

MARC ANCEL

INTRODUCTION

THERE IS PROBABLY no need, today, to justify at any length the publication of a book on social defence. Few concepts are more frequently invoked: indeed the first difficulty that arises is probably the result of the innumerable ways in which the concept is used, with varied and sometimes contradictory meanings. It might almost be said that this expression is, to some extent, a fashionable one, so that some people do not always withstand the temptation to use it, on occasion, rather casually. However, I would strongly emphasize my conviction that when all is said and done the frequency and variety with which the term 'social defence' is employed corresponds to one of the realities of our age, and that it thus serves as a vehicle or means of expression for concepts whose dynamism is henceforth undeniable.

Moreover, the reality and the strength of the social defence movement today can no longer be gainsaid. The following chapters will provide an opportunity for discovering and evaluating the scope of the movement. But I am not unaware that the very term 'social defence' often appears strange and is also frequently misunderstood, especially by lawyers brought up in the Common Law tradition or by the criminologists of the English-speaking world. Although the term is more and more widely used, especially in America, and in spite of its adoption by the United Nations in 1948, it has not yet been completely absorbed into the terminology of Anglo-American criminological studies. As will shortly become apparent, the term involves a reference to the notion of 'penal policy', another expression which does not form part of the everyday language of English-speaking criminal lawyers and criminologists. It must not be forgotten that the terms 'social defence' and 'penal policy' are of Italian and of German origin respectively: each was quickly assimilated into the penal theory of continental Europe and of Latin America. But both seem to have had some difficulty in crossing the Channel or the North Atlantic. One of the ambitions of this book, which in other respects is more restricted in its scope, is precisely to facilitate such a crossing.

Nor am I unaware that the notion of social defence still arouses a good deal of anxiety and opposition in certain circles. Such doubt or hostility is found first of all among the neo-classicists who are devoted to the restoration and maintenance of the principle of moral responsibility and of retributive punishment, which was severely shaken at the end of last century by the revolt of the positivists. Secondly, it appears in the eclectic school at the beginning of this century, who thought themselves well and truly freed from positivist doubts because they had 'cut their losses' in accepting some of the teachings of criminological science. Thirdly, there are the adherents of the 'pure law' school concerned above all to reconstitute a system of criminal law and a pure, self-sufficient legal technique. Fourthly, there are the positivists—in so far as they still exist—who are perhaps worried about possible competition and disconcerted in the face of a doctrine which, though derived in part from the positivism taught by Lombroso, Ferri, and Garofalo, has broken away from that teaching on some essential points. Finally there is opposition, in many cases, from criminal lawyers and criminologists, on whose part adherence to the doctrine of social defence would seem quite natural, but who are disturbed in their habits both of thought and of language by a movement which is not easily summed up in an over-simple formula: one which, in spite of its reaction against the abuse of legal technique, refuses to abolish criminal law in the interests of biology, medicine, or social science, and is, moreover, astonishingly dynamic.

Such defensive attitudes are, indeed, quite natural. They are also encouraging, for—notwithstanding certain criticisms more forceful than convincing—they enable us to perceive the real character of the movement: in fact it is only what exists and somehow or other threatens established positions, that provokes resistance. This is indeed the case, as it happens, with modern social defence. It is characteristic of the movement that in order to define itself and determine its field of action, it is obliged in the first place to react against several current theoretical foundations and contemporary modes of thinking and reasoning. It will be pointed out at a later stage that what really gave birth to the social defence movement was the positivist revolt. And positivism was in fact a 'revolt' against traditional criminal law, a revolt whose historical significance is comparable in many ways to the movement which found expression in 1764 in Beccaria's celebrated little treatise *On Crimes and Punishments*. The difference probably comes from the fact that after the rapid evolution of ideas and the triumph of the French Revolution, Beccaria's views received general acceptance fairly rapidly. The repressive system of the *ancien régime*, as it functioned in continental Europe, gave way to the neo-classical penal system of the nineteenth century, based on moral responsibility and exemplary punishment. Since the end of the nineteenth century, however, an even more lively reaction has set in against both the *homo delinquens* of criminal law and the *homo juridicus* of civil law. The 'publicization' and 'socialization' of private law are phenomena recognized by even the most reactionary of civil lawyers. No one any longer seriously disputes the fact that civil law has been radically transformed by the movements which brought about the emancipation of women and the development of child welfare, by the loosening—some would say the disintegration—of family ties, by mechanization, by the birth of what Édouard Lambert called a 'corporative' law peculiar to certain kinds of social activity, and by the increasing intervention of the State in opposition to the tenets of *laissez-faire* liberalism. Further, private law is influenced by modern techniques, which ignore national frontiers, and by regional arrangements or groups of States, such as the Common Market. In Western Europe, however, neither socialism, nor the concept of social solidarity, nor the internationalization of methods, nor even the authoritarian State, have called in question the bases of the civil law system as a whole. In spite of the complete transformation of the economic environment, commercial law is still taught in its traditional framework, and the teacher of civil law can consider, in turn, freely negotiated agreements, standard contractual clauses, and contracts imposed as a whole by one party on the other, without speaking of the first of these merely as a historical concept. The civil courts, for their part, continue to affirm that no one can be civilly liable without fault.

In criminal law, on the contrary, since the end of the nineteenth century, everything has been challenged. This is not always apparent, of course, from a study of the standard textbooks. But even those writers most strongly attached to the neo-classical system are aware more or less explicitly of this change. Their disquiet finds expression either in a desperate appeal for sterner methods of repression, or in an almost morbid denunciation of the weakness of criminal justice and the critical condition of criminal law, or, again, in abuse of those who advocate innovations or simply a measure of serious reform. Today, the criminal lawyer is conscious of the fact that he can no longer be just a lawyer, discussing in an abstract way the legal conditions of liability or analysing the elements of the offence on the basis of a legal definition and by exclusively legal methods. On the other hand, the informed criminal lawyer is also aware that he cannot admit that the physician, sociologist, or psychologist has the right, indiscriminately, to take his place. Modern criminology claims to study the phenomenon of crime with the help of all the human sciences. Both its conclusions and its methods, however, are still uncertain, and there remains the problem of transforming the lessons of criminology into rules of law applicable to the individual and social phenomenon which constitutes the offence. A true criminal law needs to be preserved, so as to avoid drifting into completely arbitrary methods or even into a kind of social chaos.

Notwithstanding the opinion of some who have tried to simplify the issue, it is not therefore a question of abolishing criminal law or of strictly subordinating the lawyer to the criminologist, but of making rational use, in the legal field, of the various data supplied by criminological science. The essential problem, in view of the undeniable changes which are taking place in modern society, is to achieve the elaboration of a system of criminal law which should no longer be an anachronism, should take account of human and social realities, and should try to make provision for these as clearly and efficiently as possible. Consequently, this is precisely a problem of legislative policy or, in other words and in an even wider sense, a problem of penal policy. This idea will be discussed at a later stage: for the moment it should be noted that the problem is one of organizing and directing the social reaction against crime, as effectively as possible and after a rigorous study of the question.

Thus it can be seen that modern criminal science has in fact three essential components: criminology, which studies the phenomenon of crime in all its aspects; criminal law, which is the explanation and application of the positive rules whereby society reacts against the phenomenon of crime; finally, penal policy, both a science and an art, of which the practical purposes, ultimately, are to enable the positive rules to be better formulated and to guide not only the legislator who has to draft criminal statutes, but the court by which they are applied and the prison administration which gives practical effect to the court's decision. In this connexion, penology—the importance of which I do not mean in any way to disregard—is closely bound up with penal policy.

The great difficulty comes from the fact that at the present time no one is quite sure with what data, according to what principles, and with what ends in view, this new penal system should be established, although it is called for more or less clearly on all sides and is recognized as necessary by every self-respecting criminal lawyer. From this point of view it is useless either to look exclusively to the criminological sciences or, on the contrary, to confine oneself entirely within the limits of pure law. The necessary renewal and synthesis cannot come from one side or the other alone, and it is in this connexion that the necessity, the importance, and even, one might say, the pre-eminence of penal policy becomes clear. It can be observed that in the course of recent controversies and of the interchange of new ideas, this truth has been to some extent lost sight of. Criminal law has tried to remain entrenched in its old positions in a kind of desperately defensive attitude. Vainly, on their side, have the criminological sciences tried to annex new spheres of activity and to encroach upon a domain which was not and could not be theirs. Between the study of criminological factors on the one hand, and legal technique on the other, there is room for a science which observes legislative phenomena and for a rational art within which scholars and practitioners, criminologists and lawyers can come together, not as antagonists or in fratricidal strife, but as fellow-workers engaged in a common task, which is first and foremost to bring into effect a realistic, humane, and healthily progressive penal policy. This is precisely the kind of policy that is thrown into relief and compellingly emphasized by the modern concept of social defence. Above all, this is the policy which draws its inspiration from the aims and ideals of *new* social defence in the sense given to that term in this book.

Finally, it should be understood that the twentieth-century system of criminal law still remains to be created. Such a system can only be established and perfected by the common effort of all men of good will, as well as by the co-operation of all specialists in the social sciences. The time when criminal law existed in a state of splendid isolation has gone forever: a coherent and useful system can be constructed only with the participation of criminologists accustomed to study the phenomena of crime scientifically. But we must go further: co-operation is also necessary between lawyers and specialists in the criminal sciences belonging to the different systems of criminal law in force today.

The elaboration of a penal policy of social defence, understood in the sense presently to be defined, must come into being irrespective of the traditional antithesis between the civil law systems on the one hand and the Common Law tradition on the other. Although, as will shortly become apparent, the expression 'social defence' is not as yet completely assimilated into the language of Common Lawyers, social defence as a new method of approach to criminological problems owes much to Anglo-American criminologists and in particular to sociologists from the United States. The same is even the case, I believe, as regards the much more striking contrast between Western systems of law and those of the Socialist countries. In the contemporary world, a continual 'socialization' of legal notions is taking place: logically, this ought to bring together criminal lawyers from East and West in an endeavour to achieve mutual understanding, if not, indeed, to create a new system. It is undeniable that the social defence movement, because it is firmly based on the idea of 'penal policy', can and indeed must constitute an area of mutual understanding between specialists drawn from different systems, provided that these systems are not distorted in the process and that both sides agree to respect their basic structure.

These ideas will soon be generally accepted and, for my part, I should like to contribute to this process. I would like to make clear how *new* social defence—which should not be confused with the older meanings of the term, nor with certain hazardous theories—is in truth a significant development in modern criminal science. It involves becoming aware of some deep-seated requirements of modern society, giving new thought to some important problems concerning the legislative judicial or administrative organization of the reaction to crime, and promoting certain specific reforms in a new spirit and according to a new co-ordinated ideology, knowingly accepted.

Introduction

I should like to explain *new* social defence as having a humanist significance and a dynamic content. I should like to make the movement intelligible to all who read this book in good faith, to all who seek enlightenment, and even to those who, on occasion, refuse such enlightenment from an almost instinctive distrust of trends which are still outside their knowledge. Social defence is not an exclusive school of thought: it does not aim at imposing a new dogma or establishing a single doctrine in place of all the other theories of criminal law and criminology. The movement simply seeks to bring together all those who are aware that the modern world and modern thought together shatter the framework of preconceived ideas, and it seeks to guide such persons in their search for a human renewal which goes beyond all merely technical considerations. That is why I venture to hope that even those who so far have contented themselves with a few hasty glimpses at social defence doctrines will give this book some of their attention.

The following chapters are dedicated to criminal lawyers, penologists, criminologists, practitioners of criminal law and procedure—to all those who are willing to take the trouble to understand exactly what this trend, or more precisely this *movement* is all about. May I dedicate them also to the 'pure lawyers', those 'civilians' who have too frequently lost touch with the evolution and the realities of criminal law. I have in mind those excellent jurists who, conscious of the changes taking place in the world today, seek to incorporate the substance of these changes in a rejuvenated civil or commercial law. They are fully aware of the inevitable consequences of a planned economy, of the emergence of standard-form contracts, of the appearance of new concepts, of the increasing regulation of the professions, and of the ever more perceptible presence of the group alongside the individual. Oddly enough, however, the same lawyers believe that as soon as criminal law is in question, they can content themselves with repressive notions of the most outdated and over-simplified kind. May they be led to reflect that the evolution of the modern world is a single whole and that the same social forces make themselves felt in the sphere of criminal as in that of private law. These pages are also addressed to public lawyers, who are not always sufficiently aware that these new trends which find their initial expression in the sphere of criminal law, will tomorrow take root inevitably in their own field. Again, these pages are dedicated to legal philosophers, who must henceforth reckon with the appearance or reappearance of a humanist trend in criminal law and prison administration, and to sociologists who have so far curiously neglected the social phenomenon constituted by the social defence movement. They are also dedicated to practitioners in the highest sense of the criminal law: judges, prosecutors, members of the Bar, officers of the Court, social service officials, and prison officers, all of whom should know and appreciate the fresh strength which this movement imparts to the renewal of the preventive or *reformative* activity which is the true reason for their existence. Finally, these pages are dedicated to public opinion itself, which has often been deceived by the external appearance or the technicalities of legal, procedural, or penitentiary practices which conceal the real problems and the true significance of the action jointly undertaken in reaction to crime, which is a social scourge but also a human phenomenon and against which none but honest and effective weapons should be used.

The essential purpose of the chapters that follow is to look at the new social defence movement as a work of penal policy. These pages are the result of reflections based on several years' study of the problem of social defence considered from a comparative standpoint, in the light of the modern development of different systems of reaction to crime. Evidently, the position I have thus been led to adopt commits no one but myself: I am convinced, however, that it does no more than reflect the thought of many who, avowedly or not, support this renovating tendency. There are indeed many people who, attracted by these novel doctrines, would like them to be restated now, so as to strike a balance between neighbouring points of view that are still too often divergent. Of course, I am not unaware that in seeking a common denominator, one may in the end have to fight on two fronts. Some lawyers will possibly complain that pure law is too drastically reduced to the rather modest rôle of serving as the instrument of a rational penal policy. On the other hand, some criminologists will probably criticize me for still allowing too large a rôle to the demands of pure law. A few will even regret that I have not replaced the lawyer or the magistrate by the physician or the sociologist. This risk I willingly accept, as it is indeed inevitable for anyone who tries both to remain clearsighted and to avoid overstating his case.

Chapter One

WHAT IS SOCIAL DEFENCE?

THE TERM *social defence* certainly needs some explanation. As we have already observed, the expression may seem strange to Anglo-American criminal lawyers, and, if others make increasingly frequent use of it, this is sometimes accompanied by a certain amount of misuse and distortion. Even those who use the term regularly do not always give it the same meaning. There would be little difficulty in noting deep differences and sometimes—at least in certain respects—actual contradictions in the various ways the phrase is employed. We will not indulge in the pastime, as facile and pointless as it is amusing, of listing these contradictions. But it seems indispensable to point out at least the main directions in which those who use the term seem inclined to go.

First of all, therefore, we must ask ourselves what is meant by social defence, and review in summary fashion at least a few of the meanings attributed to the expression. Obviously, the following list does not claim to be comprehensive: it deliberately leaves aside those uses which by their generality or their imprecision—however well-intentioned—have in the long run deprived the term of any intellectual validity, as it has sometimes enthralled certain neophytes whose enthusiasm outran their knowledge. Conversely, little attention will be paid to those writers who are so wholly taken up with established classifications that they refuse to allow mention of the term social defence, for fear lest its novelty might prove too dynamic.[1] Thus Mariano Ruiz-Funes, the Spanish criminal lawyer who met an untimely death, wrote that no principle has been more disfigured and distorted than that of social defence.[2] Luis Jiménez de Asúa, after declaring that

[1] Erwin R. Frey, in a closely-written article which will be referred to again later, speaks of 'so-called social defence' Strafrecht oder soziale Verteidigung? *Rev. pénale suisse*, 1953, pp. 405 ff.).

[2] *La crisis de la prisión*, Havana, 1949, p. 74: however, many ideas characteristic of the social defence movement are to be found throughout this book.

'today nobody knows what social defence is' did not wish to regard it (at one time at any rate) as having any more than a 'fleeting significance'.[3] This, however, was a momentary outburst, for in his notable *Tratado de derecho penal* de Asúa could not help paying attention to the ideas of social defence.[4] And how can we forget that de Asúa, with Ruiz-Funes, was an author or sponsor of the *ley de vagos y maleantes*, the vagrancy law enacted by the Spanish Republic in 1933—a statute which, together with the Belgian statute of 1930 (though by entirely different methods), is one of the typical instances of social defence legislation of the first half of the twentieth century? From the terminological point of view we may therefore leave aside, for the time being, writers whom we shall come across again when discussing the actual content of the doctrine. For the moment, attention will be restricted to those writers who give the term 'social defence' a certain meaning which remains to be defined.

I

One interpretation of the term social defence, fairly widespread though now wholly obsolete, is that it means the protection of society against crime, to the extent that such protection is sought by the vigorous repression of the crimes committed. It was in this context that a formula long in use referred to 'the essential needs of social defence'. So Vidal and Magnol in their classic work[5] wrote of the extreme rigour of the old penal law that 'the need for

[3] *El criminalista*, vol. X, Buenos Aires, 1952, p. 36, in a study which is, moreover, most suggestive as regards new trends in criminal law.

[4] See especially, in de Asúa's great treatise, his striking treatment of preventive criminal law: vol. II, 2nd. ed., 1958, pp. 196 ff. See also his article 'La nueva defensa social', in *La Ley* (Buenos Aires), vol. 88 (1957), pp. 693 ff., where, in spite of his misgivings, de Asúa investigates the doctrine very thoroughly.

[5] *Cours de droit crim. et de science pénit.*, 9th. ed., vol. 1, No. 15. *Cf.* the paper prepared by Dean R. Garraud in connexion with the Centenary of the French Penal Code, 'Le Code de 1810 et l'évolution du droit pénal', *Rev. pénit.*, 1910, pp. 926 ff., where the author considers that the main characteristic of this Code is that of 'having organized criminal law as a mere instrument of social defence' (p. 927). It is true that even Prins, in his first important book (*Science pénale et droit positif*, 1899, No. 462, p. 278) wrote that in allowing extenuating circumstances by reason of the slight character of the injury caused, there is an 'infringement of the rules of social defence'. More recently, in England, James A. Joyce recalled that the right of the State to take human life had been legalized 'in the name of social defence' (*The Right to Life, A World View of Capital Punishment*, 1962, p. 12). All these cases involve social protection by means of the *repression* of crime.

intimidation and for *social defence* led to an extreme severity which greatly increased the number of punishments'. Many writers have thus continued, for purposes of linguistic convenience, to give the term social defence a meaning which is synonymous with stern repression.[6]

This way of looking at things leads quite naturally to an antithesis between social defence and individual freedom, or at any rate the rights of the individual. If the expression 'social defence' is to be understood in the literal and original meaning of the words as an absolute protection for society, should we not in fact conclude that, solely concerned with ensuring the forceful protection of the community of citizens, it means achieving this, if need be, at the expense of the individual?[7] This point will be raised again later: it is noted here simply to show that according to some ways of thinking, a threat to the individual is inherent in the words 'social defence'. Thus Fontan Balestra wrote somewhat hastily that the problem of social defence had 'rather overshadowed the respect for individual rights which constitutes its natural limit'.[8] In less categorical terms, Molinario observed the existence of this problem, especially in the course of the *Premières Journées franco-latino-américaines*, held at Paris in 1948.[9] In Belgium, Braas has on a number of occasions revealed his preoccupation with a doctrine which tends, in his opinion, to threaten the rights of man, whereas in the U.S.A., Jerome Hall did not hesitate to write that the characteristic feature of the principle of social defence is its acceptance of the view that any measure needed to protect society is justified.[10] In

[6] Cf. Jean Signorel, *Le Crime et la défense sociale*, 1912: 'Let us return to the true principles of social defence and be guided by Vergniaud's celebrated remark: "The purpose of the law is to reassure honest citizens and to make the wicked tremble" ' (p. 133).

[7] J. A. Joyce, *op. cit.*, p. 53, where, in connexion with the mass executions of antiquity or under ancient law, the author mentions the use of terror as an instrument of either social defence or military power. This very well informed author, moreover, has perfectly grasped the modern meaning of the expression: see esp. pp. 201, 207.

[8] *La Mission de garantie du droit pénal*, Paris, 1950, p. 5.

[9] 'A propos de la place des mesures de sûreté dans le droit positif moderne', *Bull. de la Soc. de législ., comp.*, 1948, p. 617. The question was also raised at the *Troisièmes Journées de droit franco—latino américaines,* held at Toulouse, in 1950 (*Rev. int. de droit comp.*, 1952, p. 773).

[10] *Principles of Criminal Law*, Indianapolis, 1947, p. 350: cf. Ruiz-Funes, *La crisis de la prisión*, p. 74, and L. Jiménez de Asúa, 'L'État dangereux dans les législations ibéro-américaines', *Revue pénale suisse*, 1952, pp. 424 ff., esp. pp. 442-43.

France, Roger Merle echoes this preoccupation in a more subtle form.[11]

For those who prefer simple formulas to complex realities, it is but a short step from this viewpoint to the assimilation of social defence with an authoritarian approach to criminal law. Some have made a point of reminding us that the criminal law of National Socialist Germany was itself concerned with the pitiless affirmation of the community—the *Volk*—if need be by the suppression of the individual.[12] Others again have recalled that the Soviet Criminal Code of 1926—which could surely not be classed as a liberal enactment—itself purports to ensure by 'measures of social defence' the protection of 'the order created by the power of the workers and peasants' against any 'dangerous' activities. Does this not re-echo, in part, the language of the first theorists of social defence?

Without going so far as this, or giving such a strained political connotation to the term 'social defence', some authors fear that the concept involves a return to an arbitrary system of punishments. Saleilles used to say that in the law of the *ancien régime* the magistrate was 'an agent of social defence'.[13] At that time the judicial bench was considered not simply as an executant, but as a law-maker in its own right, collaborating with the law in its main purpose of ensuring public order and security. In that respect, discretionary punishment might well appear at first sight as a measure of 'social defence'. We remember also the anxieties of Émile Garçon—a contemporary of Saleilles—when in the course of his controversies with Prins and Liszt, and in the face of the arguments adduced by these advocates of the primitive doctrine of social defence, he stood forth as the uncompromising champion of the tradition of 1789 against the supporters of safety measures and of the indeterminate sentence. But this attitude, though

[11] 'L'Évolution du droit pénal moderne', *Annales de la Faculté de droit de Toulouse*, vol. VI (fasc. 1), 1958, pp. 133 ff. This thesis, which Merle has expanded in an exceedingly balanced and incisive fashion, was adopted by several other writers in an aggressively polemical form which robs the argument of any scientific value and which it is not proposed to discuss.

[12] K. Siegert, *Grundzüge des Strafrechts im neuen Staate*, 1934. Erwin R. Frey (*Rev. pénale suisse*, 1953, pp. 421-22) rather too summarily establishes a link between the social defence movement and the suppression of the rule *nulla poena sine lege* in the U.S.S.R. and Nazi Germany.

[13] *L'Individualisation de la peine*, 2nd ed., Paris, 1909, p. 47.

transcended both by modern conditions and by modern doctrine, still appears even among first-rate minds.[14]

Other writers, on the contrary, see in social defence a reflection, or a pseudo-scientific renewal, of the old utilitarian theories. At the beginning of this century René Garraud wrote that the idea of social defence was a very old one, which had simply undergone an attempted rejuvenation that had taken the form of presenting punishment as a reaction by the social organism against the offence which threatens its life or well-being.[15] Did not Beccaria himself, treating of the basis of punishment, refer to the right of self-defence of every individual? Beccaria, however, as a child of the eighteenth century, believed that in becoming a member of society and by virtue of the social contract, a man handed over this inherent right of self-defence to society, whose right to punish in the name of the community he thus acknowledged. This was still 'social defence' in the original meaning of the term,[16] but naturally restricted to what is useful for the preservation of society: it was this idea that Bentham was to illuminate very soon afterwards, when he sought the basis of punishment in its utility or rather in its necessity.[17]

Those who reject this interpretation of social defence will no

[14] See the rather surprising assertions of A. Mellor in his book, which is nonetheless most suggestive, on *Les Grands Problèmes contemporains de l'instruction criminelle*, 1952, pp. 223 and 224 (it should however be noted that at pp. 13 and 14 of the same work there is a more accurate impression of the notion of social defence). Warlomont himself, in an otherwise remarkable article on 'La Fonction judiciaire et les positions actuelles de la défense sociale', *Rev. de droit pénal et de criminologie*, April, 1952, writes of 'the fear, whether conscious or otherwise', of the magistracy in face of social defence which would seem, at least at first sight, to require them to 'step outside the law so as to venture forth into a discretionary—though paternalistic—area' and to 'abandon the traditional safeguards of public law, placing their trust instead in the still unfulfilled promises of the specialists'. Still more clearly, G. Bettiol ('Orientamenti generali nel diritto penale', *Jus*, 1951, pp. 451 ff.) boldly asserts that social prophylaxis leads to the concentration camp. The more important of these objections will be raised again and discussed in Chapter VII.

[15] R. Garraud, *Traité théorique et pratique de droit pénal français*, 3rd. ed., vol. 1, Paris, 1913, p. 83. Cf. Henri Joly, *Le Combat contre le crime*, Paris, 1891, who draws a close parallel between the idea of social defence and that of self-defence: it is this which the wronged individual surrenders to the State when it becomes more highly organized (pp. 17 ff.).

[16] Romagnosi, in his *Genesi del diritto penale*, 1791, gave to social defence a somewhat similar meaning: 'Il diritto penale è diritto di difesa e non puo essere altra cosa . . . la difesa sociale mira al futuro; la società ha bisogno di defendersi . . .'

[17] The same justification of criminal law and of punishment is to be found in the excellent book by P. J. Fitzgerald, *Criminal Law and Punishment*, Oxford, 1962.

longer be the individualists mainly concerned to safeguard individual rights, but those who intend to preserve the moral basis of criminal law. Referring to the Italian positivist school—which in his view aimed at reducing the penal code to the single notion of social defence and saw in this code a mere development of the sociology of crime—Saleilles wrote: 'The criminal law is indeed a policy of social defence, for such is its immediate purpose. But this policy of social defence has to be attuned to the inherent requirements of the idea of justice, and this qualification should be added to the formula used by the Italian school'.[18]

For the Positivists, in fact, the expression 'social defence' explains nothing beyond the new purpose of punishment, once this is no longer the retribution for faults according to principles or moral responsibility. This is the sense in which the term is both used and justified by Ferri,[19] and it is also the meaning that was to be attributed to it by the *Terza Scuola*, and in particular by Carnevale.[20]

Thus social defence would be no more than the survival or residuum of the positivist school. This would imply the acceptance of a deterministic approach and it is in this sense that such a writer as Bettiol[21] confronts the partisans of social defence with a refurbished neo-classical doctrine designed 'to bring criminal law back to its human origins, so as to make of it a means of safeguarding individual freedom' and to give back to the relation between criminal law and morality that tangible quality which a materialistic and laicizing tendency have caused it to lose.

In the view of many other authorities on crime, social defence would be no more than the doctrine—or rather the tendency—which in the words of J. A. Roux, 'on the hypothesis that an offence has been perpetrated, endeavours by means of measures of re-education and protection to prevent the offender's relapse'.[22]

[18] *L'Individualisation de la peine*, 2nd ed., p. 6.

[19] Ferri, *Sociologia criminale*, 3rd ed. Turin, 1892, pp. 432 ff.

[20] Carnevale, *Diritto Criminale*, Rome, 1932, vol. 1, No. 6, p. 18 and No. 16, p. 44: 'La difesa della società è l'ufficio generico della pena.'

[21] *Op. cit.*, in *Jus*, 1951, pp. 451 ff.; *id.* 'Punti fermi in tema di pena retributiva', in *Scritti giuridici in onore di Alfredo de Marsico*, Milan, 1960, vol. I, pp. 53 ff. Cf. Quintano Ripolles, 'Culpabilidad y retribución como premisas logicas de justicia penal', in *Estudios juridico-sociales*, Santiago de Compostela, 1960, p. 1032. The same point of view was likewise expressed by the commission set up in the Federal German Republic for the purpose of revising the Criminal Code.

[22] *Cours de droit criminel français*, 2nd ed., 1927, vol. I, p. 9.

So the concept of social defence would involve no more than the systematization of preventive measures. Rather along the same lines, though inspired by completely different ideas, Grispigni considered the measures of social defence applicable to persons who had committed an act defined by law as an offence, to be a means of dealing with the 'dangerousness' (*pericolosità*) of the individual in question, but quite apart from any legal sanction—i.e. the imposition of any penalty in respect of the offence committed.[23] Thus in relation to enacted law, social defence would take its place on the edge of traditional penal law with its system of punishments. Similarly, in a lapidary phrase, Jean Constant has said that the social defence school considers punishment to be no longer the sole or the best means of controlling crime, and it therefore advocates measures of social protection against dangerous offenders.[24]

Acceptance of the notion of dangerous condition, application of safety measures to individuals because of and in proportion to their individual capacity for doing harm—such would be the true meaning of the expression 'social defence'. It may indeed be observed that these safety measures have gradually become concentrated around two poles of attraction: habitual offenders and abnormal offenders. We might then be led to think that the content of the expression 'social defence' might be both defined and limited by these two kinds of measures. This indeed was the intention of the well-known Belgian statute of 9 April 1930, the so-called 'social defence law', and the same interpretation was adopted by so well-informed an author as Pinatel who—because a post-trial method of treatment was involved—had no qualms about assimilating social defence to the study of penitentiary problems.[25]

Taking as their starting-point the notion of danger, other writers tend to give the words 'social defence' a different meaning or more precisely a different flavour. So De Greeff observed that the term 'redoubtability' expresses an idea which is both original and useful: 'In a society which tries to anticipate rather than simply to punish, and to protect rather than to avenge, there is introduced

[23] *Diritto penale italiano*, 1950 ed., vol. I, No. 12-14, p. 140.

[24] *Manuel de droit pénal*, 4th ed., Liège, 1948, vol. 1, No. 6.

[25] *Traité élémentaire de science pénitentiaire et de défense sociale*, Paris, 1950, Part 2, 'Problèmes de défense sociale', pp. 380 ff.

an attitude characterized both by the determination to rid criminal justice of an undesirable element of revenge and by the intention to intervene only in so far as this is indispensable.'[26]

However, as the criterion founded on the capacity for doing harm is naturally distinct from the test of moral responsibility, some have been led to ask themselves whether the term 'social defence' does not conceal a theory by which the offender would be sought out because of his potentially dangerous condition alone. Thus Léon Cornil, *Procureur-Général* of the Belgian Court of Cassation, complained on occasion that social defence purported to consider all offenders as 'sick and irresponsible persons' for whom curative measures would be regarded as uniquely appropriate.

So, whereas some used to complain that social defence, narrowly interpreted, sacrificed the individual to the State and personal liberty to severe repression, and whereas even today some people tend to consider that social defence allegedly involves no more than the creation of a general and arbitrary system of preventive measures *ante delictum*, we have seen that others—sometimes even the same persons—accuse the social defence movement of paying attention to the morbid needs of the criminal at the expense of repression, collective intimidation, and the protection of law-abiding citizens. This is not a new reaction, for, at a Congress held in 1912, Loubat, *Procureur-Général* at Grenoble, protested against these 'new-fangled' notions which led to what was even then called 'the crisis of repression'.

II

The foregoing remarks enable a further step to be taken towards a proper definition of the *modern* significance of the term 'social defence'. In this new connotation, the expression no longer serves merely as a vehicle for the older concept of 'protection of society', but acquires its own dynamic force and evokes the idea of a certain protest against what *is*, or a particular attitude with regard to what *should be*.

For a very long time, even, we may say, for centuries, it was never questioned that pitiless punishment of the offence was the only means of controlling the phenomenon of crime. Of course,

[26] *Introduction à la criminologie*, vol. 1, Paris, 1948, p. 31.

this over-simplified notion has varied much in content from Plato to Beccaria, as will be shown in the next chapter. Moreover, as everyone knows, the object of such punishment has been—successively or concurrently—vengeance, expiation, retribution, reparation for the harm inflicted, intimidation, reformation, satisfaction of the public conscience, or the prevention of new offences. In all these cases, however, the social reaction against crime was primarily thought out in terms of punishment: the criminal must 'pay', and the other purposes of the penalty were secondary. The classical criminal law which emerged in the late eighteenth century, while rejecting the brutalities of the former régime, itself established a system of retributive punishment. To a large extent, this consisted in fitting the means of dealing with crime into a rigid legal framework: this, then, was the system of law responsible for ensuring the protection of society against crime and hence was 'social defence'.

Now in its modern connotation, social defence appeared first of all as a reaction against this exclusively retributive system. That is why the term acquired a scope—or if we prefer, an autonomy—which was new; that is why, again, it came to imply a renewed conception of the struggle against delinquency; that is why, finally, it came to presuppose the existence of a deliberate penal policy founded on data provided by the social sciences and by criminology. Such modern penal policy is based on the essential premise that, because crime is a social fact and a human act, the process of dealing with crime is not completed once the offence has been legally defined and equated with a penalty imposed by law: there remains the need to understand the crime as a social and individual phenomenon; the need to prevent its commission or repetition; the need, finally, for asking oneself what attitude is to be adopted towards the criminal, over and beyond the legal qualification of the offence.

The history of these ideas thus confronts us with two main interpretations of the notion of 'social defence', fundamentally different from one another: first the old interpretation, which still has many supporters ,who would limit the notion to the protection of society by the repression of crime; and secondly the *modern* conception, which finds expression in the excellent formula adopted by the United Nations Organization when its social defence section was set up in 1948: 'The prevention of crime and the treatment of offenders'. Prevention and treatment, it may be said, are the two dimensions that were lacking in the traditional interpretation, which likewise failed to place the reaction against crime in proper perspective: whereas in the traditional interpretation this reaction consisted wholly in the precise determination of a body of legal rules, the modern tendency is to envisage the problem in a social and criminological context. To arrange the system of protection of society with due regard to criminological facts, but bearing in mind the need to perfect a true system of criminal law—this is what we understand by the implementation of a 'penal policy'. In its modern meaning, social defence thus appears simultaneously as a new approach to the problem of crime and as a new trend in the practical decision-making which organizes the means of controlling crime.

It is essential to have a thorough understanding of the fundamental antithesis between the old and the new conceptions of social defence, and constantly to bear this antithesis in mind, for only thus can serious confusion be avoided and the precise significance of the notion of social defence, in its modern dynamic force, be appreciated. It goes without saying that the modern conception alone will engage our attention from now on.

Furthermore, it will be seen that this modern conception is not unitary or uniform, but has at least two very different aspects, which will be discussed in greater detail on page 73. In the opinion of Gramatica, for instance, social defence is definitely to be visualized as a reaction against repressive criminal law, and would even envisage substituting for the criminal law, *stricto sensu*, a non-punitive system of reaction against anti-social behaviour. Such a system would then aim at establishing a coherent body of remedies chosen with a view to the attainment of social harmony.[27]

From this point of view, social defence might even be considered in the context of political philosophy as a conception in which the State did not simply exercise the utilitarian and beneficient function attributed to it by Bentham, of ensuring the greatest happiness of the greatest number, but would go further than the mere *protection* of the citizen and organize a system designed to *ameliorate* both society and the citizens. Some time ago, Saldana

[27] 'Criminologia e difesa sociale', *Riv. di Difesa sociale*, 1950, pp. 113 ff., esp. pp. 127, 129. Cf. the same author's *Principi di difesa sociale*, Padua, 1961.

also worked out the idea of a similarly perfectionist criminal law.[28] This writer, in a vision more enthusiastic than convincing and less precise than generous, even wished to project his scheme on to the world scale and to have it administered by an international tribunal. He was thus led to envisage a system of 'universal social defence' which would replace the existing penal law by a 'law of insurance' consisting of reciprocal means of protection and safeguards.[29] Gramatica, for his part, has asserted on many occasions that such an undertaking would involve fundamental changes in the structure of the legal system and even in that of society itself.

We are here confronted with what may be termed the 'extremist interpretation' of social defence. Later on, we shall see what reservations and even opposition this interpretation has aroused, because—as may be imagined—it has provoked bitter controversy.

Whatever we may think of these discussions, which are not always free from mere verbosity but which at least illustrate the topical importance and the vitality of the concept of social defence, the fact remains that, quite apart from the extreme view just referred to, the modern concept of social defence is often considered to be a synonym for action of a non-penal nature, or at any rate for a treatment of the offender in a way that is not merely repressive. A Danish criminologist has adopted the notion of the struggle against punishment, but without giving this the negative significance favoured by Gramatica.[30] Again, as the latter very properly observed, it is impossible to overlook the great reputation and inspiring work in this field of the great Swedish specialist, Karl Schlyter, whose celebrated slogan 'Empty the prisons!' could well be adopted as a rallying-cry by the partisans of social defence. Schlyter remained within the logic of his system and his work in expressing the wish that the term 'criminal code' should be replaced by 'social defence code' or 'code of protection'.[31]

[28] This system is derived, in particular, from pragmatic penology (*Nueva penologia*, 1931). Cf. J. Masaveu, *Nueva dirección española en filosofía del derecho penal*, pp. 53 ff.

[29] *La Défense sociale universelle*, Paris, 1925; cf. 'Peine et mesures de sûreté', *Rev. int. de droit pénal*, 1927, pp. 7 ff.

[30] Louis Le Maire, *Kampen mod Straffen*, Copenhagen, 1952, who considers that crime is the expression of an abnormality requiring purely therapeutic treatment. See, for conclusive objections to this kind of approach, S. Hurwitz, *Den danske kriminalret*, Copenhagen, 1950, pp. 111-112.

[31] Stephan Hurwitz, *op. cit.*, pp. 102-103; cf. Thore Engströmer, *Festskrift tillägnad Karl Schlyter*, Stockholm, 1949, p. 10. On Karl Schlyter, see *Rev. de Science crim.*, 1959, p. 916; 1960, p. 134.

Here the concept of social defence covers an active and preventive social policy which aims at the protection of society by protecting the offender as well, and is designed to ensure that the latter should receive the treatment which is appropriate to his individual case, within a legal framework and by legal methods. Thus conceived, social defence is largely based on the substitution of treatment for retributive punishment. It need hardly be emphasized that this approach in no way denies the value of criminal law, since it is the approach which the United Nations Organization adopted and has undertaken to develop, with the consent and active participation of all its member states. In the Council of Europe, the same work has been undertaken by the European Committee on Crime Problems, since it was set up in 1957.[32] In the same spirit, the Twelfth (and last) International Penal and Penitentiary Congress —a memorable event—expressly raised the question 'of the measures which are appropriate substitutes for punishment, taking into account the necessities of a humane social defence'.[33]

Does it then follow that the concept of social defence necessarily involves the rejection of all repressive measures, and a final separation from the notion of punishment? Is it necessary to make a choice, here again, between criminal law and social defence? On the contrary, many determined advocates of social defence believe that criminal law *and* social defence should be brought together in a fresh perspective.[34] Stefan Hurwitz, indeed, sees social defence as a doctrine that would give greater weight to the repression of crime than to its prevention, and he would prefer the expression 'punishment' to be abandoned altogether, so as better to stress the fact that penal sanction is no longer associated with ignominious suffering: he considers such a change advantageous not only from the technical standpoint but also as 'the

[32] On this Committee, see *Rev. de Science crim.*, 1958, p. 922.

[33] See Marc Ancel, 'Security Measures Appropriate to a Humane System of Social Defence', in *Proceedings of the Twelfth International Penal and Penitentiary Congress*, Berne, 1951, vol. II, pp. 503-515. The same approach is to be found in the paper submitted to this Congress by Paul Cornil, on the problem of applied penal law in the light of new relevant tendencies, *ibid.*, vol. II, pp. 476 ff., and *Rev. de droit pénal et de criminologie*, Brussels, February 1951.

[34] Cf. the study by E. R. Frey already cited, 'Strafrecht oder soziale Verteidigung', *Rev. pénale suisse*, 1953, pp. 405 ff.; cf. also Marc Ancel, 'Droit pénal et défense sociale', *Rev. de Science crim.*, 1953, pp. 144 ff. See especially the conclusive reply of J. Graven in *Rev. pénale suisse*, 1955, pp. 1 ff., and cf. the discussion with Frey at the International Society for Criminology, *Bulletin* of that society, 1956, pp. 119 ff.

expression of a sound programme of penal policy'.[35] Yet he does not forget that in public opinion the idea of sanction still retains its vitality, and that the necessary social reaction may still involve depriving certain persons of their freedom or inflicting fines on them. I. Strahl, for his part, while supporting the elaboration of a system of social defence measures and a procedural reform which would make possible a more satisfactory individual approach to the situation of the particular person accused, has no intention of doing away altogether with the criminal trial as such or with the possibility of inflicting punishment.[36] The *Nordisk Kriminalistik Årsbok* (Yearbook of the Northern Associations of Criminalists), which never fails to concern itself in a sound and genuine manner with problems of social defence, contains many examples of this tendency to make room for punishment in a rational system of social defence. So Graven, who played a major and unforgettable part in the first social defence Congresses, did not hesitate on occasion to declare himself in favour of the death penalty, arguing for the necessity of its retention and even—in the case of Switzerland—its reintroduction.[37]

The expression 'social defence' is therefore subject to a great variety of uses and interpretations. As has already been observed, some writers have sought to compare—if not to assimilate—social defence both to penology and to criminology, whereas other specialists have tried to give the notion the scope of a genuine political philosophy. Again, some have asserted that social defence should postulate the criminal problem 'from a higher standpoint which would be derived from first principles, would acquire an ever-increasing ascendancy over the Criminal Code as the idea and the reality of society as such gained strength, and would command increasing attention from man considered as an individual'. The concept of social defence would therefore involve consideration of 'the problem of man and society, of their

[35] Report of the San Remo Congress, 1947, in *Respekt for Mennesket*, Copenhagen, 1951, pp. 217 ff.

[36] I. Strahl, 'La Réforme du droit pénal en Suède', *Rev. de Science crim.*, 1952, pp. 359 ff., also the same author's *Brotten och brottspåfoljderna* ('The Offence and its consequences'), Stockholm, 1952. J. Andenaes, in his study of social defence in Norway (same *Revue*, 1953, pp. 273ff.) seems to accept an identical point of view as legitimate; cf. his 'General Prevention, Illusion or Reality?', *Journal of Criminal Law, Criminology, and Police Science*, Jul.-Aug. 1952, pp. 176 ff.

[37] 'Le Problème de la peine de mort et sa réapparition en Suisse', *Rev. int. de criminologie et de police technique*, Special issue, Jan.-Mar. 1952, pp. 3 ff.

respective natures and of their relation'. This philosophical and social problem would be resolved with the help of the social sciences. With regard to the legal aspects of the problem, social defence would require above all that 'the progress accomplished in the social sciences and particularly in sociology should be amply integrated in the law'.[38] There is also a new affinity between the respective fields of social defence, criminology, and political philosophy. Still another author, in a report expressing certain extreme opinions that are characteristic of a particular interpretation of social defence, even concludes with a reference to brotherly love and the vision of this particular concept of social defence as the philosophical system where the individual and society are harmoniously inter-related for the social well-being of all.[39]

This certainly takes us a long way from a criminal policy applied solely with a view to the rational prevention of crime and the scientific treatment of offenders. Will social defence therefore get lost among these well-meaning generalizations, in which non-lawyers feel more at home than academic lawyers or practitioners concerned with criminal law? Some non-specialists may occasionally have been responsible for such pseudo-philosophical attitudes and a certain facile dogmatism. It does not necessarily follow that the term 'social defence' may not have a content and a significance which one is compelled to link up with the general system of thought that dominates the rules of law actually applied. This proposition could be demonstrated, if need be, not so much by scattered references culled from the works of recent theoreticians of social defence, but rather by the significant discussions that have taken place ever since June 1953 on the occasion of the *Journées de Défense sociale* which are arranged annually by the Comparative Law Institute of the University of Paris, with the assistance of the various university law faculties in France.[40]

[38] See the first 'Chronique de défense sociale' ('Avertissement') in *Rev. de Science crim.*, 1948, pp. 119 ff.; cf. Piprot d'Alleaume, *ibid.*, 1948, p. 801.

[39] De Vincentiis, General Report to the San Marino session (1951), *Riv. di difesa sociale*, 1951, pp. 86 ff., esp. p. 160. T. Collignon, *Rev. int. de criminologie et de police technique*, 1949, p. 80, writes that 'social defence tends to suppress the need for repression, by doing away with the cause thereof'.

[40] On these *Journées*, see *Rev. de Science crim.*, 1953, p. 540; 1954, pp. 172, 809; 1955, pp. 578, 724; 1956, pp. 162, 200, 650, 872; 1957, pp. 700, 835; 1958, p. 805; 1959, pp. 41, 125, 898; 1960, pp. 41, 125, 595, 702; 1961, p. 843; 1962, pp. 574, 801; 1963, pp. 751, 774, 779, 855; 1964, pp. 721, 801, 898.

The first of these meetings[41] considered the particularly important problem of the relation between social defence and individual freedom. Gradually, irresistibly so to speak, there emerged the idea that not only was the concept of social defence not opposed—or no longer opposed—to individual freedom, but, on the contrary, presupposed such freedom, the latter being redefined in terms of a social action ultimately providing genuine safeguards for the individual. The concept of social defence thus leads to a true judicial humanism which, while avoiding any violent rejection of the existing criminal law, aims in a consistent and resolute fashion to transform the administration of criminal justice itself. It then becomes possible to envisage social defence less as an objective doctrine than as a *commitment*, in the most modern sense of the word, meaning the deliberate acceptance of a particular approach to criminal justice, marked both by respect for the human person and by a concern to redeem for society those who must inevitably be affected by the social reaction against their acts. Of course, this generous conception goes beyond the province of criminal law envisaged as a particular kind of legal technique. However, it will be seen that this 'social penal policy' (for such, perhaps, might be the true definition of the new social defence) has no intention of disregarding either the inescapable exigencies of a legal system or the requirements of legal science.

III

So it is that the term 'social defence', founded on a certain idea of the social reaction against the phenomenon of crime, may be given a very wide meaning, which is ultimately suggestive of a new penal philosophy while remaining closely and necessarily bound up with the organization of a system of criminal law. The term may likewise be given meanings that are narrow, more restricted, and more strictly technical. As we have observed, it has even been used in opposite senses and has on occasion, here and there, been the object of distortions that were not always merely unintentional.

These several interpretations of the term 'social defence' have been mentioned simply in order to emphasize the many shades of meaning that could variously or in turn be attributed to this expression, which is today in general use. A little later, it may not

[41] See the full report of these *Journées* in the *Rev. de Science crim.*, 1954, pp. 172 ff.

be very difficult to show that many of these shades of meaning can in fact be reconciled in a single broad conception, destined to give way to distinct tendencies emanating, if truth be told, from the one basic idea. Without in any way professing to give a lapidary definition of social defence at this point—for in the light of the foregoing pages it is well to bear in mind the maxim *omnis definitio periculosa*—but after surveying, however briefly, most of the valid uses of the notion and the expression 'social defence', it appears possible to give at least a provisional answer to the question raised at the head of this chapter: what is meant by social defence?

From the unquestionable confusion of the different doctrines, as well as from the undeniable rivalry of the authors, we can already draw both a lesson and an encouragement. In effect, the term 'social defence', through all the ways in which it is used, even though they be empirical or fortuitous, emerges from the foregoing brief survey with certain salient features that enable us to place it in perspective with regard to the traditional, classical criminal law. We would recall once again, at this point, that it is intended to consider the *modern* concept of social defence, as contrasted with the older notion of the protection of society by way of repressive punishment alone. It may easily be perceived that this modern concept of social defence immediately calls to mind a few very simple ideas. In order to formulate the problem with sufficient precision in this preliminary chapter, these may now be enumerated. For the sake of brevity, it is proposed to set forth the ideas that follow in a schematic fashion, giving a summary in a synthetic form: at a later stage, perhaps, it will be necessary to draw attention to certain points needing greater elaboration or more specific treatment.

1. In the first place, social defence presupposes that the means of dealing with crime should be generally conceived as a system which aims not at punishing a fault and sanctioning by a penalty the conscious infringement of a legal rule, but at protecting society against criminal acts. There is no doubt that in this respect —which must engage our attention later—social defence recalls the positivist revolt against the traditional criminal law.

2. The intention of social defence is to carry such social protection into effect, quite naturally, by means of a body of measures that are generally outside the ambit of the criminal law as such

and are designed to 'neutralize' the offender, either by his removal or segregation, or by applying remedial or educational methods. Here again there is clearly a connexion between the ideas of social defence and the notion of 'dangerousness' which has been worked out, in particular, by the International Union of Criminal Law.[42]

3. Social defence thus leads to the promotion of a penal policy which naturally favours the individual rather than the collective approach to the prevention of crime, and endeavours to ensure 'the prevention of crime and the treatment of offenders'. Consequently, this rational penal policy aims at the systematic *resocialization* of the offender, and the importance of this term must be stressed from the very beginning.

4. Nevertheless, such a process of resocialization can take place only by way of an ever-increasing *humanization* of the new criminal law, which will have to call upon all the resources of the person concerned, seeking to restore not only his self-confidence but also his sense of personal responsibility (or more precisely, the awareness of his freedom in society) and the sense of human values. Moreover, this conception will endeavour to safeguard the offender's inherent rights as a human being, whether he is charged with an offence or actually convicted.

5. Such a humanization of criminal law and the criminal trial will not just be the result of a merely humanitarian or sentimental movement. On the contrary, the process will be based as firmly as possible on scientific understanding of the phenomenon of crime and the offender's personality. Moreover, the humanization of criminal law presupposes a humanist philosophy and a moral ideal which naturally go far beyond the boundaries of materialistic determinism. In this sense, and in this sense only, it may be said that social defence impinges directly upon the essential problem of the relations between the individual and the State. It is in this sense also that social defence differs fundamentally from totalitarianism, in so far as it considers that society can exist only through man and for man. In short, it is based on a political philosophy which tends to what may be described as social individualism.

These are the basic factors that enable us to define, tentatively at any rate, the admittedly complex notion of social defence. It should be understood at once that these several factors make their

[42] *Infra*, Chapter III.

appearance in the historical context outlined above and in this ascending order. *New* social defence, the spirit of which we should like to bring into the open, precisely involves becoming aware of these factors in their essential sequence and their natural order. To this extent also it may be said that social defence today implies, above all, a way of reflecting upon, approaching, and reconsidering the fundamental problems of criminal law in the light of a few essential ideas which form the philosophical basis of the whole system.

Chapter Two

ORIGINS OF THE SOCIAL DEFENCE MOVEMENT

IN THE HISTORY of criminal law and criminology, the social defence movement appears essentially as a modern and even—as we shall see—as a twentieth-century phenomenon. The movement indeed finds its direct antecedents in the revolutionary changes in criminal science carried out by the positivist school in the closing years of the nineteenth century. This does not mean however that the social defence movement is merely a consequence, extension, or re-edition of the positivist movement itself, and we must return to this point later. The earliest antecedents of social defence go back to a much earlier epoch. Granted sufficient leisure, it would be interesting to seek out these historical antecedents: the result would be a large volume, packed with references, illustrating the earliest manifestations of the ideas of social defence. It would then be seen that these ideas appeared very early in the history of human thought.

In a study which is exclusively concerned with the essential features of the *new* social defence movement, there is no question of drawing up such an archeological enumeration, as it were. Nonetheless, there is some reason to underline the fact that the ideas of this movement are not an artificial creation for which modern thought in the criminal sciences has been completely unprepared. In this regard a certain amount of information may be useful in order to clarify the notion of social defence itself, envisaged both as a permanent concept and in its successive variations or forms of expression. Afterwards it will be possible to explain why these ideas, although they go back such a long way, were unable to form a body of doctrine until quite recent times.

I

So as to give greater precision to the summary which follows, it will be assumed that, from the historical point of view, ideas of social defence may be said to emerge from the moment that one of three notions can be perceived: first, a concern for the protection of society over and above merely expiatory punishment; secondly, the desire to bring about the amelioration of the offender if not his re-education, beyond the infliction of a purely exemplary or retributive penalty; finally, and beyond the mere requirements of procedural technique, the desire to promote or to safeguard the concept of the human person, to whom none but a humane treatment can be applied. What should be borne in mind for the moment is that in each of these three cases the notion of social defence manifests itself by deliberately going further than the normal practice in penal matters.

There is a penetrating study of the part played by Greek philosophy in the history of this movement.[1] Without summarizing that brilliant exposition, to which I would simply refer, it should at least be specified at this point that Plato, in truth, was alone among the Greeks in perceiving the ideas which were to become those of social defence. He was among the first to understand the concept of prevention and to work out the notion that the aim of punishment should be, not the avenging of past injustice—for what is done cannot be undone—but the safeguarding of the future and the avoidance of further crimes on the part both of the offender himself and of those who witnessed his punishment.[2] Plato even attributes the dominant rôle to prevention when he desires that the laws should endeavour to turn men away from criminal acts and to punish them if such acts have been committed.[3]

Similarly, Plato perceived the idea of the protection of society against the dangerous offender. His prison system is several centuries ahead of his age, for at a time when a prison was simply

[1] R. Van der Made, 'Contribution à l'étude de l'histoire de la défense sociale' (Report submitted to 2nd International Congress of Social Defence, Liège, 1949), *Rev. de droit pénal et de criminologie*, 1949-1950, pp. 944 ff.

[2] *Protagoras*, 324; *Gorgias*, 525. [3] *Laws*, IX, 853.

a place of temporary incarceration, he wanted imprisonment to become the penalty normally applicable in the great majority of cases, if not in all.[4] Furthermore, he envisaged three institutions one of which would be no more than a place of temporary confinement, but the third, 'located in a wilderness or desert, its name suggestive of a place of punishment', would receive the incorrigible offenders. Plato, indeed, was the first to make a distinction between offenders who are capable of reformation and those who are not, or in his own significant words, 'between criminals who can be cured and those who cannot'. The second of Plato's three institutions is designed for criminals who can be reformed, and is called the house of repentance (*sophronisterion*). Criminals will be put there when it is realized that 'whoever does wrong does not do so of his own free will', that the offender merits compassion as do the sick, and that he should be treated with care.[5] Here, in an embryonic form, may already be found not merely the notion of re-educating and reforming the convicted offender, but even that of treating the offender who is considered to be curable by quasi-medical means.

The extremely venerable law of China also provides some very odd glimpses of social defence concepts. About the year 1050 B.C., a work of nine chapters on punishment put forward the desirability of a penal policy based on the reformation of the offender. The idea of repentance was invoked, and so it was decided that sentence of death would not be passed on one who committed a crime, even a serious one, by mistake, ill-luck, or as the result of fortuitous circumstances, and who unequivocally confessed his guilt. The principle is interesting because in primitive societies, as we know, the system of punishment for crime is initially conceived as an objective expiation for the act committed. The same ancient penal law of China knew the curious practice of the so-called 'beautiful stone' or veined stone which was placed at the entrance to the court. The offender was seated on this in the hope that he would 'reform' while 'contemplating the symmetry of the lines in the stone, pattern of the harmonious law of

[4] *Laws*, X, 908.

[5] *Laws*, V, 731. A few of these ideas, in particular those concerning the protection of public security and the separation of the virtuous from the wicked, are to be found in Seneca. (See especially *De Clementia*, I, 22); cf. J. M. Stampa, *Las ideas penales y criminologicas de Seneca*, Valladolid, 1950).

nature'.[6] The session on the 'beautiful stone' might last from three to thirteen days, after which the convict was employed on road-mending or similar tasks.

In the fourteenth century, Moslem law laid down that infants up to the age of seven could not be convicted of a criminal offence, and provided measures of re-education only, which were not genuine penalties, for children over seven who had not yet reached the age of puberty. As regards adult offenders, moreover, Moslem law laid down rules which might even then be described as constituting a system of social defence. Apart from the five major crimes which were defined and provided for by the Koran, the judge had discretionary powers in respect of a certain number of offences: he was bound to take into account not only the offence itself but also the conditions in which it had been committed and the personality of the offender.[7]

From the end of the Middle Ages onwards the criminal law of Europe, as it existed before the Revolutionary and Napoleonic era, provided a number of examples of the ideas of social defence. Article 176 of the famous 'Caroline Constitution' enacted by the Emperor Charles V in 1532 has often been cited as one of the embryonic antecedents of the modern 'safety measure'. This provision laid down that when a person failed to honour his bond, or after committing one crime threatened to commit another, a magistrate who considered that he constituted a threat to the safety of other persons might, 'as a precaution against the harm and damage that might be expected', order the offender to be kept in prison until such time as he provided an adequate surety or guarantee. Again, there could be mentioned the well-known 'retention clause' of the old Spanish criminal law, later enforced by a Pragmatic Sanction of 1777, which enabled those condemned to the galleys to be detained for at least a further two years at the end of their term, in cases where their liberation might constitute a disadvantage or a danger.

In most places, the criminal law of pre-revolutionary Europe instituted measures against beggars, vagrants, and persons of

[6] J. Escarra, Introduction to *Code pénal de la République de Chine, promulgué le 10 mars 1928 . . .*, Paris, 1930 (*Bibliothèque de l'Institut de droit comparé de Lyon*), a French translation of the Criminal Code of the Republic of China.

[7] Saïd Moustafa el Saïd Bey, 'La Notion de responsabilité pénale', *Travaux de la Semaine internationale de droit musulman, Paris, 2-7 juillet 1951*, Paris, 1953, pp. 122 ff.; cf. L. Milliot, *Introduction à l'étude du droit musulman*, Paris, 1953, pp. 744 ff.

evil life. As early as 1389 a Spanish ordinance subjected vagrants to compulsory labour.[8] In France, the Intendants were instructed in 1769 to establish in each of the principal administrative regions (then called *généralités*) workhouses for beggars, vagrants, prostitutes, lunatics, and persons guilty of serious misconduct. Several workhouses of this kind were opened in France, in particular one at Nancy in 1770, where the men were employed in weaving cloth and the women in spinning yarn or sewing.[9] This French establishment did no more than take up an idea which had already been applied in a striking fashion in the Netherlands, where the *Rasphuis* of Amsterdam had existed since 1596: there the men were employed as carpenters, whereas in a similar institution created later for women, the *Spinhuis*, the inmates were employed in spinning. These institutions, sponsored by men whom Thorsten Sellin has described, in a felicitous phrase, as the true pioneers of penology,[10] were based on the idea that the community should be protected against the danger represented by idle and delinquent persons and that the reformation of prisoners should be brought about by putting them to work. The movement was copied in Germany—especially in the Hanseatic towns—as it, had been in France.

Again, we may recall that in 1773 the celebrated Vilenus XIV, High Bailiff of Ghent and in many respects a pioneer of the modern pris on system, addressed to the States of Flanders a memorandum concerning 'the manner of correcting evildoers and idle persons for their own benefit and so as to make them useful to the State'. A few years later, Mirabeau—who had his own reasons for knowing intimately the miserable condition of the prisons of the *ancien régime*—proposed an amendment of the prison system that should be inspired both by the humanitarian ideas which had just found expression in the French Revolution, and by a penal policy directed towards the reclassification of offenders.[11] The whole movement for prison reform, which emerged at the end of the

[8] Francisco F. Olesa Munido, *Las medidas de seguridad*, Barcelona, 1951, pp. 34 ff.

[9] See Dr. Cœurdrain, 'Prisons de femmes á Nancy au XVIIIe siècle', *Rev. pénit.*, 1951, p. 485.

[10] Thorsten Sellin, *Pioneering in Penology, The Amsterdam Houses of Correction in the 16th and 17th Centuries*, Philadelphia, 1944; on these institutions, cf. L. Stroorant-Stevens, *Le Rasphuyz de Gand, Recherches sur la répression du vagabondage et sur le système pénitentiaire établi en Flandre au XVIIe et au XVIIIe siècles*, Ghent, 1900.

[11] Report presented to the Legislative Assembly in 1790.

eighteenth century with John Howard before finding expression in the works of Bentham and the selfless efforts of Elizabeth Fry, and in the early nineteenth century led to the first achievements of the Pennsylvania Quakers, was inspired by similar ideas. It would not be difficult to show how that movement, to a fairly large extent, embodied at least the spirit, if not the teaching, of social defence.[12]

To these trends, which were both utilitarian and humanitarian, and still in the Europe of the *ancien régime*, should be added the influence of the Christian tradition inspired by the ideas of charity and the redemption of the offender. In the writings of the Fathers of the Church we may already easily discern signs of the characteristic tendency of social defence ideas to step outside the confines of current penal practice. It has been suggested that St Augustine, in particular, was a forerunner of modern criminal science in so far as this is inspired by concepts of social defence.[13] To the same effect it can be recalled that the Council of Châlon-sur-Saône, in the year 650, conceived punishment as a real 'medicine of the soul'. And in the famous *Decretum* of Gratian there appears this characteristic phrase: *Medicinali severitate mali cogantur ad bonum*. Although often cited in support of retribution and retributive punishment, St Thomas Aquinas himself was not indifferent to this line of thought which is also to be found in certain Spanish theologians of the Middle Ages, even in their reaction against heresy at the time of the Inquisition.[14]

This idea of 'medicinal punishment', prototype of the modern notion of 'treatment of offenders', also underlies the canonical punishments where the purpose of detention was to bring the sinner to repent of his acts and to reform through a correct understanding of the seriousness of his guilt. The normal result of this attitude, in fact, was the development of a system of detention for convicted offenders that was designed as a truly corrective

[12] See H. E. Barnes and N. K. Teeters, *New Horizons in Criminology*, New York, 1946, Part V, chap. XXII, 'The Origins of the Prison System in America', pp. 466 ff.

[13] On this topic see the suggestive study by José Lopez Riocerezo in the *Revista brasileira de criminologia*, 1959, pp. 85 ff., where the author recalls that in *The City of God*, his chief work, St Augustine condemns torture, urges the sovereign to be forgiving, and asserts that 'punishment should not aim at destroying the guilty person, but at making him mend his ways'.

[14] Guallart, *La teologia penal de Santo Tomás de Aquino*, Saragossa, 1959, pp. 79 ff. J. Anton Oneca, 'La teoria de la pena en los correcionalistas españoles', *Estudios juridico-sociales*, Santiago de Compostela, 1960, II, pp. 1025 ff.

education. The Church Councils had long been concerned with this problem, and in the late seventeenth century Mabillon was able to write that 'While severity and rigour are usually predominant in secular justice, the spirit of charity, compassion, and mercy ought to prevail in the justice of the Church'.[15] A few years later, in 1703, and inspired by the same ideas, Pope Clement XI established an institution in Rome for young delinquents, over which was placed a motto calculated to inspire all those who were to demand or promote prison reform: *Parum est coercere improbos poena nisi probos efficias disciplina.*

Finally, one more current of ideas which gave an impetus to the evolution of concepts of social defence appeared in the sixteenth century, as an aspect of humanism, and reappeared in the eighteenth as a part of the philosophy of the 'Age of Enlightenment'. A special study could well be devoted to the relation between social defence and humanism alone, but on this point it will be enough to mention, by way of example, the particularly valuable contribution of Thomas More in *Utopia*, published in 1516. Resolutely opposed to the death penalty, More also ran counter to the habits of his time in urging that corporal punishments should be replaced by a form of preventive custody. Furthermore, he recalled that the Romans had utilized penalties of this kind when they sent criminals to work in the mines: *ad metalla*.[16] He also favoured rehabilitation through work, which should lead to the mitigation or even the complete remission of the penalty for those who manifest sincere repentance: 'but they which take their bondage patiently be not left all hopeless'.[17] More asserts also that the criminal should in any case be treated in a humane fashion; thus with reference to the infliction of the death penalty on a thief, for example, he exclaims: 'Therefore in this point not you only but also the most part of the world be like evil schoolmasters, which be readier to beat than to teach their scholars.'[18]

The well-known passage in which La Bruyère, writing at the end of the seventeenth century of the brutal tortures inflicted

[15] *Réflexions sur les prisons des ordres religieux*, 1690. See A. Rivière, 'Un moine criminaliste', *Rev. hist. de droit fr.*, 1898, p. 758; on the penitentiary institutions of the Church, see also J. Pinatel, *Traité élémentaire de science pénitentiaire et de défense sociale*, Paris, 1950, pp. xlv ff., and the references there cited.

[16] *Utopia*, with an introduction by John Warrington, London, 1951, p. 32.

[17] *Ibid.*, p. 102. [18] *Ibid.*, p. 23.

under the law of the *ancien régime*, expressed his indignation at the cruelties 'inflicted by some men upon other men', can be placed in the same context. The voices raised in protest during the eighteenth century against torture; the arguments of the *philosophes*, Montesquieu in particular, in favour of the alleviation of punishments and of the need to adjust the penalty to the circumstances of the offence; the criticisms voiced against the abuse of the death penalty; the abolition of capital punishment which was demanded by Beccaria and actually achieved in some of the legislative fruits of benevolent despotism;[19] the movement for penal reform which stirred Britain in the last years of the eighteenth century and made an undeniable impact although its fortunes were varied:[20] all these ideas drew at least part of their inspiration from concepts which will be found to lie at the root of the theories of social defence. In France, on the eve of the Great Revolution, the *Cahiers de doléances* of the States-General demanded a reformed criminal justice which should show greater respect for the rights of man and would lead, in particular, to an improvement in the prison system.[21] As early as 1766, however, the *Avocat Général* Servan made a speech at the Parlement of Grenoble which had a considerable impact. He adjured his audience in terms which join the Christian ideal of charity to the demands formulated two years earlier by Beccaria in his celebrated little book *Dei delitti e delle pene*.[22] 'See over your heads the image of your God, who was an

[19] See the Austrian Code of 1787 and above all the famous penal Code of Tuscany of 1786, which was inspired by Beccaria; cf. Ortolan, *Cours de législation pénale comparée*, Paris, 1841, vol. II, 2nd part, section III (the movement for penal reform in the eighteenth century), pp. 131 ff.; Faustin-Hélie, 'Introduction au traité des délits et des peines de Beccaria', in Beccaria, *Des Délits et des Peines* (French translation), Paris, 1856; J. Graven, *Beccaria et l'avènement du droit pénal moderne* (monographs published by the Law Faculty of the University of Geneva, No. 6); see also Marc Ancel, 'The Collection of European Penal Codes and the Study of Comparative Law', reprint, *University of Pennsylvania Law Review*, vol. 106, No. 3, January 1958, at p. 341 (English translation of *Introduction comparative aux Codes pénaux européens*, Paris, 1956).

[20] See the monumental *History of English Criminal Law and its Administration from 1750* by L. Radzinowicz, vol. I, London, 1948, which considers in all its aspects the movement for penal reform in England in the late eighteenth and nineteenth centuries.

[21] See A. Desjardins, *Les Cahiers des États-Généraux en 1789 et la législation criminelle*, Paris, 1883.

[22] Published anonymously at Livorno in 1764, the book had an immediate success; a French translation appeared in 1766 and an English translation was published in 1767.

innocent man accused; you who are men, be human; you who are judges, be moderate; you who are Christians, be charitable. Men, judges, Christians—whoever you are, be compassionate towards misfortune.' Of course, there were some who opposed this attitude and who defended 'tradition'. But one of the most prominent of these, Séguier, obtuse as he may have been, nonetheless admitted a few years later that 'in this troubled time, a general outcry has gone up against the criminal ordinance'.[23] So the new spirit, which was to triumph with the Revolution, first attacked an outdated and unduly repressive criminal legislation.

II

It may well be asked why these various tendencies, which had been apparent for so long, failed to establish themselves more openly in the 'great leap forward' and the great hope that marked the end of the eighteenth century. A new criminal law was about to come into being on the European continent, and yet the doctrines of social defence were not to be systematized until more than a century later, at a time relatively recent. Must it then be assumed that all these scattered yet convergent trends, whose most significant aspects have just been noted, were simply forgotten? The reforming spirits of the 'Age of Enlightenment', who had a taste for classical authorities, were fully aware that the idea of an essential relation between the individual and the State was already known to Antiquity, and that from the Greek philosophers to the humanists of the Renaissance the dignity of man had been emphasized. Christianity, in turn, while it developed the idea of the individual's personal responsibility for his fault—an idea frequently disregarded in primitive societies—had also tempered human justice with the idea of charity, which involved helping even the guilty who had sinned. Traditional pre-revolutionary law as a whole, and more particularly, what has been described as the 'general law'—*droit commun*—of the *ancien régime*,[24]

[23] In the regrettable speech in which he demanded the suppression of the *Mémoire justificatif pour trois hommes condamnés à la roue* (1786) by Dupaty, President of the Parliament of Bordeaux. On this movement as a whole, see A. Esmein, *Histoire de la procédure criminelle en France*, Paris, 1882, pp. 386 ff.

[24] See Jiménez de Asúa, *Tratado de derecho penal*, vol. I, 2nd ed., Buenos Aires, 1956, pp. 287 ff.; on the development of ideas regarding criminal justice in the 'Age of Enlightenment', see also vol. I, pp. 241 ff.

which extended throughout Europe until the last thirty years or so of the eighteenth century, had been conscious of the notion of social protection and even (to some extent) that of preventive measures. It would therefore have been conceivable that all these interconnected tendencies should result in a system which, in certain respects at least, encouraged a wide judicial discretion, an arbitrary system of penalties, and even, to some extent, the granting of facilities to the administration to prevent certain offenders, or certain individuals with delinquent tendencies, from doing harm. It would likewise have been conceivable that the philosophical movement of the late eighteenth century, humanitarian in inspiration but utilitarian in what it tried to accomplish, should endeavour to promote, along the lines of the precedents described above, a body of what were to be called, a hundred years later, 'measures of social defence'.

However, we have only to think of the exact scope of the penal reform movement in the late eighteenth century, and of the legislative and ideological conditions in which 'classical' criminal law grew up, to understand that for nearly a hundred years the essential conditions for the emergence and development of a genuine system and doctrine of social defence were sadly lacking.

The humanist tradition was, in fact, rapidly engrossed by the considerations which had led the older criminal legislation to terrorize the 'wicked' in order to deter them from wrongdoing. The older law never quite succeeded in forgetting the time when the social reaction against crime was envisaged in terms of avenging the Deity for the affront constituted by the offence, while at the same time preserving the peace of public order. And if, in a sense, this older law can be said to have carried out a penal policy of social defence, it did so in spite of itself as it were, unconsciously or more exactly perhaps as an addition, which made no essential difference to a system of repression which was altogether dominated by ideas of vengeance and expiation. Of the Christian tradition, on the other hand, the repressive system of this older law retained little more than the concepts of sin and atonement[25] and also, in the legal systems of continental Europe, the facilities of inquisitorial procedure, designed to obtain confessions from the criminal, pitilessly handed over to the judge's discretion. It follows that while we are entitled, to a certain extent and if only

[25] See Margery Fry, *Arms of the Law*, London, 1951, p. 38.

out of curiosity, to seek the earliest antecedents of social defence institutions in Antiquity or in the pre-revolutionary law, we would be ill-advised to claim that the notion of social defence emerged therefrom or was even clearly perceived therein. Again, it would be a rather serious historical error to try to assimilate the twentieth-century penal policy of social defence to the attempts at the empirical protection of the community which were to be found, ever since the end of the Middle Ages, in those European countries that remained faithful to the Roman Law tradition.

Furthermore, and above all, the philosophical movement of the late eighteenth century was set in a direction which almost inevitably made it lose sight of the exigencies and ideals of social defence. In so far as it was humanitarian, the Enlightenment reacted against the excessive cruelty of the punishments of the *ancien régime*. But it was influenced much less by the Christian ideal of charity—with which the social defence movement is permeated—than by abstract theories of natural law and even by the theory of the social contract.[26] Man—presumed to be reasonable and master of his acts, and endowed with that liberty of which Montesquieu wrote that it was the one good upon which enjoyment of all the others depended—should be protected in the enjoyment and exercise of his fundamental rights by the law, even as against the sovereign. The individual could alienate his rights only in so far as he agreed to do so for the benefit of society into which he entered, and through the social contract by which alone he might restrict his own freedom of action. Thus by the Declaration of the Rights of Man (1789) the citizen agreed in advance to undergo punishment if he infringed the social contract, but he could be condemned only if the act, freely and consciously committed, had previously been classified by the law as a crime. Therefore the legislator, reincarnation of the sovereign, must have previously decided that the particular kind of act in question constituted an offence which, once it had been properly established, would automatically involve the infliction of the legal penalty.

[26] The humanization and liberalization of criminal law was then chiefly associated with a determinedly secular and rationalizing tendency, as was indeed shown by Eberhard Schmidt, 'Die geistesgeschichtliche Bedeutung der Aufklärung für die Entwicklung der Strafjustiz aus der Sicht des 20. Jahrhunderts', *Rev. pénale suisse*, 1958, pp. 341-360.

The movement which was to produce the first theory of classical criminal law, and which may be placed roughly between 1748, the date of publication of Montesquieu's *Spirit of Laws*, and 1813, when the Bavarian Criminal Code[27] directly inspired by Feuerbach was promulgated, was therefore completely dominated by considerations of legality, of moral responsibility, and of a strictly objective conception of the criminal act.[28] Thus by a kind of interior logic, though not of course deliberately, there was a trend away from the implicit conceptions of social defence which might have existed in previous centuries. Indeed, the criminal law which achieved pre-eminence in the Codes of the nineteenth century left no room for the preoccupations of the social defence movement. The nineteenth-century attitude found its most vigorous expression in a repressive system which attributed no importance at all to the offender considered as an individual: the criminal offence was envisaged as an abstract legal entity which the legislator first defined objectively by statute, and the judge dealt with in due course as a purely objective notion, examined according to legal criteria.

Classical or liberal criminal law would thus have left the basic ideas of social defence entirely out of account. However, after the first effervescence of the revolutionary codes modelled on the French Code of 1791 which laid down a rigid system of fixed penalties, a more flexible tendency once again made room for a discretionary element. Thus the 1832 revision of the French Code of 1810 enabled the jury to make full allowance for extenuating circumstances. Again, there was the important movement in favour of the *individualization* of penalties which was to make a significant and notable contribution to the legislative developments of the nineteenth century. At the same time, the prison

[27] Eberhard Schmidt, *op. cit.*, extends the formative period of the criminal law derived from the 'Age of Enlightenment' from 1748 to 1848. Actually, its influence can be observed until the full development of the liberal system of the Victorian era. However, in the Europe of the Congress of Vienna, marked in France by the period known as the Restoration, the influence of the *philosophes* had become secondary, as it were. Feuerbach's Code, on the contrary, can be considered a turning-point (just as the Zanardelli Code of 1889 was to be a turning-point for neo-classical law): it closed the creative period of pure classical law begun with the Tuscan Code of 1786 and the French of 1791. See Marc Ancel, 'The Collection of European Penal Codes and the Study of Comparative Law', cited above, esp. pp. 346-49.

[28] On this conception see the remarkable study by R. Saleilles, *L'Individualisation de la peine*, 2nd ed., 1909, pp. 56 ff.

reform movement which emerged in the last years of the eighteenth century with the work of John Howard and Elizabeth Fry in England, leading to the 'penitentiary school' of the mid-nineteenth century associated with the names of Charles Lucas, Bonneville de Marsangy, and Ducpétiaux, revealed the possibilities and the advantages of the re-education of offenders.[29] The so-called system of 'parallel penalties' which appears in outline in the Bavarian Code of 1813, developed the idea of a choice between various measures which would be applicable, if not exactly according to the personality of the offender, then at least according to the circumstances of the offence or even perhaps to the motives which led to its commission.

The idea of reserving special treatment for juvenile delinquents, already expressed in the French Code of 1791 with the introduction of the question of discernment and the excuse of infancy, also enabled a distinction to be made between different categories of offenders. Better still, it was already possible under the 1791 Code to apply re-educative measures to a young delinquent who manifestly acted without discernment, although in principle he ought not to have been liable to any real penalty at all, since in the classical system punishment could only be retribution for an offence consciously and wilfully committed by one who was master of his acts. Now this movement, which on a more specially penitentiary basis was embodied in the French statute of 5 August 1850 on the education and supervision of young offenders, was in keeping with the fundamental notions of classical law, since the problem of discernment was primarily concerned—at any rate in principle—with the discovery of intention according to the prevailing theory of moral responsibility.

Perhaps it should be recalled that Bonneville de Marsangy, to take him as an example, was not just the inventor of the criminal record (*casier judiciaire*). Very well informed and much in advance of his time, he sought to draw up a systematic record of the previous convictions of accused persons simply because he was interested in the general problem of crime and the repetition of offences. He was perhaps the first to show clearly that an individual's present behaviour, correctly interpreted, may be the pointer to his future conduct. In this respect, Bonneville de

[29] See *Les Méthodes pénitentiaires modernes*, published by the F.I.P.P., Paris, 1955, pp. xvi ff.

Marsangy can be claimed as a precursor[30] of doctrines such as those of the preventive treatment of crime and those underlying the concept of 'preventive measures' (*mesures de sûreté*). He could even be claimed as the ancestor of the ideas which inspire contemporary research into the foreseeability of conduct, exemplified by the 'prediction tables' that are advocated in particular by S. and E. Glueck.[31] At about the same period that Bonneville de Marsangy was developing his ideas in France, Robert von Mohl in Germany tried to establish a distinction between 'preventive' and 'reparative' justice, the former being based not on the certain but the probable infringement of a legal rule.[32] In the same period, and also in Germany, Roeder[33] laid the foundations of the theory which in the late nineteenth and even more in the early twentieth century was to be adopted by the Spanish 'correctionalist' school whose most distinguished representative, Dorado Montero, went so far as to demand a *law for the protection of criminals*.[34]

If time allowed, it might thus be possible to seek in the doctrinal writings of the nineteenth century, underneath the thick shell constituted by the legalistic theory of classical criminal law, the first rather fugitive and cloistered glimpses of theories of social defence. In this connexion we could review the whole history of *indeterminate sentences*, which after Maconochie's pioneer work among convicts presumed to be utterly depraved, led to Brockway's experiments in the famous reformatory at Elmira.[35] It could probably also be shown how, from the Pennsylvania Quakers to the prison reformers of New York, there had grown up a whole movement which aimed to 'give convicted

[30] Bonneville de Marsangy, *De l'amélioration de la loi criminelle en vue d'une justice plus prompte, plus efficace, plus généreuse et plus moralisante*, Part II, Paris, 1864.

[31] Sheldon and Eleanor Glueck, *Predicting Delinquency and Crime*, Cambridge, Mass., 1959; on the prediction tables, see also Howard Jones, *Crime and the Penal System*, 2nd. ed., London, 1962, pp. 184 ff., with the references cited.

[32] *System der Präventivjustiz*, 1845.

[33] *Commentatio an poena malum debet esse* (1839): Roeder was one of the first to assert that the State was under a duty to re-adapt the delinquent to the life of society.

[34] On this movement, especially in Spain, see Jiménez de Asúa, *Tratado de Derecho Penal*, vol. I, 2nd ed. Buenos Aires, 1956, Nos. 123 and 289, vol. II, 2nd ed., 1958, Nos. 508, 541 and 542. Cf. the volume specially issued by the Faculty of Law and Social Science of the Universidad Nacional del Litoral, Santa Fé, 1962, for the centenary of the birth of D. Pedro Dorado Montero, and especially the very full study by Manuel de Rivacoba y Rivacoba.

[35] See John Vincent Barry, *Alexander Maconochie of Norfolk Island*): *A Study of a Pioneer in Penal Reform*, Melbourne, 1958.

men their chance' while ensuring more adequate protection of society against those whose release might constitute a social danger.[36]

However, even if we were to undertake this study, from which many lessons might be drawn, it would have to be borne in mind that these endeavours were carried out in a way that was both empirical and sporadic, without any preconceived ideas, without producing a coherent doctrine, and on the margin of a criminal law which continued to insist on the necessity of general prevention and of retributive punishment. This criminal law in the 'neo-classical' form of the second half of the nineteenth century perhaps found its most complete expression in the Italian Criminal Code of 1889. In a sense, this so-called 'Zanardelli Code' succeeded the French Penal Code of 1810 as the source of inspiration for penal legislation. Although the Code was enacted fifteen years after the publication of Lombroso's well-known book, it owed much more to the inspiration of Carrara's theories than to the still quite novel doctrines of positivism. After some three-quarters of a century of doctrinal contributions, criminal law was then constructed as an exceedingly dense body of legal technique, a sort of algebra[37] in which abstract reasoning took pride of place, and in which the criminal act was primarily a legal entity, objectively considered as such.

In fact, it was against this system that the ideas which emerged at the end of the nineteenth century were to react. This is not the place to dwell at length on the positivist revolution which followed the publication in 1876 of *L'Uomo delinquente* and which, in the evolution of penal ideas, was analogous in many respects to the renewal which had followed the publication in 1764 of Beccaria's little book *On Crimes and Punishments*. Nor can we dwell on the difference between this positivist movement and the work of the *philosophes* in the second half of the eighteenth century. It should be stressed, however, that it is only since the positivist revolt, and only with the help of the stirring of ideas produced thereby, that the notions of social defence could appear clearly in their true form. The fact is that the positivist movement was itself the offshoot of a scientific movement which went beyond the field of

[36] H. E. Barnes and N. K. Teeters, *New Horizons in Criminology*, 3rd. ed., Eaglewood Cliffs, 1959, pp. 325 ff.

[37] R. Saleilles, *op. cit.*, p. 8.

criminal law and strictly legal notions, so as to cover what were later to be called the social sciences.

On the other hand, first of all with Lombroso, later and more clearly with Enrico Ferri and Garofalo, the positivist movement appeared as a reaction against the doctrines, or more precisely the basic assumptions, of classical or neo-classical criminal law. Positivism challenged the idea of moral responsibility and the traditional theories concerning the legitimacy and the function of punishment. Its intention was to replace the kind of purely legal logic which inspired the disciples of Carrara by the experimental method favoured in the natural sciences. Primary importance was no longer assigned to the punishable act—i.e. the criminal offence as a legal entity—but to the criminal himself, envisaged in his individual personality, his biological identity, and his reality as a social being, deeply dependent on the environment in which he had lived. Ferri, in a striking phrase which has remained famous, declared that the delinquent had become or would become 'the protagonist of criminal justice'. The legalistic criminal justice of the nineteenth century, like the arbitrary criminal justice of the eighteenth, was inevitably shaken by this inflow of new doctrines and new ways of thought. Still more shattering, at the close of the nineteenth century, was this sudden apparition of man as an individual in the midst of all the abstract concepts of criminal law. There resulted that 'crisis of criminal law' which was soon to be noted by criminal lawyers of the early years of this century—a 'crisis' which even an authority so acutely aware of the realities of criminal justice as Henri Donnedieu de Vabres was to consider a characteristic phenomenon even so recently as 1938.[38]

With the emergence of positivist doctrines and in the wake of the disarray caused by the challenging of so many notions that seemed firmly entrenched once and for all, many changes became possible.[39] One of these changes was to be the development of the

[38] H. Donnedieu de Vabres, *La Politique criminelle des États autoritaires*, Paris, 1938; there had already been much talk at the beginning of the century about the 'crisis of repression'; see Loubat, *Rev. pol. et parlem.*, 1911, p. 434; cf. *Rev. pénit.*, 1912, pp. 658, 880 ff. See also R. Garraud, *Traité théorique et pratique de droit pénal français*, 3rd ed., vol. I, 1913, No. 88, p. 180 note.

[39] Cf. the remarks of Gemelli on the way in which Lombroso, by basing criminal science on the offender's personality, made possible the modern orientation of the criminological sciences; 'La concezione dinamica delle personnalità nello studio dei delinquenti', *Riv. penale*, 1955, pp. 8 ff.

first doctrine of social defence. This did not emerge directly from positivist doctrines—and only a superficial analysis would confound the two—but from the general movement of ideas and the various attempts at restatement that followed the emergence of positivism. The idea of social defence took shape in the last years of the nineteenth century, but the first theory of social defence did not make its appearance until the beginning of the twentieth. However distant may have been its origins, however various its earliest manifestations, it was from the beginning of this century and from then only, that social defence could form an explicit and coherent doctrine.

Chapter Three

THE MAIN STAGES OF THE SOCIAL DEFENCE MOVEMENT

THE TRUE CONCEPT of social defence came into being with the positivist movement: more exactly, it was only after the positivist revolt that a theory of social defence could be conceived and organized. This is an aspect of the history of ideas which must be accepted once and for all, but it should also be understood not only that social defence is not to be confused with positivism but also that as an independent doctrine it does not even form part of positivist theory. This should be emphasized in passing, before we examine the successive stages in the evolution of social defence doctrine.

I

All that has been said hitherto indicates that it was the existence of the positivist movement that enabled the first doctrine of social defence to emerge. In this connexion it is enough to recall in outline the key positions of that movement which were to make possible the theories of social defence:

1. The rejection of free will is not of course an essential aspect of social defence, any more than the biological or social determinism of Lombroso and Ferri involves the rejection of moral responsibility as the foundation of criminal law. Such an approach, however, presupposes that the new criminal law, in contrast with the classical criminal law, will no longer be shaped in terms of the traditional notion of *homo delinquens*, the reasonable man who is master of his acts and always free to choose between good and evil—man, in other words, as envisaged by Descartes and by the Declaration of the Rights of Man.

2. Consequently, the criminal offence itself will no longer be seen as an abstraction or a purely legal entity, but as a natural and

social fact, as a human act which needs to be examined not only objectively, in law, but also and above all in its subjective reality, namely in relation to the actual personality of the offender, which should itself be systematically examined.

3. Hence the purpose of criminal law will no longer be the punishment of fault, nor the abstract restoration of the right that has been infringed, by means of a sanction envisaged as reparation for a wrong; such a punitive sanction would no longer be designed with a view to the theoretical or ideal restoration of the rule of law, jeopardized by the criminal act. A metaphysical doctrine of repression gives way to a realistic approach designed solely to protect society against crime, and it is in this sense that the positivists were the first to make current use of the term *social defence*: the punitive function, said Ferri, becomes 'purely and simply a function of social defence'.

4. But whereas in the classical view the retributive function of criminal justice is both abstract and necessarily incomplete or approximate, the positivists assign to criminal justice the precise and practical task of protecting society against crime: they urge that this task should be carried out as thoroughly and as efficiently as possible, and they therefore react against the continual trend towards the lessening of penalties. Garofalo, who was the first to work out clearly the notion of *pericolosità*, took issue with those magistrates who, in the name of a misunderstood humanism, imposed insufficient penalties. Thus it is that mental defectives, whom the classical system placed outside the ambit of criminal law, are included therein by the positivists because of the danger they represent, and serious efforts are made to help society deal effectively with such abnormal offenders, whom the neo-classical law brushed aside by the over-simple expedient of 'diminished responsibility'.

5. The essential merit of the new criminal justice will be its preventive character. Legislation inspired by the positivist movement assigns a large rôle to the prevention of crime, first of all by attacking the social conditions conducive to crime (as with Ferri's 'substitutes for punishment'): once a crime has been committed, the main thing will be to prevent its recurrence, by means of a number of 'preventive measures' designed to neutralize or cure the offender.

6. Finally, this new criminal justice and legislation will fulfil their purpose of social protection only if guided by a thorough

understanding of anthropology and criminal sociology. Consistently, therefore, this movement for criminal law reform takes its stand on criminology, the new science which is the keystone of Garofalo's whole system, and the first result of this criminological approach is the classification of offenders into different categories, each in need of specialized treatment: this method, in turn, leads directly to a demand that criminal judges should themselves be specialists with an adequate criminological training, so that the lay jury, theoretically representative of the sovereign people, will lose its traditional rôle.

The various factors enumerated above do not constitute the whole of positivist doctrine, but they are all contained in the teaching of the Italian reformers, and it is in so far as these factors can be derived from that teaching that they pave the way for the appearance of the first theories of social defence. It should be clearly understood that the emergence of these theories comes *after* the formulation of positivist doctrine itself, for although positivism may be said to contain the seeds of the earliest theory of social defence, it does not explicitly formulate such a theory: social defence is *not* a positivist doctrine but an indirect consequence, twice removed so to speak, of that doctrine. Although the positivists, and Ferri in particular, continually use the expression 'social defence', they do not consider it as a distinct theory: for them, the expression means strictly the protection of the social group, and it was in this sense that Ferri, in the explanatory introduction to his famous draft code of 1921, could write of social defence as 'the direct and primary function of criminal justice'.

So the positivist approach alone made the emergence of a first theory of social defence possible, but did not formulate any such theory. From whom, then, did the expression first receive its own doctrinal content? In fact, that rôle was filled by the International Union of Criminal Law, and among the three founders of the Union—von Liszt, van Hamel, and Adolphe Prins—the last-named formulated the first social defence theory at the very beginning of this century. Social defence, as an autonomous doctrine, is thus indeed a twentieth-century creation.

The International Union of Criminal Law, however, was founded in 1889, and it is doubtless curious as well as symbolic, so to speak, that this body, which was directly responsible for the appearance of the first doctrine of social defence, should have been instituted in the very year of the promulgation of the Zanardelli Code, that perfect expression of neo-classical criminal law. In its initial form, the deed of association of the International Union resolutely turned its back on the assumptions of the traditional system. It boldly proclaimed that 'the mission of criminal law is the control of crime envisaged as a social phenomenon', and expressed the wish that criminal science and criminal legislation might 'take into account the results of anthropological and sociological studies'. It was openly stated that punishment was not the only means of controlling crime; careful distinction was made between occasional and habitual offenders; it was intended to seek measures which would replace short prison sentences; it was argued that the length of a prison sentence should no longer depend exclusively on the 'gravity, objectively speaking, of the offence'; finally, it was emphatically maintained that it was essential both to take account of the reformation of the offender while the penalty lasts and to render habitual offenders 'incapable of inflicting harm for as long as possible'.[1]

At the time, such assertions appeared singularly bold, as is abundantly clear from the reactions of traditionalist criminal lawyers at the time. These were being asked to perform the most difficult of tasks, which the modern social defence movement has called for ever since: a new look at what is well-established, a critical appraisal of the existing system, a revision of values in the criminological sphere. However, the birthday of the first social defence doctrine cannot be placed as early as 1889. To do this would be an exaggeration, for two reasons.

First, the principles set forth in the preliminary manifesto of the Union, though strongly asserted, did not as yet form a coherent doctrine: they simply constituted a number of claims designed as a pole of attraction for the advocates of structural reforms in criminal law and practice. In other words, they were pointers towards a future that remained inchoate. Those who had drawn up the text in question were chiefly concerned to restate the problem, to note a few essential demands, and in the light of the novel criminal science of the time to suggest a certain number of reforms whose urgent necessity had to be understood: they were

[1] On the teaching and influence of the International Union of Criminal Law, see the special issue of the *Rev. int. de droit pénal*, 1951, No. 2/3.

not in any way seeking to found a new doctrine. The Union neither was nor wished to be a 'school'.

Secondly, and as a consequence of this position, the founders of the Union sought to attract the largest possible number of adherents, even when not convinced. So the initial criminological *credo* did not long remain intact. Many who showed interest in the newly-constituted Union retained too many misgivings, so that from its first years, and throughout its existence, the Union was skilfully and subtly undermined from within by the representatives of the 'eclectic school' of the early twentieth century. In fact, this 'eclecticism' was nothing else than a more palatable form of neo-classicism, slightly ashamed of its own doctrine but strongly attached to certain 'major principles' which it considered unassailable. This movement avoided making a frontal attack on the reforms successfully accomplished by the positivist school; instead, the movement cut its losses and after a while managed to transform the Union, once a focal point of forward-looking and progressive endeavour, into a few well-intentioned flickers of activity which left untouched the venerable structure of moral responsibility and retributive punishment.

The statutes of the Union were revised at Lisbon in 1897, and less concrete formulas were adopted in order to calm the apprehensions of the 'eclectic school', which nonetheless carefully continued to take the edge off the measures proposed by the innovators. H. Donnedieu de Vabres has recalled by what assiduous and detailed efforts certain members of that school, in 1906, worked to tone down the more audacious proposals of von Liszt concerning the 'dangerousness'[2] of potential offenders. When the Union celebrated its twenty-fifth anniversary in 1914, it could pride itself on 'representing all schools of thought', but failed to perceive that to do so amounted implicitly to self-repudiation: by 1914, indeed, the Union had gone a long way from the innovating enthusiasm of 1889. If, therefore, a first doctrine of social defence existed at the time of this twenty-fifth anniversary, such a doctrine could no longer be that of the Union as a whole, but only that of one of the tendencies represented.

It may be thought surprising that the tendency in question was not that of von Liszt, who, of course, largely adopted the 1889 programme which he had directly inspired. He supported both

[2] *Rev. int. de droit pénal*, 1951, p. 197.

the introduction of conditional sentences (the suspended sentence, *sursis*, which Carrara rejected in the name of the rule of law and of retributive punishment) and the establishment of preventive measures, and he protested against short prison sentences. He called for a special system applicable to young offenders and he insisted on the need to make use of the criminological sciences, statistics, and comparative law.[3] All these claims have become commonplace today, but at that time they had a peculiar novelty and constituted in themselves a programme of radical reform. Above all, Liszt focused attention on the primary importance of the concept of a penal policy systematically directed towards the control of crime, and he also, in a way that was both temperate and relevant, denounced certain excesses which resulted from a legalistic approach. For all these reasons, active supporters of social defence cannot forget his work.[4]

Nevertheless, it was not he who laid down or formulated the first doctrine of social defence; doubtless because he himself had a different personal doctrine, which was both wider from the philosophical standpoint and narrower from the legal, but also because some of his views and certain aspects of his teaching caused him to hesitate before the postulates of the notion of social defence, even in its first form. Although he had moved away from the rigour of his own teacher, Binding, von Liszt remained over-preoccupied with purely legal technique and too deeply imbued with the spirit of the traditional criminal law to be able to elaborate a theory of social defence which could only exist, up to a point, in opposition to traditional criminal law. Although himself a determinist, Liszt nevertheless wanted to retain the idea of punishment as a legal sanction, considered essentially as a means of protection of the legal order: this paradox resulted from what Professor Hurwitz has rightly called an 'inherent contradiction'.[5] It was in the wake of this purely legal doctrine that preventive measures, instead of being considered as a more flexible, individualized aspect of a general system of penal

[3] See *La Législation pénale comparée* (published by the International Union of Criminal Law), vol. I: *Le Droit criminel des États européens*, by F. von Liszt, Paris, 1894, in particular the Introduction, p. xix ff.

[4] In particular, we should not disregard the efforts of von Liszt to replace the notion of *Vergeltungsstrafe* by that of *Zweckstrafe*. See especially 'Der Zweckgedanke im Strafrecht', *Zeitschrift für die gesamte Strafrechtswissenschaft*, 1882, pp. 33 ff.

[5] *Rev. int. de droit pénal*, 1951, p. 267.

sanctions, were analysed and established as a legal concept distinct from penalties. From the intellectual point of view the effort was remarkable, but this return to the method of abstract entities ultimately introduced more confusion than benefit in the development of the law as applied in continental Europe and the Latin countries generally.[6] Similarly, it cannot be forgotten how Liszt adopted and developed the idea of 'anti-legality' (*Rechtswidrigkeit*) which was destined to enjoy such widespread success among criminal specialists steeped in Italian and German dogmatic thought.[7]

Thus, in spite of the fact that he borrowed from the criminological sciences, von Liszt defended criminal law as a legal discipline against the anthropologists, the sociologists, and the criminologists: whence his success among certain intermediate schools of thought and among the disciples of the 'pure law' school, who tried to bring criminal doctrine back into the framework of legal science from which the positivist movement had shaken it, yet took into account some aspects of the positivist contribution. But this was not the direction taken by the earliest theories of social defence. Thus it is that the 'father' of these theories is neither von Liszt nor van Hamel[8] but Adolphe Prins. This is the doctrine of which a brief outline must now be given, so that it may be seen in its place in the modern evolution of social defence.

II

Adolphe Prins was the first apostle and most thorough interpreter of this first theory. Even in his first large-scale work, *Science pénale et droit positif* (1899), Prins assigned to social defence a noteworthy rôle in the evolution of criminal law, but it was above all in a well-known book entitled *La Défense sociale et les transformations du droit pénal* (1910) that he formulated the doctrine as such.[9] In order to

[6] The Anglo-American system (in the sense in which this expression is understood by continental lawyers) has avoided this problem and its confusions, precisely by refusing to admit that the special notion of preventive measures constitutes a distinct legal category.

[7] See the study by Jiménez de Asúa in the special issue of the *Rev. int. de droit pénal*, 1951, pp. 273 ff.

[8] On Van Hamel, see however the very suggestive study by M. P. Vrij, *Rev. int. de droit pénal*, 1951, pp. 361 ff.

[9] See Paul Cornil, 'Adolphe Prins et la Défense Sociale', *Rev. int. de droit pénal*, 1951, pp. 177 ff.

understand the development of the theories of social defence and in particular of the difference between the theories accepted today and those which were in favour at the beginning of the century, it is necessary to take a quick look at the earlier theories. This can best be done by referring to the views expressed by Prins in a work of sobriety and mature reflexion which remains the earliest classic in this field.

For Prins, the justification for the theory of social defence lay in the inadequacy of the classical idea of moral responsibility. In doctrine, the theory of moral responsibility led to an impossible choice between determinism and free-will; in practice, it led to a multiplication of short prison sentences and an ever-increasing acceptance of the notion of diminished responsibility, leaving society practically defenceless against the most dangerous criminals. Thus criminal law and criminal justice based on moral responsibility failed to provide effective protection for society. Nor did the traditional prison system, which was inspired by the same ideas, provide any better protection, for the system of solitary confinement and the supposedly curative action of the traditional type of prison had proved to be completely ineffective: this is sufficiently indicated by the considerable increase in the incidence of recidivism, especially at the close of the nineteenth century.

According to the earliest partisans of social defence, the root cause of the trouble lay in the fact that theories of moral responsibility tried to assign to criminal law an absolute and unrealizable objective: to *punish* the criminal, in the fullest sense of the word, in exact proportion to the moral fault he had committed. But the purpose of criminal justice, an essentially human process, can never be anything other than relative. Its only purpose must be to ensure in the best possible way the protection of the personal security, life, property, and reputation of citizens. This can be truly achieved, however, only if the idea of moral responsibility is replaced by the notion of the dangerousness of the offender. New means must be found to deal with this dangerousness, and these must be based not on the individual's transient act, but on his permanent state. According to this first view of social defence, the means of dealing with the criminal should even, if need be, involve depriving him of liberty for a longer period, where such action appears essential for the better protection of society. In this connexion it is particularly important to bear in mind the two fundamental categories of dangerous persons, namely abnormal or mentally deficient individuals on the one hand, recidivists or habitual offenders on the other. In order to be effective, therefore, the measures undertaken in this connexion would require the creation of new institutions, especially for abnormal offenders.

This action, however, or at any rate the predominant rôle in dealing with an individual who has committed a crime, will be reserved for the magistrates. In fact, Prins took the view that dangerousness was essentially a legal concept, as distinct from diminished responsibility, which in his view had an essentially medical character. Thus individual liberty was safeguarded even in the face of such new concepts as preventive measures—which differed from traditional punishments—and of indeterminate sentences. This indefinite aspect was in Prins's opinion desirable and even implicit in a new system which was based not on repressive justice but on the protection of society maintained as long as the dangerous condition lasted. Finally, this *judicial* action would need to be completed by preventive action of an *administrative* or more precisely a *social* character, which by trying to prevent the development of 'dangerousness' would endeavour to control this condition before it resulted in delinquent acts. Such preventive action would take the form, in particular, of town-planning schemes, slum-clearance, social legislation designed to prevent certain unfortunates from sinking into misery and despair, and perhaps above all of effective preventive treatment and appropriate education of deficient individuals.

Such, in broad outline, was the first doctrine of social defence as formulated by Prins. Considered as a whole, it will be noticed that this doctrine contains a number of features that should perhaps be underlined. The first point is that although the core of the doctrine indeed involves taking account of the offender's dangerousness, it should perhaps be made absolutely clear that this condition is envisaged exclusively from the standpoint of the State and of society, the individual's own viewpoint being practically ignored, at least provisionally or apparently. The criminal judge is faced with the question whether there exists a dangerousness which would justify or indeed require a measure of social protection. No doubt, the measure decided upon might contribute to the protection of the individual, since it would frequently be of a therapeutic nature. But the protection of the individual would be an indirect result, a kind of side-effect. The essential starting-point remains the protection of society, envisaged as the unique basis of a rational and efficient penal system.

A second characteristic result of this first doctrine was that the new theories were accompanied by a most vigorous reaction against short prison sentences and the excessive leniency of the courts. In his book, published in 1910, Prins reiterates this point several times with an emphasis typical of him. He explains that the courts are guided by humanitarian attitudes of leniency and compassion which are in fact blameworthy in so far as they are injurious to society, which is thus left defenceless: this echoes the thesis already put forward in Garofalo's *Criminology* at the close of the nineteenth century.

Finally, this reaction against the action of the courts is associated with a corresponding reaction against the inadequacies of the system advocated by the 'penitentiary school'. The allegedly reformist system of individual confinement turned out to be ineffective. Writing of persistent offenders, Prins stated that it was ingenuous to believe that by confining such offenders in a prison cell for a short period, adequate safeguards were provided for the security of the social order. Here again, a dangerous and confused humanitarianism weakened the action of the prison system, which had to guarantee the protection of society. Garofalo's influence is likewise evident in all these aspects of Prins's work.

In contrast with these somewhat negative features of his doctrine, certain positive demands are to be found. First among these was the argument that punishments proper should be supplemented by new measures specifically designed to bring about, eventually, a true system of social defence. In particular, Prins refers to the steps which had already been taken in the Norwegian Code of 1902, the Prevention of Crime Act (1908) in England, the statutes in force in Australia and South Africa, and the French statute of 1885 which introduced the system of *relégation*. However, the term preventive measures, which was to be so much employed in the specialist literature of Latin America and the continental countries, is not used in Prins's book. He does not attempt to define or promote a new legal concept: on the contrary, it is fairly characteristic of him that, in calling for measures which differed from traditional forms of punishment, he was only concerned to see such measures incorporated into new legislation, rather along the lines of *preventive detention* in England.

At the same time, the partisans of this first doctrine of social defence called for the introduction of a truly systematic classification of offenders. But here again, although Prins repeats some positivist arguments, he does not take over Lombroso's theories, and is particularly cautious as regards both the allegedly special nature of criminals and even the idea of predisposition towards crime. The importance he assigns to the real but somewhat external symptoms of dangerousness enables him, in effect, to avoid making up his mind in favour of any doctrine of the causes of crime. Thus the unanswerable assertions of a discipline which is too sure of itself and too full of its own importance, are replaced in Prins's work by the more subtle approach of a penal policy at grips with the teachings of a renovated criminal science.

If we peruse the *Bulletin* of the International Union of Criminal Law, or refer to the Congresses on criminal anthropology held in the late nineteenth and early twentieth centuries, or read Prins's book itself, we notice that the measures proposed are in fact limited to two classes of offenders; mental defectives and persistent offenders. It is also noticeable that the notion of preventive measures does not emerge clearly. All things considered, the most widely favoured solution consists of the extension of punishments or the combination with existing penalties of a form of preventive custody. It is with this in mind that Prins refers to the examples of the French statute of 1885 or the English Act of 1908. The organization of the prison system on a scientific basis, though often advocated, is in fact postponed until later. The immediate purpose is to obtain recognition of the dangerous character of certain persons, in order that steps may be taken to prevent them from causing harm for as long a period as possible.

Moreover, it should not be forgotten that, in its first phase, the doctrine of social defence attributed great importance to the maintenance of judicial institutions which would provide effective safeguards for the protection of individual freedom. In this respect, Ferri's views are rather similar, when he makes a point of showing that the dangerousness which finds expression in the commission of an offence is the only situation which falls within the competence of the criminal court, and that acceptance of this new criterion in no way imperils individual freedom, since the accused retains the protection afforded by 'justice according to law'.

As expounded in Prins's work, the doctrine of social defence nevertheless remains far from insensible to the element of social compassion: this is perhaps what distinguishes the moral climate of his doctrine from that of Garofalo. Prins wanted social defence to result in the more effective protection of the poor, the humble, and the miserable, whom contemporary society either leaves defenceless and at the mercy of professional criminals, or even predisposes towards crime.[10] But here again, the protection of the humble, that is to say of certain *individuals*, is not envisaged as anything other than the protection of a social group which should be brought about by vigorous measures of collective security.

In short, therefore, the central idea of this first doctrine of social defence was that of segregating dangerous criminals with a view to subjecting them to a severe régime. This is the form in which social defence may first be said to have become part of the enacted law. Adolphe Prins was certainly justified when he cited in support of his doctrine the French statute of 27 May 1885 or the system set up by article 65 of the Norwegian Penal Code of 1902 (which was subsequently amended to a great extent, however, in particular by a statute of 27 February 1929). This system, like that of the English Act of 1908, involved the introduction of a provisional or final measure of neutralization (*élimination*) for habitual offenders who were deemed incorrigible.[11] Punishment was no longer expected to correct such an individual or detention to amend his ways. The intention was simply to set apart the most dangerous individuals so as to deprive them of the opportunity of causing harm. The idea of an 'eliminatory' sanction was so strong that Garofalo had even proposed that such incorrigible individuals should be subjected to the eliminatory sanction *par excellence*—capital punishment. Without going as far as this, von Liszt and Carl Stooss (author of the preliminary draft of the Swiss Criminal Code of 1893) showed their attachment to the system of *élimination*,[12] whereas Prins, who was abolitionist both by his personal sympathies and by intellectual conviction, himself sought a

[10] *La Défense sociale et les transformations du droit pénal*, pp. 86, 90 ff.

[11] Cf. N. S. Timasheff, 'The Treatment of Persistent Offenders outside of the United States', *Journ. of Criminal Law and Criminology*, vol. XXX, 1939-1940, pp. 455 ff.

[12] C. Stooss, *Der Geist der modernen Strafgesetzgebung*, Vienna, 1906.

measure of 'neutralization' rather than of radical 'elimination'. In France, even Tarde appeared to favour this severe approach. Referring to individuals who lacked all moral sense, even as the result of cerebral malformation, he refused to treat them as sick persons who were outside the scope of the criminal law: 'although acknowledged to be colour-blind, a man may preserve his individual station and remain within his social group; but should he be recognized as morally deficient from birth, that is to say anti-social,[13] he must be treated as a social outlaw, as if he were a tiger which had escaped from a menagerie . . . he should be expelled and excommunicated from society. Convict settlements and prisons are in fact the expression—and hitherto have been the sole expression—of this greater or lesser excommunication'.[14] The notion of 'eliminatory methods' is thus fairly widespread. The merit of Prins is twofold: On the moral plane, he does not go to the brutal extremes of the theory of 'elimination', and he remembers that the being Tarde classifies as anti-social is, after all, a man. On the scientific plane, he incorporates the method of segregation or neutralization into a general system of criminal law and a reasoned penal policy.

The legislative movement of the beginning of the century in fact seemed to indicate that this form of approach was the right one. The measures of social defence which were introduced into statute law were exclusively determined by the idea of segregating certain incorrigible and dangerous offenders so as to subject them to a protracted or perpetual penalty. Consequently, it mattered little whether the decision applied to them was technically a penalty or a preventive measure. French law considered relegation to be 'an additional penalty of a perpetual and colonial character'. In Saleilles's view, relegation was 'directly inspired by the Italian school'. Such incorrigible offenders, he wrote,

[13] It will be noted that this word is used in a special sense which is by no means—as some have argued—the creation of the most recent social defence theorists.

[14] *La Criminalité comparée*, 1907, p. 35. This passage illustrates the acceptance—at any rate implicit—of a kind of determinism (which the same author elsewhere rejects), and also the curious mode of reasoning which, admitting the need for practical measures of social defence, still tries to make these conform to the traditional pattern of punishment, by maintaining an element of moral condemnation which is rather out of place. Such a policy of protection does not fit into a system of social defence that has been thoroughly thought out, as is the case with Prins. The same line of reasoning leads Tarde to accept the death penalty and even to attempt its justification (*La Philosophie pénale*, Paris, 1890, pp. 521 ff.).

'should be segregated and banned from society. A colony should be sacrificed for this purpose and set apart to receive those outcasts from social life who should be sent there: here is a penalty worthy of a true criminal policy, but it is certainly not a penalty as understood by the criminal law. It is only a measure of social policy.'[15] Thus legislative action, spontaneously and almost instinctively, as it were, tends to organize a *defensive reaction* against the most dangerous individuals. The first social defence movement became aware of this legislative trend, which was still to a large extent potential rather than actual, and deliberately set out to channel these tendencies into a doctrine of penal policy which could then be defined, precisely and rigorously, as a doctrine of social defence in the original meaning of the term.

III

Hitherto we have endeavoured to describe how there emerged what must be called the first doctrine of social defence, and to illustrate the form taken by that doctrine. Afterwards, and going beyond the influence of positivism and of the International Union of Criminal Law, we showed how Prins for the first time proposed a doctrinal synthesis of social defence in which the new autonomous theory was confronted with criminal law viewed both in historical perspective and in the light of contemporary reality. It was Prins who took the historic initiative of filling out the already current expression 'social defence' with this doctrinal content, so as to fashion it for the first time into the conscious expression of a certain form of penal policy. To complete the picture it would probably be necessary to show also how other writers of the same period, without really achieving such a doctrinal synthesis, could sometimes speak the same language: from Lacassagne to Tarde and Saleilles in France, not to mention writers of the same period in Germany or Italy, the choice would certainly not be difficult. There is neither place nor time for such an enumeration at this point, as for the moment it is not intended to give a complete history of the social defence movement, but merely to indicate, in summary fashion, its main stages of development. It can simply be noted that in the writings and speeches of

[15] *L'Individualisation de la peine*, 2nd ed., 1909, p. 189.

Brockway, the reformer of the Elmira institution and the long-neglected apostle of indeterminate sentences, there are numerous statements unquestionably inspired by the spirit, if not the explicit ideas, of the first theory of social defence: this was especially the case during the series of penitentiary Congresses held before the outbreak of the 1914 War. Again, although the Spanish 'correctionalist' school of the early part of the century did not formulate an explicit doctrine of social defence, its own doctrine, which must not be neglected in the history of modern penal ideas, comes close to Prins's teaching on a good many essential points and even foreshadows certain later tendencies of fully-developed social defence theories. The conclusion may therefore be drawn that if Prins was a pioneer and an innovator, he was not an isolated figure in his time, and his principal distinction lay not so much in having created a school or launched a doctrine, as in having made a reasoned synthesis, for the first time, of tendencies that were scattered and occasionally still disparate.

Prins gave such complete and representative expression to the ideas of his time that he had no disciples, properly so called, and no immediate successor. His teaching crystallized a great many trends but did not constitute a school. In Belgium, when Vandervelde and Vervaeck tried to translate Prins's ideas into practice, each in his own special field and with his own special methods, they did not openly claim to be applying a new doctrine. With them there opened what may be described as a second, tangible stage in the development of social defence, when theoretical considerations gave way to practical achievements. The nature of this second period, and the direction taken by it, must now be discussed. It will be seen that it was this second stage which, by a sort of inherent necessity, led to the doctrinal renewal of the third stage, from which the new social defence movement really emerged.

The earlier stage had already been marked by the appearance in statutory form of the first social defence measures. In a remarkable report to the Sixth International Congress for Criminal Law, in Rome, concerning the unification of punishments and preventive measures, Grispigni recalled that Luigi Lucchino, though 'a proud adversary and a severe critic of the positivist school', had introduced into the Code of 1889 various innovations corresponding to 'those which we were subsequently to term preventive measures'.[16] But it should not be forgotten that the first genuine preventive measure to be given statutory form at the end of the nineteenth century was *relégation* as provided by the French statute of 1885, which was imitated soon afterwards in the Portuguese statute of 1892, and later by the Argentinian statute of 1903, in the barely different form of deportation to the remote southern territories of that country. In 1891, Belgium readopted the old idea of administrative internment following a judicial decision, in a form which stressed the element of social defence: this was to make possible a more efficient control of vagrancy. In New South Wales, the Habitual Criminals Act (1905) introduced into the British Empire the concept of preventive detention, which was taken up in England by the Prevention of Crime Act (1908), an enactment which in many respects, as already suggested, is truly a law of social defence, although it does not use that term.[17] And there is hardly any need to recall these enactments, from the 1878 Massachusetts statute onwards, which introduced or extended the probation system in the legislation of the Anglo-American world,[18] whereas the countries of continental Europe or Latin America all in turn adopted laws relating to suspended sentences (*sursis*), in imitation of the Belgian statute of 1888 and the French *loi Bérenger* of 1891. To this legislative movement should be added the similar movement in the United States which gave statutory expression to indeterminate sentences[19] and yet another movement—also North American in origin—which by

[16] These measures concerned: the internment of dangerous mental defectives in mental hospitals (art. 46), the committal of mentally deficient persons and alcoholics to a special institution where they would remain throughout their sentence (arts. 47 and 48), and measures available with regard to children and young persons (arts. 53 to 55). See the text of Grispigni's report in *Rev. int. de droit pénal*, 1954, pp. 760-61.

[17] On the 1908 Act, seen in the light of penal policy as regards habitual offenders, see Norval Morris, *The Habitual Criminal*, London, 1950, pp. 53 ff.

[18] On this movement and on the development of the probation system in the United States, the United Kingdom, and the Commonwealth see *Probation and Related Measures* (United Nations Publications), 1951; Max Grünhut, *Practical Results and Financial Aspects of Adult Probation in Selected Countries* (United Nations Publications), 1954; *The Results of Probation, a Report of the Cambridge Department of Criminal Science*, in the series *English Studies in Criminal Science*, published by L. Radzinowicz, London and New York, 1958; Marc Ancel, *Report on Indeterminate Sentences* (United Nations Publications), 1953.

[19] See H. E. Barnes and N. K. Teeters, *New Horizons in Criminology*, 3rd ed., 1959, pp. 566 ff.; E. H. Sutherland, *Principles of Criminology*, 3rd ed., pp. 515 ff.; Thorsten Sellin, 'L'Expérience de la sentence indéterminée aux Etats-Unis', *Rev. de Science crim.*, 1951, pp. 417 ff.

a form of legislative contagion, significantly enough, led to the widespread institution of juvenile courts which were established in order to remove juvenile delinquents from the repressive system normally applied to adult offenders.[20]

These facts are unquestionable. Academic writers, however, and von Liszt foremost among them, were right in hailing Stooss's well-known scheme of 1893 as the first complete legislative embodiment of a rational system of preventive measures. Now it was only with the Swiss Code of 1937 that Stooss's project found legislative expression, and although the Norwegian Code of 1902 —certain radical aspects of which disturbed the neo-classicists of the time[21]—inaugurated the series of twentieth-century criminal codes, its innovations were still limited, and even the preventive measures which it introduced did not form a planned social defence legislation. Until the 1914–18 War, social defence measures made only a sporadic appearance in enacted legislation, in an exceptional or, we might say, experimental fashion. So in the 'incubation' period which came to an end with the First World War, the concepts of preventive measures and of social defence are expressed in academic writings and in these alone: at that time the term and even the idea of social defence had no precise significance and indeed no real meaning in the realm of applied or enacted law.

The situation was to be curiously reversed during the next phase which falls roughly between the two World Wars and which may be described as the second stage in the evolution of social defence. The theoretical controversies had not of course, disappeared, but they no longer had the liveliness or the passionate tone characteristic of the earlier period: positivist and neo-classical antagonism had lost its virulence. The eclectic approach seemed triumphant, whether in its agnostic form as in France, or in Italy in the form of a legal theory, particularly with the 'pure law' school. Almost everywhere, in this period, it is taught that the great doctrinal controversies on fundamental philosophical principles have become outmoded by a legislative evolution which

[20] See *Comparative Survey on Juvenile Delinquency*, Part I, North America, by P. W. Tappan, and Part II, Europe, by J. L. Costa (Publications of the Department of Economic and Social Affairs of the United Nations), 2 vols., New York, 1952.

[21] See the foreword by Émile Garçon to the French translation of the new Norwegian Criminal Code by du Monceau, *Nouveau Code pénal norvégien*, Paris, 1903. This introductory essay is significant not only for its scholarly interest but also by the doctrinal misgivings which it expresses.

incorporates into the law in force what is worthy of retention in the two great conflicting systems. In some circles this attitude was taken up all the more easily in so far as the times were marked by a strongly authoritarian trend, and such an approach enabled the zealots for the new political systems to shut themselves up in the mere exegesis of the written law, which was thus carefully preserved from confrontation with the requirements of natural law, as in Beccaria's day, or with the teachings of the social sciences, freely investigated, as in the time of Lombroso. So for many reasons the doctrinal controversies settled down into a middle position which reassured the 'pure lawyers', who, moreover, rightly emphasize the *via media* of the new penal legislation.[22]

The term 'social defence' certainly did not disappear from the legal vocabulary. By and large, it was even more generally used than in the earlier period. But it had lost, to some extent, the particular colouring given it by the positivists, the dynamism it acquired with Liszt, or the doctrinal significance given it by Prins. This was the time at which the term tended to oscillate between the numerous different interpretations noted in our first chapter, and its only technically precise meaning was related to a particular and restricted system of preventive measures applied to mental defectives and persistent offenders. By a strange reversal of the positions adopted in the preceding period, social defence then moved from the realm of theory to that of enacted law. This was clearly asserted by the Belgian statute of 9 April 1930, but this enactment was no more isolated in its time than was Adolphe Prins, in the doctrinal field, in his. Whereas at the time Prins was working out his first theory the legislative applications of social defence were few and far between, almost unconscious and unavowed, as it were, in the following period the doctrinal eclipse of social defence corresponded with its determined introduction into actual legislation.

We are then confronted with the particularly significant factor of the systematic absorption of preventive measures into enacted law, at any rate in the countries of continental Europe and of Latin America. It may be said that from 1919 to 1939 all new criminal legislation takes account of such measures and assigns to them a large rôle. The period between the wars saw the

[22] See Rappaport, *La media via du Code pénal polonais*, 1935, p. 227, 1936, p. 209; the same tendency is also to be found in the Greek penal code of 1951, see Elias Gaphos, *International Review of Criminal Policy*, 1952, pp. 120 ff.

emergence of a series of carefully drafted criminal codes of unquestionable technical quality.[23] This was especially the case with the Spanish Code of 1928, which, though stillborn from the legislative point of view, was nevertheless of considerable importance and influence as regards criminal science. The same may be said, especially, of the Yugoslav Code of 1929, the Italian and Danish Codes of 1930, the Polish Code of 1932, the Rumanian of 1936, and the Swiss of 1937. To these European codes may be added, in Latin America, the Peruvian Code of 1924, the Mexican Codes of 1928 and 1931, the Cuban Code curiously entitled 'Social Defence Code', the Colombian Criminal Code of 1936, and the Brazilian Code of 1940. Even where preventive measures were not formally recognized under that new technical name, even where they were not given separate treatment in a particular chapter of the code in question, a place was found for them, as in the Argentinian Code of 1922, which, without explicitly mentioning such measures, recognized at least three. Side by side with the new Codes, there are numerous examples of special statutes enacting preventive measures, as for instance in Sweden (1927), Hungary (1928), Czechoslovakia (1929), Belgium (with the well-known 1930 statute already cited), Finland (1932), Spain and Germany (1933). In the U.S.A., although the statutes in question did not mention preventive measures, and although legal writers did not even acknowledge the existence of this new category, social defence measures made their appearance. Thus the Baumes Act of New York (1926) was followed by a spate of legislation providing for the lifelong detention of persistent criminals after a certain number of convictions; and later, on the eve of the Second World War, a new and parallel legislative movement instituted the confinement of sexual psychopaths—measures adopted successively in California, Illinois, Michigan, and Minnesota.[24]

[23] On these Codes and on criminal legislation between the two World Wars, see Marc Ancel, 'The Collection of European Penal Codes and the Study of Comparative Law, reprint, *University of Pennsylvania Law Review*, vol. 106, No. 3, January 1958, pp. 360 ff., especially the bibliography cited p. 363.

[24] For the constitutionality of the Minnesota statute, see *Pearson v. Probate Court of Ramsay County* (1940) 309 11-3-270; on these statutes, cf. Sutherland, 'The Sexual Psychopath Laws', *Journ. of Criminal Law and Criminology*, 1950, pp. 543 ff.; Tappan, 'Sentences for Sex Criminals', same Review, Sept.-Oct. 1951, pp. 332 ff.; Gibbens, 'Recent Trends in the Management of Psychopathic Offenders', *British Journ. of Delinquency*, vol. II: 2, Oct. 1951, pp. 103 ff.; Glueck, *After Conduct of Discharged Offenders*, London, 1949, pp. 98 ff.

These various legislative measures were not always unaccompanied by a certain confusion. In any case they led to a 'mixed' system comprising both traditional punishments and new measures, generally called preventive measures or social defence measures. In many instances the legislation in question simply enumerated these measures without providing a systematic classification. This was so, for example, with the Polish Code of 1932, the Spanish Code of 1928, and the Cuban Code of 1936. In most of these cases, the legislation merely provided these measures for such and such a category of offenders, without any attempt to construct a complete system in which the respective spheres of application of punishments and preventive measures would be strictly defined. The Italian Code of 1930, perhaps the most ambitious of them all, still kept to solutions of a largely empirical character.

Moreover, the legislation which enacted measures of this kind was in a continual state of flux, coming into being progressively and proceeding, fairly often, by successive stages. Thus the English notion of preventive detention, introduced by the 1908 Act, went through a long period of uncertainty in England, and aroused judicial hostility, before achieving a new status in the Criminal Justice Act (1948), which enacted other novel measures for the treatment of offenders.[25]

In Sweden, preventive measures were introduced, organized, and extended in several successive stages, by statutes of 1927, 1937, 1945, and 1947.[26] In Portugal, a decree of 1936 reformed the system of relegation which dated from 1892, and filled in the fragmentary provisions of the law of 20 July 1912 (which envisaged the committal of certain individuals to a sort of workhouse), by instituting a more coherent system based on the notion of dangerousness and the classification of offenders.[27] The multiplicity of schemes, not only in Europe but perhaps even more in

[25] Lionel W. Fox, *The English Prison and Borstal Systems*, London, 1952, pp. 315 ff.; Max Grünhut, 'The Treatment of Persistent Offenders', *Journ. of Crim. Science*, vol. II, 1950, pp. 65 ff.

[26] See Marc Ancel's report on *Mesures de sûreté en matière criminelle* (Publications of the I.P.P.C.), Melun, 1950, pp. 215 ff.

[27] *Ibid*, pp. 193 ff.; cf. P. Cannat, *Droit pénal et politique pénitentiaire au Portugal*, Paris, 1946; V. A. Duarte Faveiro, *Prevenção criminal* (*medidas de segurança*), Coimbra, 1952; see also J. Beleza dos Santos, *Nova organização prisional portuguesa* (*principios e realizações*), Coimbra, 1947.

the countries of Latin America, is a sufficient illustration both of the fluctuations of these reformist movements and of their intensity.

To complete the picture, we should also take into account the movement in favour of the preventive treatment of crime, in this period and on the eve of the Second World War. This movement took up some of the ideas developed by the first theories of social defence, in particular the notion of preventive measures, the classification of offenders, and the need for specialized psychiatric departments. On the other hand the same movement already foreshadowed the new theories of social defence in the form in which these were to be developed after the 1939-45 War, stressing the ideas both of assistance by means of re-education and of the need to organize preventive treatment on the basis of a more complete study of the human personality. In France, the movement for the preventive treatment of crime was marked by the creation of the *Société de prophylaxie criminelle* and of the *Société d'hygiène mentale*, which were very active before the War under the impetus, in particular, of Dr Toulouse. The same movement made its appearance in Switzerland, where a society for criminal prevention was established, and in Belgium where it inspired the particularly fervent work of Dr Vervaeck in the period before 1940.[28] A significant echo of this trend is to be found in the work of the first International Congress for Criminology, which was held in Rome in 1938 and where one of the questions on the agenda dealt specifically with the organization of the preventive treatment of crime in the principal countries represented.[29]

This was an interesting movement, for it contained the beginnings of a doctrinal renewal based on a new awareness of the criminological sciences, apart from purely legal considerations. The collaboration which it urged between the medical and legal professions,[30] the attentive study of the offender's personality, the suggestions designed to change the rules of procedure or to make them more flexible—all these could hardly have failed soon to provoke a reappraisal of values in the doctrinal sphere. Once

[28] See Vervaeck, *Le crime et la peine*, 1934; cf. on the Crime Prevention Section of the *Ligue belge d'hygiène mentale*, *Rev. de droit pénal et de criminologie*, 1938, pp. 536 ff.

[29] See the Proceedings of the Congress, *Atti del I. Congresso Internazionale di Criminologia*, Rome, 1939, vol. V, pp. 9 ff.

[30] See P. Schiff, 'La prophylaxie criminelle et la collaboration médico-judiciaire', *Rev. de Science crim.*, 1936, pp. 479 ff.

committed to this approach, those who were anxious to go beyond the stage of administrative empiricism or of legislative experiment would probably soon have tried to give new thought to the criminal problem and to revive an active concept of penal policy which would go further than that of the beginning of the century. But this scientific movement, as well as the practical achievements of social defence in the period between the two Wars, was to be frustrated—a few years before the outbreak of war in 1939—by the violent counter-attack of ideas of repressive punishment and intimidation. This retrograde move was due to the coming to power of totalitarian régimes in various countries and to the manifestation, even in the democratic states, of an authoritarian current of opinion which imparted a new direction to the criminal law of the time. It is this antagonism between social defence and authoritarian criminal law that marks the close of our second period and also, as will be seen, the beginning of the third, when out of adversity there was finally to emerge a new social defence movement.

IV

At first sight it might have been thought that the social defence movement would be reinforced or at any rate facilitated by the advent of totalitarian systems. The Italian criminal code of 1930, which at the time was greeted as a 'fascist criminal code' and asserted by its author to be a 'political code',[31] was to introduce preventive measures into Italy in a systematic form. Furthermore, it was the Hitler régime which by a statute of 1933 established a system of preventive measures in Germany,[32] whereas another statute of 14 July 1933 introduced sterilization, imposed on certain persons for eugenic reasons. The Soviet criminal code of 1926, for its part, purported to replace the old punishments by 'measures of social defence', inspired by certain concepts, and especially by a terminology, largely borrowed from the teachings of positivism.[33]

[31] *Code pénal du Royaume d'Italie*, translated into French by P. de Casabianca, Paris, 1932. Introduction, p. xv.

[32] R. Béraud, *Les mesures de sûreté en droit allemand d'après la loi du 24 novembre 1933*, Aix-en-Provence, 1937.

[33] See L. Jiménez de Asúa, *Derecho penal sovietico*, Buenos Aires, 1947, esp. pp, 83 ff.; H. Donnedieu de Vabres, *La Politique criminelle des États autoritaires*, Paris, 1938, pp. 142 ff.; Marc Ancel, 'Introduction au système de droit pénal soviétique (De la Révolution d'octobre aux Codes de 1960)', in *La Réforme pénale soviétique*, Paris, 1962 , with the references there cited.

Any affinity between social defence and the system just described is however merely apparent, for the totalitarian régimes stressed above all the retributive and intimidating aspects of punishment. The Italian criminal code of 1930 considerably increased the severity of the penalties applied, and this, furthermore, followed upon the restoration by the Fascist régime of the death penalty, which had no part in the 1889 Code. A similar preoccupation was even more noticeable and assertive in National Socialist criminal law, which in its official doctrine exalted the protection of the community, the *Volk*.

A particularly striking example of this attitude might be found in the transformation of the 1923 Convention among the State Governments of Germany on the 'Principles concerning the application of sentences involving deprivation of liberty' (*Reichstagsgrundsätze*), article 48 of which laid down that the purpose of such application was the moral improvement of convicted offenders through work. From 1934 onwards, a new text asserted that the application of the penalty aimed at expiating the harm caused by the offence and that sentences involving deprivation of liberty should entail an appreciable element of pain, so as to prevent recidivism. Thus the notion of exemplary punishment re-emerged, and the special prevention envisaged developed into collective intimidation. A statute of 22 July 1940, further amending the said article 48, declared again in still more unmistakable terms that in the application of sentences involving deprivation of liberty the community must be protected, the harmful act expiated, and further criminal acts prevented. So the prevention of crime appeared to be no more than the consequence of a system of expiation and intimidation. Moreover, one of the exponents of Nazi doctrine went so far as to announce that retribution was essential, because the *Volk* required protection, and this should be effected, if necessary, at the cost of the life of the individual, since the safeguarding of the 'people' must take absolute precedence over private interests. Asserting that one must 'chastise in order to cure', the same writer criticized liberal criminal law for having made the re-education of the offender the central aspect of criminal law.[34]

[34] See K. Siegert, *Grundzüge des Strafrechts im neuen Staate*, 1934; Stock, *Die Strafe als Dienst am Volke*, 1933; F. Exner, *Sinnwandel in der neuesten Entwicklung der Strafe*, Berlin, 1944, pp. 24 ff.

But the current opinion that found fullest expression among the doctrinaire exponents of National Socialist criminal law was not restricted to the totalitarian states. The criminal law of the years immediately preceding the Second World War tended everywhere to acquire an authoritarian character, and the outbreak of hostilities could only encourage this tendency.[35] Even in England, during the war, there existed the system of administrative internment. The strengthening of the machinery of repression seemed to take precedence over all other considerations of legislative policy. One example, in France, is to be found in the statutes and more particularly the statutory regulations of the period immediately before the War of 1939: the reform of the rules concerning offences against State security, and the repression of treason and espionage, was carried out with such severity that France, almost alone among the countries occupied between 1940 and 1945, had no need to amend this legislation in order to punish acts of collaboration with the occupying power as one form of having dealings with the enemy. This was a general movement, and one eminent criminal scientist has pointed out the 'monstrous' increase, between 1930 and 1940, in the number of punishable acts.[36]

During the whole of this period, therefore, the idea of social defence, with that of the preventive treatment of crime, suffered an eclipse. Besides, one of the first acts of the Vichy government in the sphere of penal policy had been the suppression of the *Conseil supérieur de prophylaxie criminelle* which had been established by decree in 1936: its name had come to be suspect in the eyes of a government with authoritarian leanings. But the excesses of totalitarianism, particularly in its Nazi form, inevitably produced after 1945 a reaction against the contempt displayed by authoritarian criminal law with regard to the human personality and the preservation of individual freedom: this was particularly the case in continental Europe which had just been liberated. Furthermore, it is significant that the authoritarian systems should have displayed marked hostility towards social defence ideas, since those systems meant to return to the most primitive ideas of punishment and retaliation, which would replace the idea of re-education and

[35] Cf. the Preface by H. Donnedieu de Vabres to the 2nd edition of his *Traité de droit criminel et de législation pénale comparée*, 1943.

[36] Pompe, 'Les Trois Degrés du droit pénal', *Rev. de droit pénal et de criminologie*, 1949, p. 799.

even that of social protection, both founded on the practical application of measures of an extra-penal character. In the U.S.S.R. the pseudo-positivist period from 1919 to 1922 (date of the first Soviet Criminal Code), and the period leading up to the Code of 1926, were followed by a deliberate return to notions of collective intimidation and pitiless repression where the concept of dangerousness was itself employed for political purposes and as a weapon against the enemies of the régime.[37]

Thus the period of authoritarian criminal law was marked by a definite reaction against social defence ideas, though this reaction was in the long run beneficial to their development, for the end of the Second World War was followed by a revolt of the human conscience against the totalitarian disregard of the dignity of the human person. It was not merely a historical coincidence that the London Declaration of 1945 and the Nuremberg trials should have developed the notion of 'crimes against humanity'. Soon the Universal Declaration of Human Rights tried to embody in a formal document an assertion of those fundamental safeguards to which a free citizen is entitled in modern society, thus giving expression to the international legal conscience at a decisive turning-point in the history of the world. Although some of these high hopes have subsequently been disappointed, it is nonetheless worth pointing out the force of a movement which caused all governments to adhere, formally at any rate, to this new Declaration of Rights.

Naturally, and as it were, inevitably, this general movement of opinion enabled tendencies to emerge and develop which were to constitute the doctrine of new social defence. It is significant, in the first place, that several constitutions of the immediate post-war period purported either to abolish the death penalty[38] or to limit repressive punishment in various ways, or again to lay down the principles of a penitentiary system which should at the

[37] Article 6 of the Criminal Code of the R.S.F.S.R. (1926) provided that 'any action or omission directed against the Soviet system and harmfully affecting the legal order established by the power of the workers and peasants, is considered *socially dangerous*'. The same provision is also found in the Bulgarian Code of 1952 (art. 3) and the Hungarian Code of 1951. The political use made of the concept of dangerousness thus tends to become a characteristic feature of the criminal law of the people's democracies.

[38] See Marc Ancel's reports on capital punishment, to the Council of Europe, *The Death Penalty in European Countries*, Strasbourg, 1962, and to the United Nations, *Capital Punishment*, New York, 1963.

same time be a social action.[39] Prison reform was undertaken or resumed almost everywhere, and the term *penitentiary reform* acquired a new meaning and content, endeavouring to go beyond the practical, empirical approach of the period between the Wars and to achieve a social humanism conceived in an entirely new spirit.[40]

It was then that the expression 'social defence' once again quite naturally emerged from obscurity. But ever since the first Congress for Social Defence held at San Remo in 1947, and the decision of the United Nations in 1948 to place itself in the forefront of the movement regarding 'the prevention of crime and the treatment of offenders' it had been understood that the expression 'social defence' could no longer be used, as by Ferri, merely to designate a particular function of criminal justice; nor could it be used, as between the two World Wars, to describe the extra-penal measures which modern legislation enacted in somewhat empirical fashion for the protection of society; or even—as by Prins—to define the doctrine which strove to embody this idea of protection in a scientifically worked out penal policy. Scandinavian penal reform[41] expressly acknowledged the inspiration of an ideal of social defence that was often invoked as such and that derived a new scope from the work and authority of Karl Schlyter. Finally, it may be said that the movement which, in England, led to the passing of the Criminal Justice Act (1948) was inspired at least in large part by the same ideal, although the words 'social defence' were not used.[42]

So in the special climate of the post-war period, beyond the inhuman excesses which had disgraced this century, specialists of all countries who also felt themselves to be men of goodwill, sought to rediscover a great tradition and in a new spirit to give

[39] See in this connexion, and on the development of modern ideas concerning the function of punishment, A. Molinario, 'Les Grands Problèmes actuels du droit pénal', *Rev. int. de droit comp.*, 1949, pp. 39 ff., esp. pp. 51-53.

[40] See P. Cornil, 'Les Problèmes de droit pénal appliqué et les nouvelles tendances en la matière', *Rev. de droit pénal et de criminologie*, 1950-51, p. 489; International Penal and Penitentiary Foundation, *Modern Methods of Penal Treatment.*

[41] See Karl Schlyter, 'Les Réformes suédoises dans le domaine des mesures défensives contre la criminalité', *Rev. de Science crim.*, 1947, pp. 191 ff.; G. Simson, 'Le Traitement des délinquants d'habitude en Suède', same *Revue*, 1952, pp. 359 ff.; Thorsten Sellin, *Recent Penal Legislation in Sweden*, Stockholm, 1947.

[42] Cf. the book by Sir Lionel Fox already cited, *British Prisons and Borstal Systems*, 1952.

fresh thought to the problem of crime, envisaged as a social problem. Then the term 'social defence' naturally became a kind of spiritual link between men of different backgrounds, and between tendencies that were at the same time different and convergent. That is why the expression gained ground everywhere in a particularly vigorous fashion, to the astonishment of some and the disquiet of others. As has already been observed, even the ways in which the term was abused served to illustrate its vitality and its dynamism. Because of this widespread diffusion of the term, all could become aware—at least if they were unprejudiced—that a new phenomenon was being prepared, or coming into being, in the history of criminal ideas and indeed in the development of what at the beginning of the century was called criminal science. This phenomenon is the existence of a genuinely new social defence movement of which we should become clearly aware and which must be placed in its doctrinal context as precisely as possible.

Before doing so, one remark needs to be made. This new social defence movement first obtained a hearing at the Congresses of San Remo and Liège in 1947 and 1949, and owes much to the moving spirit of these Congresses, Filippo Gramatica, who was also the first President of the International Society of Social Defence. We shall have occasion to notice, and the duty to point out, that *new* social defence should not be confused either with the resolutions of these Congresses or, especially, with the personal views of the President of that Society: certain necessary contradictions and disagreements will have to be underlined. However, the important and useful part played by Gramatica must not be ignored. The founder of the study-centre for social defence at Genoa had the signal merit of being one of the very first to grasp the meaning and the value of the new social defence movement, and to try not only to ensure its development but also to provide it with a doctrine. It is therefore fitting that at the close of this too brief history of social defence, a fair tribute should be paid to him.

Chapter Four

THE PENAL POLICY OF SOCIAL DEFENCE AND ITS EFFECT ON CONTEMPORARY SYSTEMS

AFTER OUTLINING first the origins of the social defence movement and then the main stages of its evolution, we must place it in an accurate perspective from both a positive and a negative standpoint. However, it would be desirable further to clarify a few points concerning the practical consequences of contemporary developments. This does not, for the moment, involve examining the penal policy of social defence as such, but of determining from outside, so to speak, that policy's general effect on the different systems of reaction against crime that are at present in force. But before embarking on this rapid comparative study, we must define the penal policy of social defence as it takes shape in the final stage of its development: only through such a definition, even though it be provisional, can we understand the effect of the movement on contemporary penal systems. This chapter will examine these two points in turn.

I

It has been shown how a new social defence movement developed in the years immediately following the Second World War. This was indeed a movement of penal policy, since its object was a reorganization along novel lines of the social reaction against crime. The movement took root between 1945 and 1949, but afterwards split into two different tendencies which on certain points even became steadfastly opposed to each other. This point needs to be thoroughly understood.

Attention has already been drawn to the historical importance of the study-centre on social defence founded by Gramatica at

Genoa in 1945. This was the starting-point of the movement, which gathered momentum with the convocation at San Remo—again under the impetus of Gramatica—of the first International Social Defence Congress. International recognition was first achieved in 1948 with the institution of the social defence section of the United Nations, which admirably defined the purpose of the movement as 'the prevention of crime and the treatment of offenders'. The second Congress, which met at Liège in 1949, demonstrated the extensive interest aroused in the movement and resulted in the setting up, during the Congress, of the International Society of Social Defence, Gramatica being forthwith elected chairman.[1] It was then a case of asserting the international existence of the penal policy of social defence and of drawing up a first statement of principles. It was Graven who was mainly responsible for drafting the resolutions of the San Remo and Liège Congresses. All the supporters of a modern penal policy were then in agreement on the need to unite their efforts so as to promote the better understanding of their views and to organize a determined campaign for penal reform.[2]

Differences of opinion, however, were soon to appear, and they were not unfruitful. The Third International Congress was not due to meet until 1954, in Antwerp. In the meantime two preparatory meetings were held, one in Europe, at San Marino, and the other in Latin America, at Caracas in Venezuela.[3] At these two preparatory meetings, Gramatica and his closest followers worked out a bold theory which aroused serious misgivings among other leading members of the International Society for Social Defence. The Society's executive committee in fact grouped together all criminal lawyers and other specialists anxious to promote penal reform along humanist lines,[4] but many of them were concerned that such a reform should preserve the essential legal framework which the civilized world derived in large part, from the 'philosophic' doctrine of the late eighteenth century.

As a result, several members of the executive committee asked for a 'minimum programme' for the International Society for

[1] *See Rev. de Science crim.*, 1947, p. 561; 1949, p. 819.

[2] See *Rev. de Science crim.*, 1949, p. 823; cf. the *Bull. de la Société int. de Défense sociale*, esp. 1955, No. 1.

[3] See in particular *Rev. de Science crim.*, 1952, pp. 146 and 307.

[4] This included, in particular, P. Cornil, J. Graven, S. Hurwitz, L. Jiménez de Asúa, I. Strahl.

Social Defence.[5] It was not a case of stultifying the movement by the definition of dogma, or of converting this movement of penal policy into a 'school' of criminal law or criminology. The only problem was to draw up a body of fundamental rules which would be acceptable to *all* supporters of social defence. Afterwards, as a purely personal matter, each one might adopt more radical views, which could not then commit the society as a whole or be put forward as the *only* expression of modern social defence. This proposal was adopted, and the minimum programme, mainly drafted by Ivar Strahl, was subsequently ratified by the Society.

The programme has only to be perused for its importance to be understood: here, indeed, one is confronted with two different conceptions of the penal policy of social defence, one which may be described as radical or even extreme, and the other moderate or reformist. The first was brilliantly defended by Gramatica, the second drew its support from those who had sponsored and adhered to the minimum programme. These two conceptions must be briefly distinguished.[6]

Gramatica's personal views had already been expounded in broad outline, under the name of *subjective criminal law*, before the Second World War. From 1945 onwards, he revived and elaborated his theory in a long series of articles, monographs, reports, and speeches, the most important of which were published in the *Rivista di difesa sociale*. One of these studies, boldly entitled 'La lotta contra la pena' (The Fight against Punishment),[7] aroused a good deal of interest, but also a good many doubts.[8] The doctrine eventually found its fullest expression in the *Principi di difesa sociale*, which Gramatica published in 1961.[9]

Discussion of the theory as a whole will be reserved for a later chapter; at this point it is intended simply to note the essential

[5] See the text of the minimum programme in *Rev. de Science crim.*, 1954, p. 807, and Marc Ancel's commentary in the same *Revue*, 1955, p. 562.

[6] The confrontation of the two points of view is very well illustrated in the *Traité de droit pénal et de criminologie* by Bouzat and Pinatel, Paris, 1963, vol. I (by P. Bouzat), No. 50.

[7] *Riv. di difesa sociale*, 1947, pp. 3-15.

[8] See the report of the discussion at the *Premières Journées franco-latino-américaines* organized in Paris in 1948 by the Society of Comparative Legislation (*Bulletin* of that Society, 1948, pp. 945 ff.), on which occasion Professor L. Hugueney, of the Faculty of Law of the University of Paris, pointed out that to speak of 'fighting against punishment' was anomalous, since it was a case of fighting against crime.

[9] A French edition was published in 1963.

features of the theory. In Gramatica's view, the object of social defence is to secure not so much the protection of society as its regeneration, which is to be achieved by an amelioration or 'socialization' of the individual. Society, or the State which is its political and legal expression, is no more than a necessity *de facto*. Hence the rules of life in society are conventions, which reveals the relativity of legal rules and imposes certain limits on the State in its creation of a legal order.[10]

It may be said that so far—leaving aside certain extreme statements—this point of view is at first sight compatible with the general theses of modern social defence. However, Gramatica goes further. In his opinion, a 'law of social defence' should take the place of the existing 'criminal law'. The ultimate purpose of such a law of social defence is the integration of the individual in the social order, and not the punishment of his acts. This is where Gramatica's two fundamental ideas, *subjectivization* and *anti-social conduct*, enter the picture. The subjectivization of the law of social defence is carried out through the outward signs of the anti-social conduct of the individual in question. It is better to take the individual into account than to assume custody of his goods, and it was such a custody of goods which criminal law envisaged when it considered the criminal offence as damage. Gramatica concludes that the law of social defence requires the abolition of criminal responsibility and its replacement by the notion of anti-social conduct, but in the view of the present writer such an inference appears rather hasty or somewhat exaggerated. His doctrine also involves the exclusion of the metaphysical question of freedom and, more specifically, the rejection of the notions of criminal offence, criminal, and punishment. The 'social defence measures' which take the place of punishment depend on knowledge of the offender's personality. Hence it is no longer necessary to distinguish punishment from 'measures': the sole object of the administration of justice in terms of social defence is the 're-socialization' of the offender, and this justice is radically different as regards its organization, its agents, and its operation, from traditional 'penal' justice.[11]

At this stage we cannot enter into the details of Gramatica's theory, either in his study of the 'institutions of social defence',

[10] *Principi di difesa sociale*, Padua, 1961, chap. I.

[11] *Ibid.*, chap. II, in particular Nos. 20, 27, and 31.

of which 'anti-social conduct' is the most important, or in his concern with the system of criminal justice which he claims to organize. It is enough to bear in mind that his theory indeed purports to abolish criminal law, criminal responsibility, punishment, and the traditional system of criminal procedure.

It was this extreme doctrine that provoked the reaction of those who sponsored the 'minimum programme' mentioned above. It was against this doctrine, at the request of the authors of the minimum programme and of a few others, that the present writer endeavoured to formulate a *new* doctrine, or at any rate to work out a reformist position which would be less absolute and more moderate, which would retain the essential dynamic of social defence while turning it into a reformist rather than a revolutionary movement. This is the meaning of the expression: *new social defence*.[12]

The essential features of this doctrine, or if it be preferred, the basic tendencies of this movement, will be set forth in the three following chapters. For the time being it may suffice simply to refer the reader to the text of the 'minimum programme', but it seems desirable, nonetheless, to stress a few fundamental points.

The penal policy of social defence certainly takes as its point of departure the protection of the individual, and indeed the preeminent dignity of the human being. This policy refuses to acknowledge that the State has any absolute value, still less any discretionary powers; on the contrary, it is maintained, the State has duties towards the citizen, even though he be delinquent, and it is in this sense that one may speak of a 'right to social readaptation', or of an obligation of the State to integrate the individual in a social community which should never act oppressively towards him: recognition of the 'rights of man' is an inherent part of this system.

Any society, however, presupposes a social order, namely a body of rules corresponding not only to the necessities of communal life but to the common aspirations of the citizens. Hence the inescapable need for a legal system in which criminal law plays a major part. The protection of the individual as well as that of society depends on the proper formulation of such a criminal law, the necessity of which is no less evident than that of social life itself. Therefore there is no question of doing away with

[12] See P. Bouzat, *op. cit.*, vol. I, pp. 60-63.

either the system of criminal law as such, or the criminal offence as an act sanctioned by the legal rule, or the judge's assessment of the offender in the purely legal context, or the legal penalty: these institutions must remain. Thus the penal policy of social defence does not envisage the 'extinction of the law', but its greater perfection: more precisely, it aims at making the reaction against crime increasingly appropriate to the combined needs of the individual and society.

For the same reasons, there can be no question of doing away with the idea of responsibility, of denying man's freedom, or of simply rejecting any notion of punishment. On the contrary, it will be seen that the penal policy of social defence in fact depends on the concept of individual responsibility, the existential reality of which is one of the main elements in the system. This responsibility, based on a truly personal awareness of individual freedom, is the main driving-force of the process of social readaptation. Anti-social conduct, like dangerousness, is no more than a particular phenomenon, but the problem is precisely how to look beyond such particular phenomena so as to attain an ontological conception of the person.

Finally, it is clear that this fundamental process of social readaptation is itself related to a criminal trial and to an organized system of procedure, without which the individual would lose his natural safeguards as against the State which sanctions his offence. Of course, the traditional criminal trial has deviated from and in great part lost the sense of social morality and collective protection: it must therefore be reformed, but paying due regard to the necessary existence of a system of criminal justice based on procedural rules of law as intangible as the legal basis of crimes and punishments. It should be added that in this moderate, reformist doctrine, the criminal court necessarily retains its normal function, for a system designed to protect individual rights could not hand over to extra-judicial bodies the task of deciding the destiny of a citizen in society, as had indeed been advocated, at one time at least, by certain extreme partisans of social defence.[13]

The unfortunate consequence of this extremist tendency was the appearance of certain troublesome confusions. Various

[13] See C. de Vincentiis, *Appunti intorno al procedimento di socializzatione, Riv. di difesa sociale*, 1947, p. 285.

specialists in the field of criminal law hastened to strike down this extremist view, which lay wide open to fairly obvious criticism, before they realized that there existed another doctrine more representative of the majority of supporters of social defence. A few others, though they subsequently became aware of this majority point of view, preferred to ignore its existence or pretended to confuse the two. Their critical appraisal thus becomes a good deal less pertinent, but it can delude ignorant or ill-informed persons.

It must be asserted forthwith—although the point may have to be raised again at a later stage—that the new social defence movement claims to act within the framework of a legal system, and that it is by antithesis with the first, extremist doctrine that I have called the movement '*new* social defence'. The moderate or reformist tendency has gained the upper hand not only within the International Society for Social Defence by the adoption of the minimum programme, but also at all the international gatherings of specialists held since 1954. The third Congress which was held at Antwerp in that year marked a turning point,[14] which was further emphasized at the fourth Congress, held in Milan in 1956.[15] The fifth and sixth Congresses, held respectively at Stockholm in 1958 and at Belgrade in 1961, strikingly confirmed this.[16] The colloquium for the study of the psychiatric treatment of offenders organized by the United Nations at Copenhagen in 1958, also fervently welcomed the doctrine of 'new social defence',[17] and the study-cycle of the International Foundation for Penal and Penitentiary Problems held at Strasbourg in 1959, was to be inspired in its turn by the fundamental tendencies of the new social defence movement.[18]

[14] On this Congress, see *Rev. de Science crim.*, 1954, pp. 421 ff.; and for the Proceedings, *Actes du Troisième Congrès international de Défense sociale* (*San Marino 1951, Caracas 1952, Anvers 1954*), Antwerp, 1955 (published under the joint editorship of R. Victor, S. C. Versele and W. Calewaert).

[15] See the Proceedings of the Fourth Congress, *Atti del Congresso internationazionale sulla prevenzione dei reati contro la vita umana e l'incolumita individuale. Actes du congrès international* . . ., Milan, 1957.

[16] See the Proceedings of the Fifth Congress, *Actes du Cinquième Congrès international de défence sociale, Stockholm, 25-30 août 1958*, Stockholm, 1963; and the Proceedings of the Sixth Congress (Belgrade 1961), *Le Statut légal et le traitement des jeunes adultes délinquants, Actes du VIe Congrès international de défense sociale*, Belgrade 1962.

[17] See *Rev. de Science crim.*, 1958, p. 679.

[18] Mario Pisani, 'Concerning "new social defence",' *Jus*, 1957, pp. 471 ff.

It has been asserted that all the important gatherings of specialists in the fields of criminal law and criminology that have taken place for the past ten years are sufficient evidence of the evolution and the progress of notions of social defence[19]: but this refers to *new* social defence alone. This will become clearer when we consider the effect on existing systems of enacted law of the modern penal policy which is the core of the new doctrine.

II

An endeavour may now be made to assess the precise influence of modern social defence ideas on the main systems of criminal law in force in the world. A rapid survey of the main points will have to suffice, for a thorough study would involve fairly lengthy treatment: our present intention is merely to give a geographical outline of the social defence movement, which will serve to complement the equally summary historical outline that has already been provided.

There is no need to dwell on the concept of a legal system, or to take sides as regards the number and structure of the main systems involved: the present work is not a treatise on comparative law, and at this point it is enough to refer to specialized works.[20] All comparative lawyers agree in distinguishing at least five main types of national laws, grouped together in specific systems by reason of their origin, their historical development, and their methods of application. These five broad divisions are the systems of continental Europe and Latin America, the Anglo-American system, the system of the Middle East, that of the Far East, and that of the socialist countries.[21]

The system of continental Europe and Latin America is the system of *Civil Law* as opposed to the Anglo-American *Common Law*. The former is based on the tradition of Roman law, and essentially comprises codified systems of law in which great importance is attributed to legal definitions, abstract notions, legal technique, and legal dogma. Ever since the advent of classical penal law and during the whole of the nineteenth century, the

[19] On the importance of the 'moderate' position defended by J. Graven and Marc Ancel, see H. Mannheim, *Pioneers in Criminology*, London, 1960, Introduction, p. 35.

[20] See Gutteridge, *Comparative Law*, 2nd. ed., 1949.

[21] The legal systems of the new countries of Asia and Africa should be left out of account for the moment, until they finally acquire a fully organized form.

civil law system has been dominated by the theoretical preoccupations chiefly developed by the Italo-German school from Feuerbach to Mittermaier, Beling, and Binding, and from Romagnosi and Carmignani to Carrara.[22] It is this special atmosphere which accounts for the fact that the new notions of penal policy should have been not only discussed at great length but also subjected to a process of theoretical definition and classification. Specialists in criminal science accordingly gave a special meaning to the new expressions *social defence*, *penal policy*, *dangerousness*, *preventive measures*. The penal policy of social defence is to some extent the creation of the Romanist system against which, moreover, it reacts. No astonishment should be caused by the fact that the ideas of social defence have been welcomed—or, on the contrary, debated—especially in Italy, in the Latin-American countries, in Belgium, in France, in Switzerland, and, as will soon be apparent, in the Scandinavian countries. These ideas seem to have been less well understood by German criminal lawyers, who are at present preoccupied by a return to the traditional notion of retributive punishment.[23]

As regards legislation, that is to say from the standpoint of reforms accomplished by new statute law, the social defence movement—after the earliest experiments in the late nineteenth century which were limited in scope—began to have a real influence with the Norwegian Code of 1902, and more especially during the period of codification between the two World Wars (1919-1939).[24] On the European continent, as we have already observed, this was the time of the *via media*, of compromise between classicism and positivism. This period was marked by the legislative recognition of preventive measures, the establishment of a dualist system which made provision both for punishment, as traditionally understood, and for the novel concept of such measures as the development of new individualized methods of dealing with offenders, different from those used in the preceding century, and the attribution of wide discretionary powers to the criminal courts.

[22] However, the importance of writers such as Carnot, Blanche, or Faustin-Hélie in France, and Haus in Belgium, should not be overlooked.

[23] See however Fritz Bauer, *Das Verbrechen und die Gesellschaft*, Munich, 1957.

[24] See Marc Ancel, 'The Collection of European Penal Codes and the Study of Comparative Law', reprint, *University of Pennsylvania Law Review*, vol. 106, No. 3, January 1958, at p. 365, §3.

On the Continent, this trend is illustrated by the Codes of Yugoslavia (1929), Italy and Denmark (1930), Poland (1932), Rumania and Switzerland (1937), and some time later, by the Greek Code of 1951. The same period also saw the enactment of special statutes, among which may be mentioned, in particular, the Belgian social defence statute of 1930 and the Spanish *ley de vagos y maleantes* of 1933. In Latin America, certain reforms were inspired at least in part by positivist ideas (Mexico, 1929; Cuba, 1936) which were often followed by a return to neo-classical ideas or at any rate to a 'pure law' approach (*tecnico-juridico*) inspired by the Rocco Code of 1930 (Mexico, 1931; Brazil, 1940).[25] The new Codes were in most cases inspired by a kind of eclectic progressivism which showed awareness of some of the claims put forward by social defence (Argentina, 1922; Peru, 1924). Other Codes have been described as inspired by a penal policy[26] indistinguishable from that which serves as a vehicle for the ideas and the institutions of modern social defence (Uruguay, 1933; Colombia, 1936).

Although the Scandinavian countries are traditionally included within the Civil Law system, it may be said that from the Norwegian Code of 1902 to the Swedish Code of 1962, and in particular as regards criminal law, they occupy a unique position which is in many ways intermediate between the continental system as a whole and the Common Law system.[27] Thanks to the generous idealism of Karl Schlyter, Sweden went so far as to envisage the enactment of a 'Code of Protection' instead of a Criminal Code.[28] In any case, the attention paid to the individualized treatment of offenders, the organization and perfecting of a flexible body of preventive measures, reform of the prison system in the direction of the social readaptation of convicted offenders, the merging of probation with the practice of imposing suspended sentences, the system of day-fines and that of child welfare councils: all these are enough to show the extent to which the Scandinavian States are aware of the new social defence doctrines. The Greenland statute of 1954 is the most advanced example of this.

[25] To which must be added numerous draft Codes, many of them remarkable, which provoked some very interesting discussion.

[26] The expression comes from Jiménez de Asúa.

[27] This sufficiently appears from a comparison of the Danish Code of 1930 with the Italian code of the same year.

[28] On this movement, see *Rev. de Science crim.*, 1957, pp. 938 ff.

At the opposite pole from the Civil Law system, the Common Law system seems naturally unwilling to accept notions of social defence. It has already been observed that the terms 'preventive measures' and 'penal policy' are barely recognized. The expressions 'individualization' and 'social readaptation' are not given the same meaning as on the Continent. In the United Kingdom and the United States there has been no attempt to formulate a dogmatic theory of the double track or of dangerousness. Neo-classical doctrine as understood on the Continent is practically unknown in the Common Law world, and positivism has had no real influence. Moreover, it was in England that Lombroso found one of his most steadfast opponents in the person of Goring.[29] Liszt, Prins, and Rocco are also ignored by English criminal theory, and the work of the American sociologists is poles apart from the theoretical movement which enabled the penal policy of social defence to be built up on the European continent.

This, however, is only a matter of externals. More precisely these remarks apply only in the sphere of abstract theory. On the practical level, and even in the field of penal philosophy, the ideas and even more the aims of the social defence movement have had a definite influence and have to a large extent been adopted in the Commonwealth as in the United States: that is a truth of a sociological kind. This must be realized—as comparative lawyers have urged—by going beyond apparent reality in order to comprehend the true significance of the system of law in question and in order to grasp, from one system to another, what C. J. Hamson rightly calls the equivalence of institutions.[30]

Although superficial analysis might lead to a different conclusion, the Common Law system was in reality more naturally ready to accept the concepts of modern social defence than was the Civil Law. The former has always been a system of judge-made law, where apart from the crime of murder,[31] the criminal court has so broad a power to order individualized treatment in

[29] Goring, *The English Convict: A Statistical Study*, London, 1913; on Goring, see E. D. Driver, in *Pioneers in Criminology* (ed. H. Mannheim), London, 1960, pp. 335 ff.

[30] See C. J. Hamson, 'La Notion de légalité dans les pays occidentaux', in *Rev. int. de droit comp.*, 1958, esp. p. 6.

[31] At least until the Homicide Act (1957), which provides for different degrees of murder.

a particular case as to make the Romanist concept of extenuating circumstances quite unnecessary. The division of the criminal trial into two distinct phases (conviction and sentence) which is called for by many supporters of social defence on the Continent at the present time, is traditional in England and favours not only a sanction adapted to the individual offender but also an examination of his personality.[32] The Common Law system also knows long-established sanctions of a non-repressive nature and procedures calculated to afford the offender a second chance, without even a nominal sentence being pronounced, as in the case of suspended sentences in Europe. Nor should another tradition be forgotten—that of the radical prison reformers, who from John Howard to the Gladstone Committee went much further than the 'penitentiary school' in continental Europe, hampered as it was by its dogmatism. Finally, the United States, a Common Law country, was the pioneer both of indeterminate sentences and of juvenile courts.

In this atmosphere and on this favourable terrain, the ideas of social defence were effective by virtue both of their dynamic force and of their profound significance, even when they had received no official recognition. The evolution of the probation system, from the work of John Augustus in Boston in the mid-nineteenth century down to the great English statutes of the late nineteenth and early twentieth centuries, were already a premonition. The Prevention of Crime Act (1908) did not merely lay down a means of neutralizing the dangerousness of a potential offender—preventive detention—but also organized the Borstal system whereby England stepped into the vanguard of penal policy as regards the re-education of young offenders. The movement has continued, and not only in the field of prison reform, where Sir Alexander Paterson and Sir Lionel Fox were successive innovators of international renown:[33] a whole series of new provisions have been enacted concerning the responsibility of children and young persons

[32] See on this point the very apt remarks of J. M. Canals, 'Classicism, Positivism and Social Defence', in *Journ. of Criminal Law, Criminology and Police Science*, March-April 1960, pp. 541 ff.

[33] Paterson, who was appointed Prison Commissioner in 1922, had a decisive influence in the transformation of prison sentences into re-educational treatment. Sir Lionel Fox, who became Chairman of the Prison Commissioners, continued Paterson's work, and was Chairman of the European consultative committee of experts set up by the United Nations, and of the European Committee on crime problems set up by the Council of Europe.

or of abnormal offenders,[34] whereas the Criminal Justice Act (1948) has been described as in certain respects a 'social defence statute'.[35]

In the United States, indeterminate sentences (which Thorsten Sellin has described as fulfilling a function similar to that of 'preventive measures' on the European continent)[36] and juvenile courts have made rapid headway against all obstacles. From the Baumes Laws of New York (1924) to the provisions regarding sexual psychopaths that have been enacted in several States since 1938, a movement has grown up, sometimes in a form that is rather over-simple, in favour of seeking new means of social protection. The extraordinary extension of the notion of parole, and of innovations such as the Youth Authority, which was soon followed by an Adult Authority, are evidence of practical research directed towards a remodelled penal policy. The Model Penal Code of the American Law Institute[37] itself shows signs of a concern for what must surely be called 'social defence'. The most recent account of American criminal law confirms this impression, and American sociological or criminological literature of the past few years is much concerned—if only implicitly—with what we should call problems of penal policy.[38]

It would be beyond the scope of this survey to pursue the enquiry throughout the Commonwealth. However, there are

[34] See the various statutes which preceded the Children and Young Persons Act (1933), and that statute itself. See also the Mental Deficiency Act (1913), and the Mental Health Act (1956), which is not a criminal but a social protection statute.

[35] The Criminal Justice Act (1961), amended and completed the 1948 Act in the same direction. The Homicide Act (1957), introduced the notion of diminished responsibility. A like inspiration is to be found in the remarkable report published by the Home Office in February 1959 under the significant title: *Penal Practice in a Changing Society*.

[36] *Rev. de Science crim.*, 1951, p. 440.

[37] *Model Penal Code. Proposed official Draft*, Philadelphia, Executive Office, American Law Institute.

[38] See in particular Paul W. Tappan, *Crime, Justice and Correction* (1960); R. C. Donnelly, J. Goldstein and R. D. Schwartz, *Criminal Law (Problems for Decision in the Promulgation, Invocation and Administration of a Law of Crime)*, New York, 1962; *Crime and Correction (Law and Contemporary Problems)*, Duke University, Durham, 1958. Nor must we forget the part played in England by writers such as Mannheim, Grünhut and L. Radzinowicz, and especially the remarkable work which the last has inspired in the Department of Criminal Science at Cambridge, where the recent creation of an Institute of Criminology should give a further impetus to the movement—and by publications like the *British Journal of Delinquency* (which since 1960 has become the *British Journal of Criminology*). Again, for the implicit recognition of the concept of penal policy—the *raison d'être* and value of the system of positive criminal law—see P. J. Fitzgerald, *Criminal Law and Punishment*, Oxford, 1962.

useful pointers in the evolution of penal conceptions in Canada (particularly by comparison of the Criminal Code of 1955 with that of 1893), in New Zealand, in Australia, and even in South Africa, where a commentator in Pretoria has said that it was to be regretted that the criminal law of South Africa had not, like other countries 'accepted the principles of social defence'.[39]

Nor can we dwell at length on the systems of the Middle and Far East. It may be noted, however, that the Lebanese Criminal Code of 1941 and the Syrian Code of 1949, influenced by the '1930 system', tried to establish an organized system of preventive measures. More recently, at the instigation of the United Nations and on the model of the Section created there in 1948, 'social defence services' have been instituted in Iraq, Jordan, Morocco, the Sudan, and the United Arab Republic.[40] As regards the Far East, it should be recalled that even the Japanese Penal Code of 1907, though of neo-classical inspiration, showed the influence of the teachings of the International Union of Criminal Law. Since 1945, Japanese criminal law has been in contact with the Anglo-American system, from which it borrowed, in particular, the probation system. But American influence was not the only one to make itself felt, or rather, it was combined with the more general influence of the modern penal policy of social readaptation. During the celebrations marking the fiftieth anniversary of the 1907 Code, which had been profoundly modified since the end of the Second World War, Dean Kimura was able to stress the part of social defence in the criminal law of contemporary Japan, and to point out that this movement, initially conceived in terms of the unilateral protection of society, had now come to mean 'the defence of society against crime through the defence of the criminal' and that 'the present trend of criminal legislation in Japan is towards this new conception of social defence'.[41] Being so far removed geographically, this explicit ratification is all the more significant.

[39] *Penal Reform News* (Organ of the Penal Reform League of South Africa), No. 47, April 1959, p. 17.

[40] See 'Some aspects of the organization of social defence services in selected Arab States', article prepared at the request of the United Nations Secretariat by the Social and Labour Department of the Secretariat-General of the League of Arab States, in *International Review of Criminal Policy*, No. 19, June 1962, pp. 51-53.

[41] Kameji Kimura, 'Evolution et tendance du droit pénal japonais (À propos du cinquantième anniversaire du Code pénal japonais)', *Rev. de Science crim.*, 1958, pp. 65 ff., at p. 70. Cf. Shigemitsu Dando in *Archiv für Strafrecht*, 1959, pp. 357 ff.;

Something remains to be said concerning the so-called Socialist States or people's democracies. Here again appearances should not be trusted. Ostensibly, the first two Soviet Codes, the Criminal Code of 1922 and that of 1926, are of positivist inspiration. Certainly they were influenced by Enrico Ferri's draft of 1921: they did not mention either guilt or punishment, their sanctions were described as 'measures of social defence' and criminal offences described as 'socially dangerous acts'. But the principle of moral responsibility was repudiated only so as to bring the new criminal law into line with Marxist materialism. The delinquent was nonetheless a 'guilty' person subject to severe sanctions designed as retribution for any crime against 'the dictatorship of the workers and peasants'. At bottom, such law was not positivist but political, making use of threats and sanctions in order to secure the construction of socialism.[42] This was the meaning of the celebrated 'socialist legality', which rejected as a bourgeois principle the rule *nullum crimen, nulla poena sine lege*. Notwithstanding the terminology employed, this Soviet criminal law was not a law of social defence: on the contrary, it will be seen that social defence is fundamentally opposed to the system of accusation by analogy.[43]

Moreover, from 1930 onwards Soviet criminal law abandoned any positivist tendencies. In 1934, the term *punishment* replaced that of *social defence measures*. The Stalinist era, marked by the Constitution of 1936, was also that of pitiless repression and expiation: no one has forgotten the spectacular trials by which Stalin liquidated both his enemies and his rivals. The suppression of the death penalty soon after the Second World War, in 1947, though ephemeral (capital punishment was restored in 1950), marked the beginning of a humanization and softening of the repressive system. This movement really got under way after Stalin's death in 1953. With greater freedom than previously existed, lengthy and arduous discussions prepared the criminal

---

Makino, 'Interrelation of a Code of Criminal Procedure and Criminal Policy', in *Keisei, Japanese Journal of Criminal Law and Criminology*, vol. 8, No. 2, June 1960, pp. 1 ff. and p. 224.

[42] See Marc Ancel, 'Introduction au système de droit pénal soviétique (De la Révolution d'Octobre aux Codes de 1960)', in *La Réforme pénale soviétique*, Paris, 1962, pp. xi ff.

[43] In his *Principi di difesa sociale*, 1961, Gramatica himself is unequivocally in favour of retaining the rule of law untouched.

law reform carried out by the 'Fundamental Principles' which the Supreme Soviet adopted on 25 December 1958 and by the Codes of the R.S.F.S.R. of 22 October 1960 (Criminal Code and Code of Criminal Procedure).[44]

This reform returns to the notion of the strict legal definition of crimes and punishments. New safeguards are granted to the defence in criminal trials, where the court's power to treat each case according to its distinct and individual character is increased. Attention is paid to the social object of punishment and to the re-education of convicted persons. Special measures of a non-punitive character are provided for those delinquents who are mentally ill and for young offenders.

Thus, in their turn, the latest Soviet criminal law reforms show the influence of the penal policy of social defence. Nevertheless it is the return to traditional concepts of retributive punishment, responsibility and fault, that is stressed.[45] Soviet criminal doctrine still rejects the concept of dangerousness and stubbornly confuses preventive measures as understood in the West with police custody or the concentration camp. To the extent that they do not constitute a return to the neo-classical system of the late nineteenth century,[46] the reforms of 1958-1960 are principally aimed against the excesses of the Stalinist system. Furthermore, an analysis that is both inadequate and distorted by certain ideological preconceptions pictures social defence (and also the Welfare State!) as an offshoot of American capitalism.

A quite different situation exists in Yugoslavia, which is evolving a national communism free from subjection to Soviet Russia. The Criminal Code of 1948 closely followed the 1926 Code of the R.S.F.S.R., but after the break with the Cominform in 1950 Yugoslavia adopted, in 1951, a Criminal Code of great interest and very considerable originality.[47] This Code was carefully revised in 1959, being deliberately orientated towards certain

[44] These two Codes (together with the statute regarding judicial organization and a general Introduction) have been published by the Centre français de droit comparé under the title: *La Réforme pénale soviétique*, Paris, 1962.

[45] The *punitive* aspect of the reform was emphasized by the statutes of 1961 and 1962, which, in particular, extended the death penalty to certain economic crimes; see *Rev. de Science crim.*, 1961, p. 854.

[46] The expression comes from van Bemmelen.

[47] See Vassalli, 'Il nuovo Codice penale jugoslavo', in *Annuario di Diritto comparato*, 1953.

principles of new social defence. Some of the most distinguished of Yugoslav criminal scientists note this by emphasizing the positions adopted with regard to young offenders, mentally deficient persons, the social rôle of penal sanctions and of criminal justice, individualization of treatment, and the resocialization of offenders.[48]

In this way the new criminal law of Yugoslavia, while remaining resolutely 'socialist', occupies a position in some respects half-way between the Soviet system and Western systems: this illustrates the vigorous penetration of ideas of social defence in an environment which doubtless differs greatly from that in which these ideas were evolved, but which is concerned with the problem of human progress.[49]

[48] See *Le Droit pénal nouveau de la Yougoslavie*, published by the Institute of Comparative Law, Paris, 1962.

[49] See the preface by N. Srzentić to the Serbo-Croat translation of the present work, *Nova druzvesita Odbraira*, Belgrade, 1963; cf. the report by Professor Zlatarić of Zagreb to the Colloquium held at Bellagio in April 1963 on Mentally Abnormal Offenders; see the record thereof by Guy Houchon in *Rev. de Science crim.*, 1963, pp. 605-618.

Chapter Five

CRITICAL ASPECTS OF THE DOCTRINES OF SOCIAL DEFENCE

FROM THE FOREGOING CHAPTERS, and from what has been said of the origins and the main stages of the social defence movement, it is now clear enough that the new conception of social defence, in evidence since 1945, involves shades of interpretation and even intellectual positions that are fairly diverse. But it is not very difficult to realize that these shades of interpretation—probably unavoidable in so vast and complex a movement—are fruitful in the long run, for they prevent the social defence movement from immuring itself in a dogmatism that is contrary both to its origin and to its purpose or spirit. There would therefore be little point in underlining the differences of opinion between the various partisans of the movement, or to divide them into 'extremists' and 'moderates', as seems to be the inclination of some criminal scientists who look at social defence from outside. All these methods are inadequate and even inaccurate in that they overlook the basic core of common doctrine that exists among the same partisans of the movement. It is this community of doctrine that must be identified: the task is a difficult one, and appears to have repelled those who might have tried to systematize the new tendencies. The effort must however be made, boldly and without hesitation.

How is this essential community of doctrine to be defined or identified? It has been said that every thesis can be defined in terms of its antithesis, and the truth of the maxim is all the greater in the case of any new scientific or philosophical theory which first appears as a reaction against outworn or earlier tendencies. A new doctrine exists at first only by way of contrast with the theories that it disputes or seeks to replace, and this is peculiarly true of social defence. We have already observed that the movement emerged as a result of the positivist revolt, to the extent that positivism had led to a reconsideration of the problems of criminal law, and to the extent that a penal policy based on the lessons of experimental science had been substituted for a purely legal edifice. This is without any doubt the most immediately apparent aspect of social defence, and might be described as the critical side of the doctrine. It is this element of the doctrine, for example, which made Émile Garçon stop short of acceptance or which caused Raymond Saleilles to hesitate, and which today perturbs certain criminal scientists who for various reasons are attached to neo-classical ideas.

However, although this critical aspect is clearly apparent, its importance should not be exaggerated: this temptation, to which some have succumbed, must be avoided if social defence is not to be reduced to a few over-simple propositions. Above all, therefore, it is necessary to establish the doctrine of *new* social defence not only in relation to classical criminal law but also in relation to positivism, to the doctrines of the International Union of Criminal Law, and even to the theories of Prins. Finally—however delicate the task may be—it is necessary to state precisely in what ways the *corpus* of new social defence doctrine, which we are trying to identify, should not be confounded with theories peculiar to such and such an author who, speaking in his own name, cannot claim to express the general or representative view of the movement. Certain enthusiasts, and occasionally certain neophytes who are still poorly informed, have gone too far in trying to fit the concept of social defence into too narrow a framework and into a body of doctrine which, while claiming a very broad philosophical basis, becomes technically too narrow from the point of view of penal policy. Here again, it is desirable to conclude on this point by stating clearly in what respects the teachings of Gramatica, as expounded in 1961 in his *Principi di difesa sociale*, cannot in the present writer's opinion be considered to express the *whole* of social defence doctrine. The theory of social defence set forth in this work will likewise be *new* in that it will be clearly distinguished from the views of Filippo Gramatica on various matters of principle.

These topics will be dealt with in turn in the present chapter. Only thereafter will it be possible in a later chapter to examine the constructive aspects of the new doctrine, to seek out its constant factors, to understand its reformist approach, and to define the positions adopted, which essentially illustrate or characterize the movement.

I

As we have just pointed out, the antithesis between the new doctrine of social defence and the traditional conceptions of classical law and criminal justice is as evident and as frequently stressed as it is sometimes misunderstood. To avoid being mistaken about the precise nature of the modern social defence movement, it is vital that the true extent of this antithesis should be appreciated. This involves first of all going back to the three possible basic interpretations of criminal justice. What is here involved is not so much a historical sequence of events properly so called, as a logical progression in the evolution of ideas regarding the nature, the function, and even the legitimacy of criminal justice.

The first conception of criminal justice is religious, and consists in imposing expiation on the criminal, who is guilty because he has offended the deity. The crime arouses the divine wrath, which only expiatory punishment can appease. This conception makes its appearance as soon as society becomes sufficiently well-organized to have outgrown the stage of private vengeance, which is thus replaced by divine vengeance. In this primitive stage of legal development, law merges fairly easily with religion and the administration of justice with the priestly function. The application of the penalty thus takes on a sacrosanct character typical of 'this theocratic period which is to be found in the history of almost all peoples'.[1]

The second conception of criminal justice is more specifically political. It no longer pursues religious ends, and its sole purpose is to keep the peace and public order by asserting the authority of the sovereign, in whose name justice is henceforth exercised. Historically, this conception coincides with the establishment of centralized government, and it is the sovereign who substitutes collective for individual vengeance. Criminal law, as such, is progressively enacted while private justice gives way to public

[1] R. Garraud, *Traité théorique et pratique de droit pénal français*, 3rd ed., vol. I, p. 109; cf. Jiménez de Asúa, *Tratado de derecho penal*, vol. I, 2nd ed., Buenos Aires, 1956, No. 58 ff.

justice, just as punishment inflicted by the community is substituted for privately inflicted punishment.[2] And so it was that under the legal order in force before 1789 (*ancien droit*) criminal lawyers took pleasure in repeating that men were forbidden to exact vengeance, which can be exercised only by the sovereign or his officers.[3] In England, during the first creative period of the Common Law in the twelfth, thirteenth, and fourteenth centuries, the notion of criminal justice was particularly prominent, finding its natural expression in the work of the itinerant justices, representatives of the king or the Curia Regis: it was in this period that there grew up the concept of the King's Peace.[4] A similar idea took root throughout the 'general law (*droit commun*)' of continental Europe, at the close of the feudal period,[5] leading to the stern repression of any attack on the order established by the sovereign, and to the appearance of punishments and tortures calculated to strike terror into criminals. Justice was then a 'political' concept in the first meaning of the term.

The third conception of criminal justice is essentially a legal one, and comes into prominence precisely at the time when the second or political conception begins to disappear. It is no longer a case of fighting crime by turning the criminal into an outlaw, but of subjecting him to a legal rule which defines as a matter of law both the offence committed and the penalty to be applied. There is here a shift from the sphere of arbitrary policy to that of legal regulation. Especially vigorous in the late eighteenth century, this conception produced the movement in favour of the legal

[2] See P. Bouzat and J. Pinatel, *Traité de droit pénal et de criminologie*, 1962, vol. I, Nos. 23 ff.

[3] See Vidal and Magnol, *Cours de droit criminel et de science pénitentiaire*, 9th ed., vol. I, p. 15, No. 2, with the reference there cited.

[4] Originally, the King's Peace was the special protection with which the sovereign favoured certain persons and certain places, so much so that this protection disappeared at the king's death until a new King's Peace was proclaimed by his successor. But the idea gradually became established as a general and permanent institution, so that Blackstone could write (*Com.* IV, 350) that 'the King's majesty is, by his office and dignity royal, the principal conservator of the peace within all his dominions' (Cited by J. W. Cecil Turner, *Kenny's Outlines of Criminal Law*, 18th ed., Cambridge, 1962, p. 127).

[5] Von Liszt rightly shows how, from the thirteenth to the sixteenth centuries, there developed a 'conception which makes crime and punishment matters of public law'. This old-established conception was 'revived with greater vigour after the interruption of the earlier period', *Lehrbuch des deutschen Strafrechts* (vol. I, p. 25 of the French translation published in 1911 under the title *Traité de droit pénal allemand*); cf. Jiménez de Asúa, op. cit., Nos. 97 ff. ('El derecho comun de los paises europeos').

character of crimes and punishments, the campaign against the arbitrary powers of judges, the institution of new penal sanctions, each carefully differentiated and applied by law to a particular criminal offence, objectively defined. The criminal offence becomes a legal notion and the appropriate penalty a legal sanction imposed by a judge who is bound by strict rules of law.[6]

It should be borne in mind, however, that these three different conceptions or phases in the history of criminal justice are interconnected, and above all that they share certain common features. In fact, all three conceptions depend on the acceptance of certain metaphysical principles, and all likewise tend to the establishment of an 'absolute' criminal justice. Whether it is a case of expiating a sacrilegious act, intimidating the criminal, or punishing him according to law, the three conceptions all aim at a complete and final reparation for the offence considered as an objective entity, and they likewise all depend on the appreciation of the crime and the criminal from an objective standpoint. It is on these abstract patterns that the classical law of the early nineteenth century bases its reasoning, and we are then confronted with a *homo delinquens* who bears a fairly close resemblance to the *homo economicus* and indeed to the *bonus paterfamilias* of the civilians. But in this respect there is no breach between classical penal law and the phases described earlier. On the contrary, classical law continues these earlier phases, provides them with a systematic framework, and integrates them in a legal order which simultaneously expresses and defines them. The theocratic conception sprang from an esoteric and occult body of learning; the political conception was based on authoritarian and arbitrary repression: in its turn, the legal conception derived from a system which, without disputing the foundations of the older attitudes, provided them with a legal technique and philosophy. As between the third conception and the first two any reform, however important and decisive, took place only to the extent that the new 'legalistic' order guaranteed the rights of man, that abstract being thrown up by the Social Contract and the Revolution.[7]

[6] See Bettiol, *Diritto penale*, 5th ed., 1962, pp. 31 ff. (*Presupposti filosofico-politici e principi della scuola classica*); cf. Cuello Calón, *Derecho penal*, 13th ed., 1960, vol. I, pp. 267 ff.

[7] See James Heath, *Eighteenth Century Penal Reform*, Oxford University Press, 1963.

The reform movement in the late eighteenth century no doubt resulted in the rejection of the repressive apparatus of the *ancien régime*, inherited from the old European 'Common Law', but in fact the new approach did no more than give legal form to a renovated system in which collective intimidation and repressive punishment still held pride of place. At this point we should call to mind what has already been said concerning the origin of social defence, and how, as has been observed, the eighteenth-century movement could not logically lead to a genuine system of social defence. Montesquieu was indeed the first to perceive the importance of the notion of penal policy, but he did so through his research into the art of legislation. It should not be forgotten that in his view the law was the essential safeguard of the natural rights of man and especially of the most precious of those rights—individual liberty.[8] Montesquieu is thus linked both with ideas of natural law and with the theory of the social contract, according to which the free citizen consents to the limitation of his inalienable rights, but only by way of an agreement freely entered into with the community as a whole. In so far as it restricts that liberty, therefore, criminal law can only proceed from the legislative act as 'the expression of the general will'. The same idea found a strenuous advocate in Beccaria, who considered that fixed punishments were its logical consequence. A fixed penalty, its scope and force determined by the law alone, was the corollary of indictment according to law, strictly interpreted and automatically applied without the least discretionary authority being left to the judge. The same principles inspired Jeremy Bentham when he advocated codification and tried to perfect a theory of legislation.[9]

This 'legalistic' theory linked up with and strengthened another movement in penal philosophy, initially discernible in a few references in the work of William Eden,[10] subsequently expounded

[8] See J. Graven, 'Montesquieu et le droit pénal', in *La Pensée politique et constitutionnelle de Montesquieu—Bicentenaire de l'Esprit des Lois* (Published by the Institut de droit comparé de la Faculté de droit de Paris), Paris, 1952, pp. 209-254.

[9] Bentham's work, first published in French under the title *Traité de législation civile et pénale*, was enthusiastically received in France at a time when a general codification was being undertaken in that country. On Bentham and his historical importance from this point of view see Gilbert Geis, 'Jeremy Bentham', in *Pioneers in Criminology* (ed. H. Mannheim), London, 1960, pp. 51 ff.

[10] *Principles of Penal Law*, 1771; cf. L. Radzinowicz, *History of English Criminal Law . . . from 1750*, vol. I, 1948, pp. 301 ff.

for the first time by Romagnosi,[11] and reaching its culminating point in the doctrinal edifice of Feuerbach, who assigned to the State the task of establishing the rule of law. Consequently, crime becomes above all an infringement of the legal order, an infringement that should be anticipated and prevented by the institution of repressive punishment, designed to 'paralyze' the potential offender by means of the *psychologischer Zwang*. Bentham, with less dogmatic severity but a greater awareness of the human realities and of what is socially effective, in his turn based traditional punishment on the image of the potential offender, faced with the threat of lawful punishment, weighing up the risks of a criminal enterprise.

In following this line of development, a system based on the idea of legality simply became legalistic. A purely legal doctrine and philosophy took the place of the social and political theories that inspired Montesquieu and Rousseau. The concept of civil society, of a human community envisaged in humanist terms, was replaced by that of a legal order defined and organized by the *lex scripta*. Crime was henceforth envisaged as an abstract attack on the legal order, and punishment as the means of effecting reparation through the restoration of the legal order that had been disturbed. Therefore crime was no longer a social phenomenon—as for Montesquieu and Bentham—but a legal entity, like punishment itself, which thereafter became a proper object of legal argument.

Thus orginated that classical criminal law, which from Feuerbach to Carrara was destined to develop into a legal doctrine well enough adapted to an era in which man's freedom to act was taken for granted, and he was acknowledged to be both the master of his acts and responsible for them. In the social context, collective prevention of crime, and retributive punishment, seemed eminently satisfactory notions: Carrara had no difficulty in connecting this liberal criminal law, retributive in character, with a conception that was religious in origin and in which Christian civilization recognized the ideas both of divine justice and of a

[11] *Genesi del diritto penale*, 1791. Having proclaimed that criminal law is '*diritto di difesa e non può essere altra cosa*' he goes on to say that the threat of punishment acts as *contra spinta criminosa*. This view resembles—and even anticipates, in some degree—Feuerbach's well-known doctrine of 'psychological coercion': this is so, even as regards the terms in which Romagnosi's doctrine is expressed.

lawful and necessary sanction for the fault committed.[12] We are thus led to that 'absolute' element which is characteristic of classical criminal law, where the concepts of the legal order, and of the function or legally definitive character of punishment, soon came to be accepted as undisputed and unquestionable dogma. Von Liszt, writing at the very end of the nineteenth century, was doubtless both fully aware of the teachings of the emerging science of criminology and preoccupied with the need for a renovated and actively conscious penal policy. Much of his work, however, is exclusively concerned with salvaging certain concepts —the legal order, 'legalism', the legal approach to punishment— in the face of the scientific reaction that derived from positivism. For von Liszt, considerations of penal policy and the *Zweckgedanke im Strafrecht*[13] were associated with an affirmation that the object of punishment was the preservation of the legal order and the maintenance, if not the renewal, of the *Rechtswidrigkeit*.[14]

That is why von Liszt's views, which had the advantage of allowing for some of the contributions made by the new theories, were to have a considerable influence on lawyers in the first half of this century. Some of his opinions were bandied about as naturally—it might almost be said automatically—in the early twentieth century, as were those of the rights of man and of the rule of law (in Beccaria's sense) a hundred years earlier. Many writers, including even some of the most eminent and original such as Jiménez de Asúa, still follow in the wake of this ideology.[15]

[12] So Carrara, who is always careful to avoid any confusion between law and religion, would limit the judicial function to an assessment of the malignity of the criminal's act: the judge would not be entitled to consider the malignity of the person who committed that act. For the modern criminal scientist, this is indeed a curious distinction, as Grispigni has very properly pointed out (*Diritto penale italiano*, 1950 ed., vol. I, p. 72).

[13] See F. von Liszt, 'Der Zweckgedanke im Strafrecht', *Zeitschrift für die gesamte Strafrechtswissenschaft*, 1882, p. 33. An Italian edition was published in 1962 under the title *La teoria dello scopo nel diritto penale*.

[14] This is the famous concept of *antijuridicité*, 'antilegalism', which has played so large a part in criminal theory, both in Europe and in Latin America, since the turn of the century. See Jiménez de Asúa, 'L'Antijuridicité', *Rev. int. de droit pénal*, 1951, pp. 273 ff.; cf. Delitala, *Il fatto nella teoria giuridica del delitto*, 1930, and Petrocelli, *L'antijuridicità*, Padua, 1947. See also, for the dogmatic conception of the criminal offence-Jiménez de Asúa, *Tratado de derecho penal*, vol. III, Nos. 961 ff.; cf. Bettiol, *Diritto penale*, 5th ed., 1962, pp. 163 ff.

[15] See especially 'La Mesure de sûreté; sa nature et ses rapports avec la peine,' *Rev. de Science crim.*, 1954, No. 1, pp. 21-38. The tenacity of these views among Latin-American jurists may be gathered from the very interesting proceedings of

The fact is that this kind of reappraisal of neo-classical criminal law leads to an ideological dogmatism which is equally characteristic of all the doctrinal positions adopted in the course of the past seventy-five years, from the Terza Scuola to the 'pure law' school, and this despite particular variations that need not concern us here, although they are often significant in connexion with legal technique or comparative analysis.

The primary characteristic of the social defence movement is a refusal to accept the metaphysical conceptions that form the basis of traditional criminal law, and it is this which explains the hesitation and indeed the instinctively negative reaction of those who adhere to the various neo-classical and eclectic theories. In other words, social defence proclaims its mistrust of the 'absolute' approach to criminal justice, that is to say of the view that crime and punishment are purely legal entities which can be dealt with exclusively by reliance on legal knowledge and legal technique. The antithesis between traditional criminal law—both in its liberal, neo-classical form and in the more modern guise of the 'pure law' theories—on the one hand, and social defence on the other, springs from the fact that social defence is anti-metaphysical and refuses to confine itself within an exclusively legal framework. By its history and its original vocation social defence thus has a fundamental affinity with the positivist movement. To the extent that positivism implies a philosophy and a metaphysical basis of its own (even though this be denied), the two movements are of course far apart, but they draw together in so far as positivism relies on the experimental method, pays attention to the social sciences, is founded on a clear-sighted approach to social problems, and spontaneously rejects the kind of conceptualism which is the final result of the doctrines of classical criminal law.

In the light of the foregoing remarks, the contrast between social defence and classical or neo-classical criminal law may be illustrated from three different points of view.

1. In the first place, social defence implies the vigorous and even systematic rejection of all metaphysics, or in other words of all that is based on *a priori* legal reasoning. As has been observed,

---

the criminal law colloquium at Buenos Aires in August 1960; see *Jornadas de derecho penal*, Buenos Aires, 1962 (published under the supervision of L. Jiménez de Asúa).

such an approach was already apparent in the teaching of Prins and remains characteristic, in many respects, of the new social defence. The movement still asserts today, as it did fifty years ago, that the object of criminal justice is not to set up an *absolute* standard, precisely adjusted—in the abstract—to the harm caused or the harmful intention. Social defence stresses the need clearly to separate criminal law not only from morals, but also from philosophy. Recalling that for Kant the affirmation of metaphysical moral standards finally led to his recognizing retaliatory punishment as 'the only just solution',[16] social defence refuses to treat crime as a purely legal notion and the criminal sanction as the legally-necessary consequence of an infringement of the established order, and likewise refuses to consider that the purpose of the punishment (or other sanction) is the abstract restoration of that legal order. According to the teaching of modern social defence this classical theory is of a largely mythical character and is based, to a large extent, on a mystical concept of punishment. It is not claimed that such theories are incorrect in themselves or intellectually untenable, but simply that as regards practical experience and in the field of applied criminal justice, which is above all dealing with human beings, other basic principles should be relied on and different methods adopted.

This point must be stressed. Social defence teaches that criminal justice is necessarily relative, and that its function is not to judge an isolated act in accordance with abstract rules, but to cause one man to be judged by other men. The fact is that human justice, administered by human beings, is incapable of instituting a system that is fully and genuinely retributive. The magistrate, who has the task of judging, is not confronted with the metaphysical problem of good and evil, but with the individual and concrete instance, restricted to the act that has been committed on a specific occasion by a particular person. Therefore the task of human justice is not to seek the means of punishment which, according to some absolute criterion, might compensate for the offence committed or might be deemed to restore the legal *status quo*: its task is to decide what sanctions would effectively make

[16] It has been remarked that Kant himself, however valuable and high-principled his philosophy, returned to 'atavistic emotional impulses, as soon as it had to do with matters of penal laws' (Von Hentig, *Punishment*, chap. III, cited by James Heath, *op. cit.*, p. 10, No. 2).

possible both the re-education of the criminal (and later, possibly, his rehabilitation) and the protection of society.[17]

2. Consequently, the social defence movement sees crime as a human phenomenon, as a manifestation or expression of the personality of its author, the particular human being who committed the offence in question. He is no longer the abstract *homo delinquens* of the classical theorists, or Lombroso's 'born criminal', whom the latest social defence doctrine rejects, while also adopting a non-committal attitude as regards the notion of a well-established and scientifically identifiable 'criminal type'. Whether a man's conduct is good or evil, he is always a specific person whose acts can be explained only to the extent that one learns to understand his personality. Hence the need to examine the criminal's personality and to substitute a subjective approach for the objective approach favoured hitherto. At the very least, it should be recognized that the *objective* conception of the criminal offence, defined by law, needs to be supplemented by the inescapable *subjective* element—the author of the criminal act.

A problem we shall soon discuss is that of responsibility, one of the three pillars of the classical theoretical structure, which stands on the threefold basis of the rule of law, moral responsibility, and repressive punishment. In the classical system, however, the idea of moral responsibility is once again merely a basic principle and not a realistic, human, and vital concept. In a system of retributive punishment the notion of moral responsibility takes the form of a presumption: because man is held to be free, he is deemed to be responsible, and it is because he is responsible that he incurs *punishment* for his fault. In this context moral responsibility is a theoretical prop, *ratio poenae*, rather than an element or expression of the individual personality of the author. The classical notion of responsibility begins with this presumption, which serves to justify the system in the abstract. Afterwards, the question whether there is responsibility in the particular case is of course considered by the court, *in concreto*, but only once. For the adherents of social defence, on the contrary, the concrete problem of responsibility is

[17] See Marc Ancel, 'Grundtankarna hos rörelsen för Socialskydd' (Les Idées de base du mouvement de défense sociale), in *Nordisk Tidsskrift for Kriminalvidenskab*, 1955, pp. 99 ff. This study has also been published in German under the title 'Die geistigen Grundlagen der Lehren von der Sozialen Verteidigung', in *Monatsschrift für Kriminologie und Strafrechtsreform*, 1956, *Sonderheft* (special issue for the IVth International Congress of Social Defence), pp. 51 ff.

a continuing problem and is furthermore, as will shortly be observed, the mainspring of the process of rehabilitation. Through its conception of personality, therefore, the doctrine assigns to the supposedly 'classical' notion of individual responsibility an importance and a tangibility, so to speak, which, paradoxically enough, sharply distinguish social defence from a neo-classical doctrine in which responsibility plays an inadequate rôle.

3. As regards the practical working of the system, that is to say its application by way of legislative, judicial, or administrative reforms, the new theory envisages criminal justice mainly as a form of social action. Consequently, it is not a question of organizing such a system of criminal justice in terms of the automatic allocation of penalties fixed by law. Even more emphatically, it is not a case of giving the court a discretionary power to intervene in the name of higher authority with a view to the restoration of an ideal system. In the first years of this century Prins already stressed the essentially relative character of human justice in the criminal sphere,[18] and it is this relativity that is always borne in mind by the adherents of social defence. So the criminal judge is no longer held to be a kind of legal oracle[19] or thought of as the representative of a society which would identify itself with the court's exercise of its repressive function. And the social defence movement does not consider that there is no more to be said once the court has applied the relevant legal provisions to a particular act legally qualified as an offence. Finally, according to this view the proceedings are not deemed to be concluded as regards the offender himself once no further appeal is possible and the offender, properly convicted and sentenced by due process of law, has served his sentence and thus—according to the old expression—'paid the price' for his crime. Crime is a human and social problem, it is not so easily forced into the strait-jacket of legal regulation. It is not claimed, however, that the criminal judge should not decide cases according to law and should refuse to apply the penalty laid down. On the contrary, we recognize that

[18] *La Défense sociale et les transformations du droit pénal*, Brussels, 1911.

[19] It may be recalled that this was Montesquieu's expression. It led him to insist on the need for fixed penalties (*Esprit des Lois*, Book VI, chap. III) as were to be prescribed by the French penal Code of 1791, and also to refuse any form of statutory interpretation, for it is the letter of the law, nothing else, that should be applied. A prohibition of this type was incorporated in the Bavarian Code of 1813, which was inspired by Feuerbach and was thoroughly imbued with the principle of legality.

this is an essential part of his task, and the point must be stressed, but we deny that the human and social problem presented by a particular criminal act can be wholly resolved by the abstract working of a distributive conception of justice.

That is why the social defence movement, at the time of its emergence, exactly coincided with what has been termed, ever since the beginning of this century, the 'crisis of repression', the 'crisis in criminal law', or 'the crisis of criminal justice'.[20] This so-called 'crisis' is in fact no more than the increasing awareness of the inadequacies of the purely repressive doctrine of neo-classical criminal law, which purports to solve by abstract and exclusively legal methods a problem which, whether we like it or not, goes beyond the restricted sphere of statutory rules in general and criminal law in particular. One of the basic tasks of the social defence movement, perhaps indeed its primary vocation, was to become fully aware of how poorly legal institutions are adapted to phenomena which can henceforth be understood in all their complexity, thanks to the development of the social sciences. This attitude is comprehensible and explicable only as a reaction against that classical, repressive penal law which has for too long disregarded the human realities.

We are here concerned with the fundamental elements of social defence doctrine, in so far as these stand over against the theory which has prevailed since last century and which may be described as the official theory of criminal law. Following the extraordinary movement of criminal law reform at the close of the eighteenth century, whose merits it would be absurd to deny, academic lawyers produced a remarkable doctrinal synthesis of a dogmatic theory of criminal law. Using strictly legal criteria, they defined and analysed the notions of crime and of punishment. They argued as if the social reaction against crime were a purely legal problem, referable to juridical science alone. Once again, it is not denied that this was a necessary reaction and that the work accomplished was of value, especially for the countries of continental Europe. But we explicitly deny that this approach is adequate:

[20] Apart from the studies already noted on this subject, see an article by F. Grispigni, 'La Crise de la justice pénale', *Rev. int. de Criminologie et de police technique*, 1953, pp. 4 ff, where the author emphasizes that 'this crisis is due precisely to the fact that we are no longer certain, at the present time, what are the nature and function of punishment, and its relation with preventive measures'. Cf. on the same 'crisis' Laignel-Lavastine and Stanciu, *Précis de Criminologie*, 1950, pp. 242 ff.

in effect, it was not enough simply to abandon the extreme aspects of the former *droit pénal commun* and to proclaim the twin principles of the rule of law and of moral responsibility. Montesquieu, Voltaire and Beccaria on the Continent, W. Eden in England, had not lost contact with social reality: the evolution of neo-classical theories during a period which was, moreover, remarkably fruitful for criminal science[21] eventually produced a legal formalism which became self-justifying and self-sufficient. The upshot of this approach (which had beneficial results for the teaching of penal law) was a tendency to forget that the criminal is also a human being and that punishment is inflicted on a creature of flesh and blood. Social defence firmly recalls this to the attention of those who find it convenient not to remember the fact.[22]

II

Indispensable as it is to specify why and in what way the modern theories of social defence are opposed to the doctrines of classical or neo-classical criminal law, it is equally essential to understand the antithesis between social defence and positivist theory.[23] It could even be said that failure to perceive this clearly has caused many writers to give inaccurate definitions or descriptions of the social defence movement, which they see as embodying a kind of outdated positivism: they then proceed to demolish this misleading image with an ease that may satisfy them but is in truth quite ineffective and devoid of intellectual significance. On this point, therefore, it is necessary to emphasize a contrast that is all the more meaningful in that it does not prevent the new social defence movement from acknowledging its historical indebtedness to positivism or from asserting that this alone made possible the initial formulation of the new doctrine.

Schematically, it may be said that positivism and social defence (in its modern or 'new' form) are opposed to each other from at least five different points of view, which must now be dealt with in turn.

[21] See Marc Ancel, 'The Collection of European Penal Codes and the Study of Comparative Law', reprint, *University of Pennsylvania Law Review*, vol. 106, No. 3, January 1958, p. 351.

[22] As also to those lawyers who claim to pay no attention to criminology: see O. Kinberg, *Les Problèmes fondamentaux de la criminologie*, Paris, 1960, No. 26 ('La Criminologie mal vue des esprits conservateurs').

[23] See Marc Ancel', 'Social Defence', *Law Quarterly Review*, 1962, pp. 497 ff.

(a) First of all, the new doctrine of social defence firmly rejects the determinism of the positivists. It accepts neither Lombroso's biological fatalism, nor Ferri's concept of social necessity, nor even the idea of an inherent or congenitally criminal nature: the latter view is sometimes canvassed by certain advocates of the preventive treatment of crime, mental health specialists or disciples of a criminal typology built up on the *a priori* classification of offenders. From the very first, Prins had insisted that the philosophical discussion concerning the existence or non-existence of free-will should be kept strictly separate from the rational organization of social action against crime. It will shortly become clear that on this point the new social defence movement takes a different view from that of Prins, for in fact it admits a very broad measure of individual freedom. Without overstating the case, it might almost be said that new social defence takes free-will as its philosophical starting-point, were it not for the fact that the movement is non-committal with regard to a problem which remains outside the sphere of applied penal policy and is based on completely different factors. There appears to be complete agreement on this point, and even the most extreme spokesmen of one wing of the social defence movement, such as Gramatica, have expressed themselves quite unequivocally on the matter.[24] In any event, as will be observed later in connexion with the positive aspects of the new social defence doctrines, the penal policy of social action (which these doctrines presuppose) is largely based, perhaps not on the *theoretical* notion of responsibility—which is outside the practical sphere of social action—but at least on the recognition, use, and development of the innate feeling of responsibility that is necessarily part of every man, including the criminal.[25] The mere statement of this essential rule sufficiently emphasizes the fundamental antithesis between the new theories of social defence and the deterministic theories of positivism.

(b) Of course, social defence considers that the classification of offenders is of the greatest importance. But the movement is

[24] See various statements by this author, since his momentous article 'La lotta contra la pena', in the first issue of the *Riv. di difesa sociale*. The same author, however, in his *Principi di difesa sociale*, (1961), appears to merge, to some extent, the concept of individual responsibility in those of 'anti-sociality' and dangerousness. This will be discussed later.

[25] See Marc Ancel's study, 'Responsabilité et défense sociale', *Rev. de Science crim.* 1959, pp. 179 ff.

chary of the tendency, widespread since the close of the nineteenth century, to divide the authors of criminal acts into the neatly-segregated and preordained categories of habitual offenders, occasional offenders, and those guilty of *crimes passionnels*. It may well be scientifically correct and useful to seek to establish such categories, but according to the new social defence movement a criminal act is above all the expression of an individual personality.[26] In our view, the criminological problem consists not so much in fitting the offender into a preordained framework, but rather in enquiring and explaining why that particular individual, in such-and-such a set of circumstances, with such-and-such a physical make-up, committed that particular act. This approach is indeed all the more necessary in that we refuse to explain the act exclusively in terms of background, constitution, or social environment. Modern criminologists place particular emphasis on the idea of the dynamic of crime, in other words on seeking the individual reasons which, at a particular moment, set in motion the commission of the criminal action.[27]

[26] See in this connexion E. de Greeff, *Introduction à la criminologie*, vol. I, Paris, 1948, and *Âmes criminelles*, Paris, 1949; see also the various articles in a symposium entitled *Autour de l'oeuvre du Dr. E. de Greeff*, 2 vols., Louvain, 1956. Cf. *Traité de droit pénal et de criminologie*, by P. Bouzat and J. Pinatel, Paris, 1962, vol. III (*Criminologie*, by J. Pinatel, esp. p. 377.) Cf. O. Kinberg, *Les Problèmes fondamentaux de la criminologie*, Paris, 1960, pp. 123 ff, 213 ff.

[27] Cf. B. di Tullio, *Trattato di antropologia criminale*, Rome, 1945, chap. 4, pp. 183 ff., and *Principi di criminologia clinica*, 3rd ed., 1963; E. Altavilla, *La dinamica del delitto*, 2 vols., Turin, 1953. See also Stephan Hurwitz, *Criminology*, London, 1952, Part IV, 'The Criminal Situation', pp. 359 ff., and 'The Deed,' pp. 368 ff. E. Mezger, speaking of the 'dynamic conception of crime', contrasts this notion with the anthropological, psychopathic, biological, and sociological conceptions which study, in a static way, one aspect only of the phenomenon of crime, whereas the dynamic conception includes both the act and its author: this approach, says Mezger, is a natural one, shorn of all mystery and related solely to direct experience—to the facts (*Kriminalpolitik und kriminologische Grundlage*, 2nd ed., Stuttgart, 1942, p. 164). Exner has shown how the same characteristics may be found both in the delinquent and the non-delinquent; one should not therefore be looking for an inherently criminal quality, but seek to discover the concurrence of forces or factors which will bring this criminal tendency into being and lead to the commission of a criminal act (*Kriminologie*, 3rd ed., 1949, p. 174); it is on this basis that new classifications comprising genuine scientific safeguards could be sought. Furthermore, it may be noted that the criminological system worked out by S. and E. Glueck (in which follow-up studies were used to produce the famous prediction tables) is based on the idea that criminal behaviour in the broad sense, as distinct from the commission of particular acts classified by law as criminal offences, should be taken into account. See *After Conduct of Discharged Offenders*, 1949, chap. 6. See also O. Kinberg, *Les Problèmes fondamentaux de la criminologie*, Paris, 1960, esp. chap. 10, 'Étiologie de la délinquance', pp. 172 ff.

(c) Consequently, the doctrines of the new social defence movement not only serve to revive the notions of free-will and responsibility, but likewise reintroduce successively into penal policy and criminal law a group of moral values of which positivism claimed to be unaware. The positivists did not wish to take into account any but purely scientific factors.[28] The new social defence movement, in readapting and giving fresh thought to the idea of responsibility from the point of view of the individual human being, evidently has to look for the feeling of moral obligation in that individual, and therefore tries to stimulate the idea of his duty towards his fellows, as well as encouraging him to become aware of a social morality to which he is necessarily subject. In this way, whether we like it or not, the idea or feeling of fault is reintroduced into criminal law, although this is no longer the objective or abstract conception of fault recognized by classical criminal law.[29] Indeed, the approach favoured by the social defence movement is as far removed from

[28] Bettiol went so far as to remark that the preconceived rejection by positivist doctrine of the idea of moral freedom constituted a serious methodological error: *Diritto penale*, Palermo, 1945, p. 42. Cf. *ibid.*, 5th ed., 1962, pp. 67 ff.

[29] See E. de Greeff, *Introduction à la criminologie*, vol. I, Paris, 1948, pp. 3 ff.; cf., for a slightly different approach, *Les Instincts de défense et de sympathie*, Paris, 1947, pp. 180 ff.; 'La Double Orientation de la criminologie', in papers of the Semaine Internationale de Strasbourg (*Les Orientations nouvelles des sciences criminelles et pénitentiaires*), Paris, 1955, pp. 14 ff.; cf. *L'Homme et son juge*, 1962; see B. di Tullio, *Trattato di antropologia criminale*, Rome, 1945, p. 558. We are aware that a certain trend in modern criminology, by speaking of the offender's personality, has tried to reintroduce the idea of responsibility into the system of dangerousness itself: according to Mezger the offender would be at fault in the traditional sense of the term, and hence would legitimately undergo punishment, because he acquired dangerous habits or did not withstand his natural tendencies, save, however, for certain tendencies considered unchangeable and for which punishment would not be incurred (*Deutsches Strafrecht*, 1949 ed., pp. 483-85). Whence the idea of 'fault in the conduct of life' for which the *Reichsgericht* found a place, inflicting even death sentences on certain psychopaths on the ground that the community was entitled to expect that those of its citizens whose personal constitution made them particularly dangerous should make a correspondingly greater effort to counterbalance their natural disposition. See in particular the decisions (R. G. St. 71, 179, R. G. St. 77, 28) cited by E. Heinitz in his study 'Strafzumessung und Persönlichkeit', *Zeitschrift für die gesamte Strafrechtswissenschaft* 1950, pp. 57 ff., where, moreover, the author very properly points out that one cannot at the same time advocate the reduction of the offender's punishment on the ground that he cannot help his condition, and increase the severity of the sanction on account of the special danger which he represents for society. See also, for a similar point of view, the interesting study by da Silva Correia, 'La doctrina de la culpabilidad en la formación de la personalidad, *Revista de Estudios penales* of the University of Valladolid, vol. III (1945-1946), pp. 23ff. This current

the positivists' legal or objective view of responsibility as from the purely moral responsibility advocated by the classical theorists.

(d) This feeling of responsibility, of obligation, or of culpability, does not, however, have a uniformly powerful impact on the individual. The new social defence movement tries to achieve a balance between the individual and society, in a rational penal policy based on the idea that society itself has obligations towards the citizen. Respect for human dignity, or the need to safeguard individual freedom—which is the first condition of the individual's exercise of his rights and the development of his personality—thus leads to the maintenance of a system founded on the rule of law, to the establishment of judicial rules of procedure, and to an instinctive distrust for the institution of an administrative system of preventive measures which might be arbitrarily laid down *ante delictum*. According to the new social defence movement, therefore, preventive measures can no longer be considered—as is maintained, for example, by Grispigni[30]—as being inherently of

---

of ideas is symptomatic of a renewal of criminal doctrine on the basis of criminological studies. It may be noted, however, without denying either the importance or the interest of this approach, that the idea of culpability in the offender's potentially dangerous condition retains an abstract and indeed fictional element, leading to the reintroduction of metaphysical notions into the sphere of the study of personality, which is essentially a concrete, not an abstract enquiry. See *contra* O. Kinberg, 'La Psychiatrie criminelle sans métaphysique', *Rev. de Science crim.*, 1949, p. 513. More modestly, but perhaps more effectively, the new social defence movement does not rely on a theoretical notion of responsibility, but takes as its point of departure the feeling of responsibility that every human being normally possesses: it is the purpose of the treatment of social readaptation to revive such a feeling of responsibility (together with a measure of self-control) when this has been lost or become defective. The English penologists are fully aware of this, and without relying on any *a priori* theory they place great emphasis on the sense of responsibility in the context of the penitentiary system. See Lionel W. Fox, *The English Prison and Borstal Systems*, London, 1951, especially p. 71. The Borstal system is based to a large extent on the active cultivation of personality, especially since the characteristic change involved in the substitution of the Borstal Training Act (1948) for the Borstal Detention Act (1908). For this aspect of the Borstal system, see, in addition to the aforementioned work of Sir Lionel Fox (pp. 368 ff.,) that of Margery Fry (*Arms of the Law*, London, 1951, pp. 136 ff.,) and the same author's 'The Effect of the Criminal Justice Act on the Borstal System', *Journ. of Criminal Science* (Published by the Department of Criminal Science, Faculty of Law, Cambridge, under the supervision of L. Radzinowicz and J. W. C. Turner), vol. II (*A Symposium on the Criminal Justice Act, 1948*), London, 1950, pp. 60 ff.

[30] *Diritto penale italiano*, 1950 ed., vol. I, p. 141; to the same effect, Manzini, *Trattato di diritto penale italiano*, vol. II, 1934, ed., p. 175.

an administrative character and not based on statute or judicial decision save for reasons of practical convenience. On the contrary, such measures should henceforward not only be subject to the rule of law, but also—as a general rule and save for strictly limited exceptions—to judicial control. Preventive measures of this kind are the active instruments of a penal policy which is certainly inspired by the findings of social and criminal science, but which is seen above all as a social action directed against crime, an action of which criminal law itself is one of the means.[31]

(e) The consequence is that although social defence derives its inspiration largely from the teachings of modern science and more especially of the social sciences, the movement is not characterized by the kind of 'scientific dependence' in which positivism wished to place not only criminal law but even penal policy. In this respect, social defence is chary of a kind of 'scientism' which is today outmoded. The social action which is advocated goes further than purely scientific research or merely legal technique: social defence aims at recovering the pristine meaning of 'policy' as the art of government, and therefore seeks to found a new penal policy which involves laying the foundations and stating the objectives of an enlightened struggle against the phenomenon of crime. The movement seeks to state the conditions for safeguarding society as a whole by ensuring, first of all, the respect and protection of the individual person. This programme of action, which thereby aims at achieving a better policy of social welfare, is in many respects none other than the reflection or even the expression of a more clearly stated, better understood, and more widely accepted social morality.

(f) The twofold battle that is waged by the social defence movement should be well understood. The movement criticized the neo-classicists (inspired by Carrara or by the Italo-German school of 'legal dogmatists') for having held that crime was nothing but a purely legal problem and that the struggle against crime was a problem for the lawyers alone, so that a well-designed system of legal rules and general prevention would be enough to protect society against delinquency. Experience has demonstrated the vanity of such a claim. But then the opposite contention was advanced, to the effect that, criminal law as such

[31] See *Stato di diritto e misure di sicurezza* (Studies of the Criminal Law Colloquium eld at Bressanone in 1961), Padua, 1962.

having allegedly failed, the field should be left open to medical and social action of a preventive nature in which the lawyers would have no place. The imperialistic monopoly of the criminal law was thus to be succeeded by a criminological imperialism, ill-defined and probably all the more dangerous, preoccupied solely with practical efficacy. Crime would be outside the judicial sphere, and the protective safeguards of criminal law and procedure would be bypassed by discretionary action against the symptoms of criminality. This unexpected consequence of the theories of recurrent criminality for a while threatened all those who adhered steadfastly to the supremacy of the rule of law. Just as the Nazi *Täterstrafrecht* was the caricature of a certain kind of criminal typology,[32] so inordinate reliance on preventive legislation of the kind typified by the Spanish *ley de vagos y maleantes* left the door wide open to all sorts of administrative abuses.[33] And doctrines which seemed at first as far removed from any political considerations as Sutherland's 'white collar crime' have been properly criticized for the confusion which they introduced into the notions of the rule of law and of due process.[34]

In some respects, the Criminological Congress of 1950 marked the apogee of this trend: in seeking a 'criminological definition of crime', the criminologists seemed to be issuing a challenge to the lawyers. It is significant, however, to note that it was one of the greatest of criminologists, Étienne de Greeff, who recommended that the Congress should return to—or preserve—the legal definition.[35] We are entitled to think that this acceptance is not entirely unconnected with the spread of social defence ideas, in so far as they encourage mutual understanding among the different social sciences and seek to preserve the balance between law and criminal science. The last two international Congresses for social

[32] On the *Tätertypen* in National Socialist doctrine and on the discussion of this theory, see S. Hurwitz, *Criminology*, pp. 294 ff.

[33] Cf. J.-B. Herzog, 'Les Lois de vagos y maleantes (Chronique de défense sociale)', *Rev. de science crim.*, 1953, p. 354.

[34] See especially the critical comments of Paul W. Tappan, 'Who is the Criminal? in *Amer. Sociological Review*, 1947, pp. 96 ff.; and (for a restatement of this criticism), *Crime, Justice and Correction*, New York, 1960, pp. 7 ff. G. B. Vold, *Theoretical Criminology*, New York, 1958, at pp. 248 ff.

[35] *Proceedings of the Second International Congress on Criminology (Paris, 1950)*, vol. VI, Paris, 1955, general report, 'Criminogénèse', by É. de Greeff, p. 300.

defence[36] have provided fresh evidence in favour of this proposition. The social defence movement may indeed congratulate itself on having, on the one hand, withstood the 'imperialism' of the criminologists, and on the other, successfully incited the lawyers to a greater degree of modesty. As a distinguished criminologist recently put it, the 'cold war' atmosphere has thus given way to an *entente cordiale*.

III

In order, however, to bring out the salient features of social defence even from the merely critical point of view with which we are at present concerned, it is not enough simply to note in what way the movement differs from classical or neo-classical criminal law on the one hand and from positivism on the other. In fact—and this is a more difficult question—it is essential to grasp in the first place just how the new social defence movement differs from the older trend associated with the name of Adolphe Prins, and secondly in what respects the modern movement should not be confused with certain tendencies which are no doubt very up-to-date and sometimes striking but which, however interesting they may be, do not express that 'common core' which we are seeking to identify.

It has been stated that, in Prins's view, the problem of free will was irrelevant. The new social defence movement has doubtless no intention of reviving nineteenth-century philosophical controversies concerning determinism, but recognizes, like Prins, that this is a philosophical problem and as such is outside the sphere of penal policy or of criminal law properly so called. On the other hand, however, it has been noted that a modern penal policy almost necessarily presupposes the freedom of the individual, or at any rate cannot disregard the reality of the individual and social sense of personal responsibility. The scope of such a penal policy is therefore not restricted to those who might be subject to irresistible biological, mental, or social pressures. Investigation of the human act and of the 'trajectory of crime' goes further than this. The new doctrine even holds that if a person commits a crime

[36] Stockholm Congress, 1958 (*Actes du Cinquième Congrès international de défense sociale*, Stockholm, 1963) and Belgrade Congress, 1961 (*Le Statut légal et le traitement des jeunes adultes délinquants. Actes du Sixième Congrès international de défense sociale*, Belgrade, 1962.)

because he is not master of his acts, then the primary aim of any treatment of social readaptation should be the restoration of such self-mastery. Therefore the problem of responsibility should no longer be neglected[37] as with Prins, but on the contrary reintroduced as an individual concept of responsibility on which the reaction against anti-social conduct would be centred.

Moreover, it may easily be seen that the measures proposed by Prins, which to a considerable extent were embodied in the Belgian Social Defence statute of 9 April 1930, were mainly of a negative character. At the risk of appearing to play with words, such measures might be described as chiefly concerned with the passive defence of society. The aim was to 'eliminate' or 'neutralize' the offender, and the mentally deficient or abnormal person was dealt with not so much with a view to treatment as to prevent his causing harm. New social defence, on the contrary, is essentially positive and active, concerned not to wait until the danger has passed, but to combat it in order to eradicate it. Whence the extensive development of curative and educational measures in recent years. Whence also the idea that even in the case of habitual or persistent offenders, who were formerly presumed to be incorrigible,[38] it is desirable to make an attempt at re-education, to try to apply, in turn, a progressive system of detention, release for a trial period, and finally a genuine method of treatment. So we move away from the fatalism that was characteristic of the old French system of *relégation* of 1885.

For the same reasons, the problems which preoccupied Prins now seem, quite rightly, rather limited in their scope. He was largely responsible for confining or appearing to confine social defence within a framework of measures designed to deal with either persistent or abnormal offenders. Today, social defence is

[37] In the opinion of Juan del Rosal (*La Personalidad del delincuente en la tecnica penal*, Valladolid, 1949, p. 128), Prins's doctrine in fact led to a 'determinism in disguise'; moreover, del Rosal denies that the test of 'social dangerousness' alone could provide an adequate basis for a system of criminal law. See however the remarks of J. Pinatel, *Traité de droit pénal et de criminologie*, vol. III, 1963, especially p. 490 ff. Cf. *La Responsabilité pénale* (Papers of the Colloquium on Penal Philosophy organized by the Institute of Criminal and Penitentiary Sciences at Strasbourg in January 1959), Paris, 1961.

[38] See Cannat, Gayraud, Vienne and Vullien, 'Le Problème des relégués', *Rev. pénit.*, 1950, pp. 72 ff.; cf. Cannat, *Nos frères les récidivistes*, Paris, 1942; Norval Morris, *The Habitual Delinquent*, London 1951; C. Germain, *Le Traitement des récidivistes en France*, 1953.

concerned with a much wider and more varied range of measures. Above all, it is now asserted that the re-education of children and young persons, and the similar measures very recently adopted with regard to 'young adults', necessarily come within the scope of social defence. In many respects, indeed, the spirit of re-education and help in which the rules of criminal law concerning children are applied is most truly characteristic of the teaching of new social defence.[39] So the limits laid down by Prins's original doctrine have been greatly exceeded, and his intellectual tendency (despite an acute sense of social compassion) to envisage the main activity of social defence in terms of the protection of society through the neutralization of the offender, has also been left behind.

Nearly all these differences between modern social defence and the doctrine of Prins are in fact explicable in terms of a novel approach to the controversial question of the 'potential dangerousness' of the offender. It was the International Union of Criminal Law which took over from the positivists the idea of dangerousness (*periculosité*, *pericolosità*) first worked out by Garofalo. Prins's whole doctrine is ultimately based on the contention that the 'danger' (*redoutabilité*) represented by the delinquent should be taken into account, first by the legislature, next by the judge, finally by the prison authorities. The influence of this idea in modern legislation is well known: it has been incorporated, for example into the Cuban Social Defence Code of 1936, the Italian Code of 1930, and the Swiss Code of 1937. It was in the order of things that the International Society for Criminology should devote to this concept a whole group of studies[40] among the series of international lecture courses, the organization of which is such a useful feature of its work, and that the subject should be considered, almost inevitably, at all the modern Congresses. At the same time, however, it is clear that the notion of 'dangerousness', if not out of date as such, has nevertheless been considerably modified since the heyday of the International Union of Criminal Law.[41]

[39] On this attitude, see J. Dublineau, 'La Surveillance éducative des jeunes délinquants en milieu libre', *Rev. de Science crim.*, 1952, pp. 53 ff.

[40] See *Deuxième cours international de Criminologie de 1953*, Paris, 1954.

[41] Modern criminologists lay stress on the complex causal factors that produce the criminal act: anti-social conduct thus results from the interplay and combination of various forces: see S. and E. Glueck, *Unraveling Juvenile Delinquency*, New York, 1950, p. 281. Cf. W. Healy, *The Individual Delinquent*, 1915; W. Healy and A. Bronner,

The idea that certain individuals are dangerous in themselves and are immediately identifiable as such, now seems inadequate. If the human act, and in particular the criminal act, is the expression—or at any rate *an* expression—of the criminal's personality, then it is the latter which should first be considered, for it is, so to speak, both the alpha and the omega of the problem. Besides, one is immediately aware that it is no longer enough to think that the problem of crime can be resolved simply by means of a distinction between 'dangerous' personalities and those which are not. In any case, there will be found to exist a large 'marginal' category of offenders whose actions cannot be explained simply in terms of the active expression of a pre-existing dangerousness. It is enough to state the problem and raise the question in order to realize that we are far removed here from the conception of dangerousness on which Prins's doctrine was based, or as understood by the Belgian social defence statute and the Spanish or Latin American *Leyes de vagos y maleantes*.[42]

If this is so, it will be acknowledged that doctrines which seek to perfect a modern, scientific, and effective penal policy are bound to transcend the views of Prins and of the International Union of Criminal Law. Perhaps it would be better to say that such progressive doctrines are obliged to react against the first system of social defence, which led to the simplification of the problem in a way that is today inadmissible. Between the two World Wars, both in the U.S.A. and in Europe, there was already a large-scale legislative movement to impose the preliminary investigation of offenders before trial. This principle, first applied to young offenders, has been progressively extended to adults, and the importance or value of the medical, psychological, and sociological

---

Delinquents and Criminals, their making and unmaking, 1926; Cantor, *Crime and Society*, 1939; M. Vamberg, 'Criminality and Behaviorism', *Journ. of Criminal Law and Criminology*, 1941, pp. 158 ff.; see also S. Hurwitz, *Criminology*, p. 210. Cf. Di Tullio, *Trattato di Antropologia criminale*, 1945, and Enrico Altavilla, *La dinamica del delitto*, 2 vols., 1953. On the 'total' nature of the personality envisaged in relation to its various constitutive factors, see F. Exner, *Kriminologie*, Berlin, 1949, p. 27. On dangerousness, see and compare the discussion in O. Kinberg, *Problèmes fondamentaux de la criminologie*, Paris, 1960, pp. 43 ff., and J. Pinatel, *Criminologie*, p. 409, respectively; Houchon, 'Les Problèmes posés par l'évolution du concept criminologique d'état dangereux', in *Annales de la Fac. de droit de Liège*, 1961, pp. 543 ff.

[42] On these enactments, see J. B. Herzog, 'Chroniques de défense sociale' in the *Rev. de Science crim.*, 1953, pp. 354 and 711.

study of the criminal is no longer seriously questioned.[43] This matter will be raised again later. It should at least be observed at this stage that this represented a success—even a conquest—for the doctrines of social defence. But it should also be noted that in thus concentrating on the assessment of the criminal personality in its dynamic aspect, that is to say in the social and individual context, the new doctrines draw apart from the earlier theories: the latter took a static view, as it were, of the potentially dangerous character of a particular person, and proposed to deal with this by measures of protection that were both simple and brutal.

IV

We have just spoken of the subjective approach and of the increasing importance of this tendency in modern penal concepts. The word brings to mind some of the theories put forward by Gramatica, who wrote a book on 'subjective criminal law',[44] while his more recent work also shows the influence of this tendency.[45] But the very idea of a 'subjective criminal law' itself raises certain difficulties, for we may well ask ourselves straightway what are or should be the limits of this subjective approach. Is it merely a case of paying increasing attention, in evaluating the criminal act, to the offender's motive?[46] Is it a case of abandoning or transforming the old notion of intention, abstract and objective, which played so prominent a part in classical or neo-classical penal doctrine, especially in France, and is today thought by many people to be distinctly outdated?[47] If that is what is meant by subjectivism,

[43] On this investigation of the personality, see especially the *Premier Cours international de Criminologie*, Paris, 1953; 'Huitièmes Journées de défense sociale', *Rev. de Science crim.*, 1960, p. 595 ff. (more especially the report by Prof. Levasseur, p. 621); *Actes du Premier Congrès français de criminologie*, 1961.

[44] *Principi di diritto penale soggettivo*, Turin, 1934.

[45] *Principi di difesa sociale*, 1961.

[46] On the ever-increasing attention paid to the question of motive in modern criminal law, see H. Donnedieu de Vabres, *La Justice pénale d'aujourd'hui* (first ed.), p. 31; cf. Jerome Hall, *General Principles of Criminal Law*, Indianapolis, 1947, pp. 161-62; Stefani and Levasseur, *Droit pénal et criminologie*, 1957, No. 175; J. Constant, *Manuel de droit pénal*, 7th ed., vol. I, Liège, 1959, No. 119; P. Bouzat, *Traité*, vol. I, 1963, No. 173.

[47] See J. Lebret, 'Essai sur la notion de l'intention criminelle', *Rev. de Science crim.*, 1938, pp. 348 ff. Cf. the *Code pénal annoté* of Émile Garçon, 2nd ed., by Rousselet, Patin and Ancel (art. I, t. I, No. 82). R. Merle, *Droit pénal général complémentaire*, Paris, 1957, pp. 226 ff.; cf. Glanville Williams, *Criminal Law (The General Part)*, 2nd ed., 1961, No. 21, p. 48; *Kenny's Outlines of Criminal Law*, 18th ed., by J. W. C. Turner, Cambridge, 1962, p. 31, No. 5.

then it would be fairly easy for agreement to be reached among all those who are inspired by the new doctrines of social defence.

It would seem, however, that one kind of subjectivism, perhaps including that favoured by Gramatica, would like to take things further. Would not this approach then involve taking account of the criminal's 'will to act', in a renovated penal policy? But then there immediately arises the question of the extent to which such an enquiry into criminal intention should be admissible. It would be out of the question to return, by some detour or other, to the excesses of the eighteenth-century *ancien droit*, which purported to punish the mere intention to commit crime, apart from any actual attempt.[48] Even more inadmissible would be any concession towards the kind of excesses which were the outcome of National Socialist criminal law when it claimed to establish a *Willensstrafrecht*.[49] We know something of the outcome of such views and of the violation of human rights that can result from the totalitarian investigation of a merely suspected criminal purpose.

It would probably be unjust to accuse Gramatica or certain of his disciples of going as far as this, for he himself was at pains to point out the differences between his 'subjective criminal law' and the *Willensstrafrecht* of Nazi Germany.[50] More particularly, those who are directly indebted to Gramatica's arguments do not fail to point out that the effect of his doctrine is to reject not only the old classical notion of intention, but even the sanction for the 'criminal mind' (*mens rea*) in the old sense: social defence, in this view, would thus reject the very idea of repression, and would postulate only an active process of social readaptation to which the offender would actually have a right. From this proposition there would ultimately be deduced, not only the elimination of punishment in so far as this involved suffering imposed on the convicted person, but also the disappearance of even the notions

[48] See the case cited by Jousse (*Traité de la justice criminelle de France*, 1771, vol. III, p. 697) concerning a man of good family who, on confessing that he had thought of killing Henri II, King of France, was 'thereupon condemned to be decapitated, which judgement was carried out'.

[49] See H. Donnedieu de Vabres, *La Politique criminelle des États autoritaires*, 1938, pp. 93 ff.

[50] See in particular the article, already cited, 'La lotta contra la pena', (The fight against punishment), *Riv. di Difesa sociale*, 1947, No. 1. Cf. *Principi di difesa sociale*, 1961. On this conception of Gramatica, see the comments by Jiménez de Asúa, *Tratado*, vol. II, 2nd ed., Nos. 531 and 541. For another view of subjectivism, see the remarks by O. A. Germann, *Das Verbrechen im neuen Strafrecht*, Zurich, 1942.

of crime and the criminal. These words—together, of course, with the term 'criminal law' which conjured up the idea of repression—would in the end be banished from the terminology of social defence. Some advocates of this extreme trend even went so far as to maintain that the process of social readaptation must on no account cause the anti-social individual 'any harm'.[51]

Hopefully, we might have expected that such isolated statements would be condemned by Gramatica himself in the doctrinal synthesis which he was preparing for publication at about that time. On the contrary, the *Principi di difesa sociale* adopt most of these extreme opinions. Elsewhere we have drawn attention to the signal merits of this work while criticizing its conceptions. In his book, as we are obliged to repeat unequivocally, the founder of the Study Centre at Genoa in 1945 expounds what is simply a personal doctrine, at variance with the generally accepted body of ideas common to the social defence movement as a whole. It is not a pleasant task, of course, to have to contradict a writer for whom one has a high regard, or to be obliged to stress the contrast between the view officially held and proclaimed by the International Society for Social Defence on the one hand, and the opinions of its President on the other. However regrettable this may be, it is necessary to assert clearly, at this stage, that the views of the new social defence movement and the doctrines of Gramatica here follow different paths.

This divergence has been demonstrated in the previous chapter,[52] and need not be repeated. Gramatica, as we know, wishes to suppress the terms 'crime', 'criminal', and 'punishment'. He wants to replace the unlawful act, which lies at the foundation of modern criminal law, by the social, biological, and psychological personality of the individual in question: in his view a concept of anti-social conduct (*antisocialità*), envisaged in subjective terms, becomes the key to a system which excludes any ideas of punishment and imposes on the State the duty to reintegrate the individual socially, while denying it the right to punish him.[53] Thus social defence would take the place of the system of criminal law, instead of becoming integrated with it.[54] But it must be stressed

[51] C. De Vincentiis, Report to the social defence session held at San Marino in September 1951, *Riv. di Difesa sociale*, 1951, pp. 85 ff.

[52] See footnotes (6) and (8), p. 73.

[53] *Principi di difesa sociale*, § 9.

[54] *Ibid.*, § 13.

once again that the whole purpose of the new social defence movement is directed towards the incorporation of its ideas into the existing system according to the principle of sound penal policy. This is shown by the standpoint adopted in the 'minimum programme' of the International Society for Social Defence, by the present orientation of that society, and by the discussions and resolutions of its most recent Congresses. In this connexion, the contrast between modern penal policy and neo-classical criminal law should not be misunderstood: the new social defence movement is equally critical of theories which purport to do away with criminal law altogether in so far as this constitutes a body of legal rules. As was very properly observed by Strahl, who was the principal draughtsman of the 'minimum programme', the new social defence has had to fight on two fronts.[55] It is indeed significant that the programme in question clearly speaks of the theory and foundations of *criminal law*.[56] It should not be forgotten that the expression 'criminal law', tirelessly repeated, was used deliberately, and that special attention was devoted to the theoretical basis of criminal law, described by Graven as 'the cornerstone of the whole edifice' of the doctrine of social defence.[57]

It is therefore quite inaccurate to claim that the doctrines of new social defence presuppose the suppression of the concepts of criminal law and crime, and the refusal to define the criminal as someone who can be called to account in the criminal courts for acts classified by the law as offences. In the next chapter it will be seen how the social defence movement in its positive aspect, after emptying certain notions of their legal content, steadfastly supports the maintenance of a conception of the rule of law which involves respect for the rule *nulla poena sine lege*, a proper system of legal procedure, and the handling of criminal cases by the criminal courts as the normal course of events. At this point we should note the importance which the 'minimum programme' assigned to the notion of *légalité*—which may be broadly translated 'the rule of law'—as traditionally understood since the late eighteenth century. I would therefore disagree with Frey's contention that

[55] 'Rörelsen för Socialskydd', in *Svensk Juristtidning*, 1955, pp. 28 ff.

[56] For this Programme, see *Rev. de Science crim.*, 1954, p. 807, and Marc Ancel's commentary, same *Revue*, 1955, p. 562.

[57] In his article, 'Droit pénal et défense sociale'; see next note.

social defence doctrines may be reduced to *un droit pur de l'auteur*, that is to say a wholly elastic and subjective body of 'rules' exclusively referable to the author of the criminal act: this would lead in the end to the complete disappearance of criminal law as a system of legal rules.[58] For the same reasons, we refuse to accept that modern penal policy should aim at substituting a system of social defence (so called) for the existing system of criminal law, as is claimed by Gramatica. On the contrary: reversing his thesis, we maintain that the essential purpose of modern penal policy should be to integrate the ideas of social defence into criminal law. Similarly, we cannot accept Gramatica's illusory proposal to suppress the traditional terminology in these matters. In the systems of criminal law currently in force which accept the notion of the 'rule of law', *lato sensu*, and in which, precisely, the advocates of social defence intend to stimulate a fruitful reformist trend, it is clear that any prohibition of the terms 'crime' and 'criminal' would be in contradiction to the clear-sighted realism on which the new social defence movement prides itself. What this movement hopes to promote, on the contrary, is a penal policy that should adopt a new approach towards both the criminal act which is classified as such by the law, and the offender, who whether we like it or not remains the individual human being who has committed an act which the law qualifies as criminal.

It is necessary to go still further, and to realize that although the social defence movement is not concerned with repression in the traditional sense, and although it adopts an attitude which may be described as anti-repressive or at any rate non-repressive, this does not on that account involve abandoning punishment as such. Of course, the birth of the movement at the close of the last century was directly related to the manifest inadequacy of the traditional concept of punishment, both on scientific and on social grounds. Jean Graven, who must often be referred to in

[58] E. Frey, 'Strafrecht oder soziale Verteidigung?', *Rev. pénale suisse*, 1953, pp. 405 ff. Some of these assertions have been repeated more recently in a lecture which is analysed in the *Revue pénitentiaire* (*Bull. de l'Union des societés de patronage de France*), 1963, pp. 281 ff. This lecture, which will be mentioned again later, shows that some neo-classical theorists remain poorly informed of the realities of the new social defence movement. Juan del Rosal, in his book *Personalidad del delinquente en la técnica penal*, Valladolid, 1949, had expounded a much more subtle theory of the *droit pénal de l'auteur*. J. Graven dealt with these accusations in his magnificent reply to Frey ('Droit pénal et défense sociale', *Rev. pénale suisse*, 1955, No. 1).

order to understand and define the modern doctrine of social defence, has indeed written that 'the failure of the purely repressive or punitive system, traditionally founded on exclusively abstract legal principles, cannot today be denied'.[59] That is why the main or initial task of the social defence movement was the development of a system of measures that should be distinct from existing punishments and better adapted to controlling the danger constituted by delinquent persons. But only a certain positivist approach, no longer in vogue, could maintain that the lessons to be drawn from criminology involved the total disappearance of punishments and their replacement by preventive measures. The difference and contrast between punishments and safety measures, or on the contrary their possible unification, will be discussed later. For the moment it is enough to note carefully that social defence, after realistic analysis of the individual social phenomena from which it starts, admits that punishment, as a means of effectuating a penal policy, ought not to be rejected *a priori*.[60] The view is doubtless taken that tomorrow punishment will not have the importance it had yesterday, or even that which it retains today. It is also thought, no doubt, that the notion of 'general prevention', as applied to punishment, has been greatly exaggerated. Recent studies, however, and in particular a most suggestive article by Andenaes, have demonstrated that the existence of general prevention could not simply be denied today.[61] Moreover, it is not without good reason that punishment has everywhere been retained in the criminal law actually in force in this second half of the twentieth century. It can even be observed, indeed, that although the modern law applied to juvenile delinquency rejects the idea of repression in favour of re-education, the possibility of applying to delinquent juveniles a penal sanction in the true sense of the word has nevertheless been retained practically everywhere, even if only for exceptional cases. And if this is the case

[59] *Op. et loc. cit.*

[60] See Marc Ancel, 'Responsabilité et défense sociale', *Rev. de Science crim.*, 1959, pp. 179 ff.; cf. the article by J. Graven on 'L'Activité du groupe médico-psycho-juridique de Genève. Colloque sur la responsabilité pénale', same *Revue*, 1961, pp. 325 ff., together with the proceedings, previously cited, of the colloquium on penal philosophy held at Strasbourg in January 1959, published under the supervision of J. Léauté under the title *La Responsabilité pénale*, Paris, 1961.

[61] 'General Prevention, Illusion or Reality?', *Journ. of Criminal Law, Criminology and Police Science*, vol. 43, No. 2, July-August, 1952, pp. 176 ff.

with regard to juveniles, it remains even truer of young adult offenders.[62]

The explanation for this is simple, and results from the taking into account of the criminal act itself as an expression of the criminal's personality. If the sanction applied to the offender is conceived in terms of treatment, which has to be individualized according to his character and deep-seated needs (and not on the basis of external criteria such as his previous criminal record or the objective circumstances of his offence), then it is desirable to discover what kind of steps would have the best results from the social standpoint. So it is clear in any event that the infliction of a punitive sanction will remain the most appropriate criminological measure for certain categories of offenders. One should remain sufficiently clear-headed to realize that in certain circumstances the sanction in question might be a short term of preventive detention. This certainly does not mean that the social defence movement, from the pioneer days of Liszt and Prins, has been mistaken in the campaign it has waged against short prison sentences. We should not, of course, give up the search for an alternative to short sentences, which remain the common coin of the criminal courts but have been shown time and time again to have harmful effects from the social point of view.[63] However, careful study of the personality of criminals and of the 'dynamic of crime' ineluctably leads to the conclusion that punishment in the proper sense of the term, of brief duration but in an exemplary form, may still have some re-educative value in the case of certain offenders and certain offences, which might be termed 'occasional offences' (*infractions occasionnelles*). Besides, it is interesting to

[62] See *Seuils d'âge et législation pénale—Contribution à l'étude du problème des jeunes adultes délinquants*, published by the *Centre d'études de défense sociale* of the Comparative Law Institute of the University of Paris, under the supervision of the *Procureur-Général* Besson, Paris, 1961. See also the Proceedings of the Fifth International Congress for Social Defence of 1958, *Actes du Cinqième Congrès international de défense sociale*, Stockholm, 1963, and the Proceedings of the Sixth Congress of Belgrade in 1961, *Le Statut légal et le traitement des jeunes adultes délinquants. Actes du Sixième Congrès international de défense sociale*, Belgrade, 1962.

[63] See in particular *Twelfth International Penal and Penitentiary Congress (The Hague, 1950) Proceedings*, Berne, 1951: Section III, 1st question: 'Short term imprisonment and its alternatives (probation, fines, compulsory home labour, etc.)', vol. II (Records of the meetings, pp. 222 ff., and vol. V (general and national reports of section III); see also the papers of the *Société des Prisons*, report by Cannat, 'Convient-il de supprimer les courtes peines de prison?', *Rev. int. de droit pénal*, 1951, pp. 573 ff.; cf. C. Germain, *Eléments de science pénitentiaire*, 1959, pp. 62 ff.

observe that the Criminal Justice Act (1948), which in many respects represents a new approach to penal policy and so—as cannot be emphasized too often—is broadly speaking, though unwittingly, a 'social defence statute', provides not only for corrective training but also introduces a largely punitive institution, under the name of 'detention centre', described by British penologists themselves as a kind of 'psychological shock'.[64] Because the social defence movement tries to maintain a realistic approach, it has no intention of abandoning the possibility of resorting, if need be, to the psychological shock of punishment.[65]

For that matter, we should not overlook the fact that most of the alternatives suggested to replace short prison sentences consist of a series of obligations or prohibitions imposed on the offender who thereafter undergoes non-institutional treatment. In particular, measures prohibiting him from engaging in certain activities or from frequenting certain places—and it is well known that preventive provisions of this kind are widespread in modern legislation—have to be accompanied by sanctions in the case of infringement. Neither probation nor a fine will always be adequate, so that it will be necessary in the long run and at one remove, so to speak (that is, *after* the failure of a measure which does not involve detention), to fall back on a punitive sanction, and in practice on a prison sentence. In that case it would be peculiarly unrealistic, and a vain play upon words, to pretend that even a sanction which involved detention should not be described as a punishment: a 'social defence code' of this kind would surely pave the way to a new version of what French lawyers call *la révolte des faits* (against codified law).[66]

[64] On detention centres, see L. W. Fox, *The English Prison and Borstal Systems*, London, 1952, pp. 341 ff. For the rather similar institution of the attendance centre, see John Spencer, *Howard Journal*, vol. VIII, No. 3, 1952, p. 146, and *British Journal of Delinquency*, January, 1951, pp. 230 ff.

[65] See the interesting observations of W. F. Roper, 'The Attitude to the Prisoner', *Howard Journal*, vol. VIII, No. 3, 1952, pp. 158 ff., where the author, professionally engaged in penitentiary treatment and largely inspired by ideas of social defence, stresses the salutary effect that punishment may have, and its effective rôle as a curative factor. He writes that this constitutes 'an opportunity, just as shocks may be in psychiatric practice. The important thing is to know how to use this opportunity in the way necessary for the individual case . . . The real verdict on punishment is not that it is wrong in itself, but that it is wrong to use it without great care and without proper treatment' (p. 160).

[66] The origin of this expression is to be found in the work of G. Morin, *La Révolte des faits contre le Code*, Paris, 1920. It is well known that in the economic

That is why the 'fundamental body of doctrine' common to the new social defence movement as a whole rejects certain interpretations of an extreme kind, facile enough it is true, which purport to replace the precise concepts actually in existence by much vaguer notions based on the general idea of anti-social conduct. As has been said above, such an approach would presuppose a breach with those human and social realities that social defence, on the contrary, flatters itself on reintroducing into the criminal law. Furthermore, such an attitude would replace the old fictions by new conventions of thought and language which would exercise a no less baleful influence. New and unexpected taboos would make their appearance (for instance, the non-recognition of the terms *crime* and *criminal*). Again, and even more easily, such an extreme approach would make do with certain subversive theories which would serve only to mislead those persons who might not be sufficiently aware of the possibly inadequate and unsatisfactory nature of such theories.

For similar reasons, as well as for others which are more profound, we cannot accept Gramatica's rejection of the notion of moral responsibility. This is probably the most serious source of conflict and also perhaps the most tenacious, so that it needs to be clearly explained.

We have already observed that, in Gramatica's view, a subjective notion of anti-social conduct is the foundation of the system. This notion replaces the traditional notion of responsibility which he deems outmoded.[67] According to the doctrines of new social defence, on the contrary, the individual and collective sense of responsibility is a psychological and social reality to which the greatest attention should be paid and which, above all, can

---

sphere modern criminal law, which lays down an ever-increasing number of prohibitions and duties, almost inevitably leads to a corresponding increase of punishments in the form of fine and imprisonment. On this topic see the reports of the Sixth International Congress for Criminal Law at Rome, and in particular the most suggestive general report by M. P. Vrij, *Rev. int. de droit pénal*, 1953, pp. 126 ff. Many modern criminologists continue to propose, quite rightly, that the punishments currently applied to the negligent motorist should be replaced by measures of which the most far-reaching would be the suppression of his driving licence. But if the motorist nevertheless continued to drive, in defiance of the prohibition, what adequate sanction would there be apart from punishment in the traditional sense, and who would seriously deny that in such a case the threat of punishment might be effective?

[67] *Principi di difesa sociale*, chap, II, pp. 32 ff.; chap. III, pp. 63 ff.

be used to implement a penal policy. It is doubtless advisable not to adopt a metaphysical approach to the problem of responsibility while going further than the traditional view in which that concept merely served as a basis for a 'presumption of imputability'. The doctrine of new social defence goes further than the prudent agnosticism of Prins and the hesitations of some of his followers.[68] The period of sterile opposition between the concepts of culpability and dangerousness is no more. Psychologists and medical practitioners have drawn our attention to the permanence and the force of the immanent sense of responsibility. Others have pointed out the difference between determinism in the positivist sense and the individual pressures which may influence a person's freedom of action without suppressing it altogether.[69] Finally, so experienced and well-informed a criminologist as Pinatel endeavours to develop and to elucidate the notion of 'proneness to lapse' (*labilité*), infinitely more subtle than the former conceptions of predisposition towards crime (and even of 'constitutional', inherent delinquency) or of the offender's lack of foresight: he seeks to reconcile the two notions of dangerousness and responsibility, which yesterday appeared antagonistic.[70] Pinatel's theory of the criminal personality is certainly far removed from Gramatica's doctrine of the anti-social personality.

Along the same lines, the new social defence movement, in so far as it tries to promote a penal policy that should be both scientific and effective, claims not to maintain but to *restore* the concept of moral responsibility, which it seeks to free both from metaphysical notions accepted *a priori* and from all purely legal formalism. In fact, it is because the individual human being believes himself to be free, and is so thought of by others, that he should be considered as such, even though the individual treatment of the criminal is founded on the anomalous or defective form in which that freedom found expression in that particular case. The notion of responsibility thus appears as the essential

[68] See in particular Paul Cornil, 'L'Impasse de la responsabilité pénale', *Rev. de droit pénal et de crim.*, 1961-1962, pp. 637 ff.

[69] Pompe, Kempe and Baan, 'Le Problème de la responsabilité criminelle', in *Autour de l'œuvre du Dr É. de Greeff*, vol. I, *L'Homme criminel*, Louvain, 1956, pp. 73 ff.

[70] J. Pinatel, 'Responsabilité pénale et criminologie', in *La Responsabilité pénale* (*Travaux du colloque de Philosophie pénale de Strasbourg, 1959*), Paris, 1961, pp. 157 ff.; P. Bouzat and J. Pinatel, *Traité de droit pénal et de criminologie*, vol. III, *Criminologie*, by J. Pinatel, 1963, pp. 490 ff.

mainspring in the treatment of social readaptation, and remains or becomes in any event the fundamental justification for the sanction that has been applied. Far from wishing to treat delinquents as sick and irresponsible, as has sometimes been casually asserted, social defence takes the view that every individual, even though he be 'guilty' of a crime, is nevertheless a human being and hence fundamentally a free agent, who in a rational system of social protection must be called to account for his faults. In many cases the practical problem will be to give him or restore to him that moral freedom which has been affected, if not annihilated by internal pressures or his incapacity to resist. It is in this way that a treatment of social readaptation, in the full sense of the term, will operate to ensure 'the prevention of crime and the treatment of offenders' which remains the ultimate purpose of the new social defence movement. We may therefore conclude with assurance, on this point, that this doctrine of penal policy cannot be understood, let alone justified, without constant reference to the idea of human responsibility, and that is where we differ radically from some of Gramatica's basic doctrines.

There is one last distinction to be drawn between new social defence as a scientific movement of penal policy and certain theoretical tendencies of an improvised nature, generous in their inspiration but completely unscientific. The social defence movement has suffered in certain respects from the somewhat hasty, unreflective, and over-enthusiastic adherence of various 'disciples' who were perhaps attracted above all by a novel phraseology. Moreover, the movement has been a pole of attraction for people who were concerned about penal reform and hoped to find in social defence a convenient weapon that could be turned against the lawyers. Such people seized upon a few striking slogans while sometimes remaining ignorant of legal realities and of the essential function of legal technique. They believed they could venture boldly into the arena of criminal law reform while neglecting indispensable basic knowledge. A few criminologists and medical practitioners, though highly qualified in their own fields, have also succumbed to such temptations. Others again have apparently lost sight of their initial legal training and have thus seemed content to bask in the glow of a generous and manageable set of ideals. We should not hesitate to affirm, here and now, that the penal policy of social defence, in so far as it tries to bring about a useful reform of criminal law, can be properly understood and usefully developed only by those who possess an adequate knowledge of criminal law. Only criminal scientists who are aware of the demands of juridical science are entitled to require that certain notions be emptied of their legal content: in specialized fields of knowledge, as in life in general, we can only presume to rid ourselves of what we actually possess. The qualified supporters of the new social defence movement should remain vigilant in this regard. The task of keeping social defence within the framework of criminal science, where its place was first marked out by Prins, is one that should never be lost sight of by those who work to ensure the evolution and success of this doctrine.

Such are the reasons that compel the partisans of new social defence to fight on two fronts—if not indeed on three. This is not an embarrassment to them, and the various criticisms that have to be met and overcome tend to demonstrate the sound basis of a middle-of-the-road, moderate doctrine which is nevertheless not eclectic in the sense in which this term was used at the beginning of this century. In any case, the advocates of social defence are concerned not to be assimilated to the followers of the extreme doctrine which is represented—brilliantly, it is true—by Gramatica. Experienced criminal scientists are today aware of the differences between the two schools of modern social defence. The best-informed treatises on criminal law or criminal science are proof of this, as are numerous criminological studies on the international level.[71] Writers in this field generally approve the part which this moderate approach, as expounded above, can play in modern criminal science.[72] No better tribute can be paid to new social defence.

[71] See especially J. Constant, *Manuel de droit pénal*, 7th ed., Liège, 1960, vol. I, Nos. 14 and 15; P. Bouzat and J. Pinatel, *Traité de droit pénal et de criminologie*, 1963, vol. I, No. 50; R. Vouin and J. Léauté, *Droit pénal et criminologie*, 1956, pp. 109 ff.

[72] P. Nuvolone, 'Les Sanctions pénales dans la pensée d'Enrico Ferri et dans la période historique actuelle', in *Rev. pénale suisse*, 1956, pp. 345 ff., esp. p. 347; A. Beristain, in *Revista de estudios penitenciarios*, 1962, pp. 5 ff.; G. Levasseur, review in *Rev. de Science crim.*, 1954, pp. 428ff.; A. Légal, review in *Rev. int. de droit comp.*, 1954, p. 842, and 1963, p. 608; E. R. Aftalion, foreword to *La nueva defensa social*, Buenos Aires, 1961; N. Szrentić, foreword to *Nova druzventa Odbraira*, Belgrade, 1963; J. M. Canals, 'Classicism, Positivism and Social Defence', in *Journ. of Crim. Law, Criminology and Police Science*, vol. 50, No. 6, 1960, pp. 541 ff.; H. Mannheim, *Pioneers in Criminology*, London, 1960, Introduction, p. 35; cf. by the same author, *Group Problems in Crime and Punishment*, pp. 202-209.

Chapter Six

THE DOCTRINE OF NEW SOCIAL DEFENCE IN ITS POSITIVE AND CONSTRUCTIVE ASPECT

IN THE PRECEDING CHAPTER we tried to give an account of what may be described as the critical aspect of the new social defence doctrine, and we were thus led to examine the theories, conceptions, and tendencies to which the movement is *opposed*. At the same time, we tried to distinguish between certain extreme interpretations and the body of common thinking that brings together the various supporters of a doctrine whose unity does not lie in any kind of dogmatic uniformity. So we were able to perceive what social defence is *not*. But the picture would be neither complete nor accurate if we did not now endeavour to explain what the doctrine *is*, and try, in the present chapter, to bring out its positive elements. This we will now attempt, without in any way intending to expound in detail what may be called the technique of social defence, or to present a synthesis of 'principles of social defence', in the way in which this expression was understood by, for instance, Gramatica.

It has already been explained that the *new* social defence doctrine does not seek to abolish the whole system of criminal law as such, but tries, on the contrary, to reorganize the existing system along the lines of a rational penal policy. The doctrine therefore includes not only various suggestions for reform, but likewise a kind of reappraisal of basic values concerning criminal law and criminal procedure. In this chapter we shall not attempt to draw up a complete inventory of what the rational penal policy of social defence ought to comprise, for this would involve a survey of nearly all the heads of criminal law and procedure. Our present task is simply to place social defence in perspective as a dynamic movement, so as to understand the changes it is actively seeking to promote.

The positive contribution of the new social defence movement appears to depend on three essential factors. First of all, social defence involves a certain process of 'de-legalization', that is to say, emptying certain conceptions of their purely legal content, yet without doing away with the legal order in the proper sense of the term. Secondly, the new social defence doctrine finds active expression in a new attitude towards the criminal, which provides the basis for realistic social action against the phenomenon of crime. Lastly, new social defence draws ideological inspiration from a certain moral attitude and aims ultimately at a humanist conception of penal policy. These three points must be dealt with in turn, before defining more completely the place of the new social defence movement with regard to the essential problem of responsibility.

I

The first and perhaps the clearest attitude taken up by the social defence movement—even if it is not the most important—is a reaction against the *legalistic* excesses of the neo-classical school. This is in many ways a starting-point, which serves to illuminate many aspects of the doctrine, helping to place it in the proper perspective of penal policy rather than of pure law.[1]

The term 'de-legalization' (*dé-juridicisation*) is of course a distressing neologism, but is nevertheless used intentionally. This is not only because the word expresses a particular intellectual reality more completely than would any other existing term (convenience of expression never justifies the misuse of language): the fact is that this new term enshrines a new, rather unusual element in the history of ideas concerning criminal justice, and brings out most clearly the significance of that element. It is essential, however, to define the term with the greatest possible precision.

For nearly two centuries, reforms in the field of criminal law have involved the transformation not only of enacted law but also

[1] See G. Levasseur, on '*La Défense sociale nouvelle*', by Marc Ancel, *Rev. de Science crim.*, 1954, p. 428; I. Strahl, 'Rörelsen för Socialskydd', *Svensk Juristtidnig*, 1955; cf. the discussions on the occasion of the twenty-fifth anniversary of the *Revue de Science criminelle et de droit pénal comparé*, concerning the theme of the relation between criminal science and comparative law, in the same *Revue*, 1962, pp. 216 ff.

of the theories which served to support, justify, and explain such law. The movement for reform, or in some cases the evolution of the existing system (or merely its extension) normally found expression within the framework—and in the terms—of criminal science considered as a legal discipline. At the close of last century however, a different approach threw light on the wider and more significant field of the emergent criminal sciences, alongside the province of criminal law itself. The former 'auxiliary disciplines' of criminal law first became autonomous and then tried not only to develop their independent character in relation to rules of law, but to assert their superiority. So it was that from the beginning of this century onwards, and in particular between the two World Wars, there were numerous doctrinal attempts to reintroduce purely legal concepts into the criminal sciences and to preserve inviolate the domain of pure law. These attempts have already been noted, and there is no need to go over the same ground again. There was thus a twofold movement, which sought on the one hand to transform criminal law from within, and on the other hand to influence it from without, with a view to producing new syntheses or new results.

The movement of ideas which sprang from the positivist controversy, the theories of criminal prevention that emerged before the second World War, the academic disputes provoked by the Criminological Congress of 1950, and its perhaps over-hasty search for a definitive methodology of the criminal sciences[2] gradually led members of the legal profession to show themselves increasingly aware of the importance of the social sciences in the study of the phenomenon of crime. Generally speaking, however, none of these movements radically affected the attitude of lawyers. Almost all the reformers took into consideration the terminology and concepts of criminal law, and the success of the theorists of pure law was largely due to their implicit rehabilitation of purely legal notions.[3] However, the natural aim of the social defence

[2] See the papers of this Congress, which on matters of detail were often remarkable: *Proceedings of the Second International Congress on Criminology* (Paris, 1950), 6 vols., Paris, 1951-1953. Cf. Bouzat and Pinatel, *Traité de droit pénal et de criminologie*, vol. III, *Criminologie*, by J. Pinatel, 1963, pp. 9 ff.

[3] See in this connexion Petrocelli, *La dirección juridica italiana en la ciencia del derecho penal* (Publicación de los seminarios de la Faculdad de derecho de la Universidad de Valladolid), 1950, which shows that the 'pure law' school is essentially a lawyers' reaction, constituting a trend rather than a school of thought in the true sense of the term.

movement from its inception has been to promote the idea of the penal policy that would adopt an approach broadly similar to that taken up by Montesquieu when he sought to investigate 'the spirit of the laws'. Such an approach does not of course involve the disappearance of criminal law, but this ceases to be autarkic, as it were: in particular, criminal law ceases to appear as an end in itself. According to this rational view of penal policy directed towards the social struggle against crime, criminal law undoubtedly appears as one of the most important aspects or instruments of such a penal policy, but is no more than an aspect or instrument. So the principles, notions, and theories of criminal law, even the most fundamental of them, exist and justify their existence only in so far as they contribute to the ultimate social purpose acknowledged by the penal policy as this is understood.

This explains, fundamentally, why the social defence movement from its inception has stood out against all forms of *a priori* legal reasoning. This term evidently means, in the first place, the abstract or objective notions of the classical theorists, but also extends to the 'metaphysical' interpretation of criminal law. These various points have already been sufficiently covered in these pages and need not be discussed further. But the durable element in social defence doctrine, to which the permanence and continuity of the movement bear witness, is a lucid attempt to break through legal forms or, if need be, the conceptions underlying those forms, so as to attain the social reality which alone can provide a basis for the new penal policy. That is why the social defence movement leads to the 'de-legalization' of certain concepts and of certain aspects of reaction to crime.

It would be easy enough to show how classical criminal law, and even in very large measure the enacted criminal law actually in force, are based on legal fictions and often make an almost gratuitous use of purely legal technique, in such a way that concepts of criminal law ultimately cease to correspond with social realities. Here again, this is not the place to enter into details. We may recall in passing, however, that the natural corollary of the rule *nulla poena sine lege* is the fiction *ignorantia juris haud excusat.* Such a presumption is probably inevitable in any organized and highly developed society that is based on legal foundations and proclaims its adherence to the rule of law. It must not be forgotten, however, that in Beccaria's view as in Bentham's the legal basis of crimes and punishments meant that any citizen could know at any moment what acts were prohibited by law and what was the punishment he might incur if he infringed such a legal prohibition. In calling for a Code the Frenchmen of 1789 somewhat ingenuously imagined that the free individual, whose 'imprescriptible rights' would be guaranteed by such a document, would refer to it directly and even read it aloud to his assembled household in the evenings, so as better to instil the civic virtues among his children and dependants. Where is this ideal vision today?

It would appear that a common-sense distinction ought at least to be drawn between those natural offences that every man—or every civilized man at any rate—immediately recognizes, and what Garofalo called 'artificial offences'.[4] The present proliferation of administrative regulations accompanied by criminal sanctions, the ever more complex network of legal obligations and prohibitions that hedge in the economic activity of every individual, render almost absurd the claim that anyone can be immediately aware of the rules which apply to his situation. In the course of a colloquium on the problem of individual rights, where the new ideas of social defence were very properly evoked, an enlightened magistrate spoke of the genuine distress experienced by the criminal judge who felt himself compelled by law to impose a repressive penalty for some purely technical offence of which—as he well knew—the 'guilty' person could not be aware either morally or socially.[5] The operation of criminal justice then rests, both in fact and sociologically, as it were, on a fiction laid down or accepted as the foundation for an alleged system of general prevention. However, still from the sociological point of view and by an inevitable reversal of the situation, this kind of general prevention is quite ineffective because members of the community do not consider that the kind of act in question is really an offence or that the punishment incurred carries social reprehension.[6]

[4] The same idea appears in the distinction drawn by Blackstone, in particular, between *mala prohibita* and *mala in se*.

[5] Colloquium of French Law Faculties held at the Faculty of Law of Aix-en-Provence (28-29 December 1953): see a record of this gathering in *Rev. de Science crim.*, 1954, No. 1 (January-March), p. 208, which includes a summary of the excellent introductory report by Professor A. Légal, which fairly takes account of social defence doctrines.

[6] See Enrique R. Aftalion, *Derecho Penal económico*, Buenos Aires, 1959. Cf. Donald R. Taft, *Criminology*, 3rd ed., New York, 1956, p. 388, where the author sees in the development of 'economic crimes' a characteristic feature of modern criminal law.

This point may be illustrated by the development of criminal sanctions for economic offences.

In other fields again, the persistence of various fictions stultifies the normal evolution of criminal law and in particular prevents that adequate relation between legal rules and social facts, without which any repressive system becomes ineffective. Is it then surprising that the adherents of social defence should protest against the fiction of the 'transferred culpability' of accomplices, and against the consequences that may be drawn therefrom by certain criminal lawyers or judicial decisions? In practice, such an over-simple explanation of the rules with regard to aiding and abetting criminal offences appears both dubious and inadequate: its main drawback is that the judge who is responsible for interpreting the law is once again prevented from perceiving the real human and social nature of the problem, which is that of participation in the criminal offence.[7]

It is doubtless even less surprising that the new doctrine should query the traditional theory of intention, seen as the author's mere knowledge that his act infringed a legal rule. The French courts, spurred on by Émile Garçon, have deduced numerous principles from this doctrine. Looked at more closely, however, the doctrine amounts to little more than a duty to obey the law, coupled with an 'irrebuttable presumption' that everyone in fact knows what the law is. It would be tempting to take issue with this doctrine in rather the same way that certain French authors, such as Planiol, criticized the civil law concept of cause.[8] In

[7] On the shortcomings and limits of the French theory concerning the 'borrowed guilt' of an accomplice, see R. Merle, *Droit pénal général complémentaire*, 1957, pp. 185 ff.; Vouin and Léauté, *Droit pénal et criminologie*, 1956 ('the archaism of the French theory on participation in the criminal offence'); Stefani and Levasseur, *Droit pénal général et criminologie*, 2nd ed., 1961, Nos. 294 ff. On the problem as a whole, see the papers of the Seventh International Congress on Criminal Law (Athens, 1957). First question: 'Modern trends regarding the notions of author of the criminal act and of participation in the criminal act', summary record in *Rev. de Science crim.*, 1958, pp. 195 ff. *Proceedings* of the Congress (Publication of the International Association of Criminal Law), Athens, 1961, pp. 79 ff.

[8] The traditional notion of cause—distinct from motive—has been attacked as imprecise and useless. In fact, between the two World Wars, the notion of cause was only saved from oblivion by a new approach on the part of certain academic writers, especially Josserand and, above all, Henri Capitant: the new analysis either brought the idea of cause close to that of motive, almost to the point of merging them, or else made cause equivalent to the purpose of the contract between the parties. On the evolution of this controversy, see J. Carbonnier, *Droit Civil*, vol. II, 2nd part,

actual fact, the criminal law theory referred to above enabled classical and neo-classical criminal law to take no account of motives, that is to say of those personal reasons which would have introduced into the investigation and judgement of the offence a subjective element distrusted by traditional doctrine. Through the concept of motive, it is the offender's conscious personality, as a whole, that would invade the sphere of that abstract criminal law which wished to take the offence alone into consideration. In this respect, besides purely theoretical notions and legal fictions, social defence tries to take into account an element of human reality, and this effort has borne fruit in most modern systems of legislation.[9] It is significant that a notable feature of modern criminal law is precisely the ever-increasing importance attributed to motive in the evaluation of punishment, in addition to criminal intention or *mens rea* as traditionally understood.[10]

It would be just as easy to show how concepts of criminal law in general use, such as the theory of attempts, for instance, rely increasingly on pure law, to the ultimate exclusion of the direct observation of social reality. The Codes of the later nineteenth century, which were very elaborate from the technical standpoint, were considered to improve on the French Criminal Code of 1810 in that they provided reduced penalties for mere attempts. Academic writers on criminal law took pains to distinguish carefully between the commencement of the criminal act itself and merely 'preparatory' acts. The objective factor then held pride of

---

1957, pp. 378 ff., H. L. and J. Mazeaud, *Leçons de Droit civil*, vol. II, 2nd ed., 1962, pp. 214 ff.; Ripert and Boulanger, *Traité de Droit Civil*, vol. II, 1957, Nos. 274 ff. In fact the civil courts of first instance have often deliberately confused cause and motive (*motif*), just as the criminal courts of first instance also frequently persist in confusing intention with motive (*mobile*). The influence of social defence ideas on civil law might well be studied . . .

[9] On the distinction between the neo-classical theory of intention and the concept of motive, see Émile Garçon's *Code pénal annoté*, 2nd ed., vol. I (art. I, Nos. 66 ff., and in particular Nos. 77 ff.). From the comparative standpoint, it is curious to note that this 'civilian' conception is practically analogous to that of the Common Law, which also makes a distinction between (abstract) intention and (concrete) motive: see Glanville Williams, *Criminal Law, The General Part*, 2nd ed., 1961, No. 21. Cf. Jerome Hall, *General Principles of Criminal Law*, 2nd ed., pp. 86 ff.

[10] See P. Bouzat and J. Pinatel, *Traité de droit pénal et de criminologie*, 1963, vol. I, No. 174; Stefani and Levasseur, *Droit pénal général et criminologie*, 2nd ed., 1961, Nos. 172 ff.; and, in spite of his general attitude, R. Merle, *Droit pénal général complémentaire*, 1957, p. 227.

place, and neo-classical doctrine seemed to take the objective approach for granted. Carrara's celebrated illustration of the impossibility of making a clear distinction between a *univocal* act (which begins to carry out the criminal act and is therefore punishable), and an *equivocal* act (which is merely preparatory and so not punishable), points to the danger of getting enmeshed in theoretical formulations.[11] The Courts, however, which are closer to real life and which are aware—sometimes in spite of themselves—that there is such a thing as dangerousness (*périculosité*) ultimately preferred the subjective test: they have not hesitated, on occasion, to treat mere attempts as the first stage in the accomplishment of the offence and to punish them accordingly. The courts thus paid attention to what has been called (by Gunzburg in particular) the 'trajectory of crime'.[12]

Moreover, it was in this field that pure law, taken to extremes, produced the theory of the 'impossible crime', leading to subtle distinctions which provoked endless argument concerning absolute impossibility on the one hand, and an allegedly 'relative impossibility' on the other. Here again—in France at any rate—the rational approach favoured by the penal policy of social defence prevailed, and the theory of 'impossible crime' was abandoned.[13] In the Italian Code of 1930, by a refinement of legal subtlety, this kind of case was dealt with by a mere preventive measure directed against the dangerousness created by the author of the harmful act, who could not in law be guilty of the act and

[11] See Carrara, *Programa*. Attention has frequently been drawn to this author's hesitations and changes of front in the face of this difficult distinction: see Bettiol, *Diritto penale*, 5th ed., 1962, p. 447. The Italian Criminal Code of 1930, breaking away from the technical complexity of the Code of 1889, has abolished this distinction and now relies on the more concrete notion of *idoneità* (art. 56). See R. Pannain, *Manuale di diritto penale*, 3rd ed., 1962, vol. I, 255; A. Santoro, *Manuale di diritto penale*, 1958, vol. I, No. 433. On the controversies and the comparative law in this field, see J. Constant, *Manuel de droit pénal*, 7th ed., Liège, 1959, vol. I, No. 287 ff.

[12] See on these problems the interesting work of Gunzburg, *La Trajectoire du crime*, Rio de Janeiro, 1941. On recent decisions of the French courts in this field, see Légal's remarks in *Rev. de Science crim.*, 1952, p. 439, and 1959, p. 842, where the author notes that in determining whether the criminal action has actually begun, the courts pay particular attention to 'the psychological attitude of the individual concerned'.

[13] Here again, after some hesitation, the subjective approach prevailed and was indeed explicitly recognized by the French statutory provisions concerning abortion (art. 317, Crim. Code, amended by a decree of 29 July 1939); the *Cour de Cassation*, however, applies this approach in other fields such as theft: Crim. 14 June 1961, Bull. 299; see Légal's remarks in *Rev. de Science crim.*, 1962, p. 89.

hence could not incur punishment.[14] This represented a new victory for the theories of social defence, a victory which could have been won more cheaply and more rapidly if it had been realized that the obstacles to be overcome, if not legal fictions in the true sense of the term, were at any rate derived from the socially undesirable abuse of the techniques of pure law.[15]

Many other examples could be cited. But enough has been said to throw light on what is meant by 'de-legalization'. At the same time it may be asserted once again that while new social defence distrusts legal fictions and the undesirable use sometimes made of the technique of pure law, the movement is not on that account trying to abolish criminal law. This point would appear to have been sufficiently discussed in the previous chapter.

One ought to even go further, and note that since the social defence movement considers that the new penal policy should protect the individual as well as society, all conceptions which purport to abolish the criminal code should be rejected out of hand, more especially the view that would suppress the particular provisions of the code in favour of a concise general part enumerating the various measures which the court might apply when it found that a particular individual showed signs of dangerousness or anti-social behaviour. At one time, no doubt, positivist doctrine made similar claims, and these views were taken up in Soviet Russia during the neo-positivist period that preceded the elaboration of the Criminal Code of 1922 or even, to some extent, that of 1926. At that time the call was for a criminal law without special provisions and without degrees of punishment.[16] But these endeavours failed even in Russia, where the reforms of 1958-1960 indicated a return to the principle of the legal basis of crimes and punishments.[17]

[14] Art. 49: the same approach is to be found in the Cuban Social Defence Code of 1936, which lays down that where the means employed by the would-be offender are totally inadequate to the accomplishment of the offence, the judge may decide that there is a case of dangerousness to which, instead of punishment, a preventive measure will be applied (art. 26, E).

[15] See Arturo Santoro, *op. cit.*, Nos. 434 ff.; Ranieri, *Manuale di diritto penale*, vol. I, pp. 354 ff.

[16] See Marc Ancel, 'La Règle *nulla poena sine lege* dans les législations modernes', *Annales de l'Institut de Droit comparé de l'Université de Paris*, 1936, pp. 245 ff., pp. 262-64, and the references cited. Cf. the same writer's *Introduction au système de droit pénal soviétique*, 1962, p. xv, with the references cited.

[17] See *La Réforme pénale soviétique* (publication of the *Centre français de Droit comparé*), 1962. Tomaso Napolitano, *Il nuovo codice penale sovietico*, Milan, 1963, pp. 65 ff.

Some writers would have us believe today that the doctrines of social defence have the same scope or are implicitly tending towards the same goal. At the beginning of the century, neo-classical theorists took issue with the social defence tendencies of the International Union of Criminal Law in the name of the very concept of criminal law. It is likewise asserted that the result of taking into consideration the biological or sociological concept of crime is to enable the State to intervene in respect of any person who is reputed to be dangerous.[18]

Other writers again are afraid of the term 'de-legalization', which in their view indicates the intention to do away with the juridical character of law. Against this state of affairs, every well-trained lawyer reacts straight away,[19] for his rôle is to defend the law and not to attack, suppress, or diminish it. Such a reaction would indeed be an ingenuous one were it not, on the contrary, extremely skilful. A few unrepentant neo-classical theorists such as Quintano Ripolles and certain South American writers are determined to reject the new social defence movement as a whole and in its crudest form.[20] They seize upon the tendency towards 'de-legalization' in order to confound the whole movement with Gramatica's doctrine. But better informed criminal specialists are aware of the need to distinguish between the struggle against excess of legalism on the one hand and the destruction or suppression of criminal law on the other. The object of condemning 'pure law', i.e. excessive reliance on legal technicality,[21] or the perils of a kind of legal imperialism in the criminological sphere, is to mark out the boundaries of the province of law, which are to be treated as inviolate. It should be emphasized once again that without the rule of law, which presupposes a legal system, there can be no protection of the individual, and social defence is concerned above all else with protecting the individual, irreplaceable human being.

[18] See the article already cited by E. Frey, *Rev. pénale suisse*, 1953, pp. 419 ff.

[19] See Roger Merle, '*L'Évolution du droit pénal moderne*', in *Annales de la Faculté de droit de Toulouse*, vol. VI, (part 1), 1958, pp. 133 ff.; cf. the remarks of R. Merle and L. Jiménez de Asúa on the occasion of the 25th anniversary of the *Revue de Science criminelle et de droit pénal comparé*, Paris, 1961, in same *Revue*, 1962, pp. 308 and 317.

[20] Quintano Ripolles, 'La evolución del derecho penal moderno' in *Anuario de derecho penal y ciencias penales*, 1957, pp. 283 ff.; cf. *Jornadas de derecho penal*, published under the supervision of L. Jiménez de Asúa, Buenos Aires, 1962, *passim*.

[21] See A. Légal in *Rev. int. de droit comp.*, 1963, p. 603.

The thesis which, understandably enough, is criticized by the neo-classical school is not the doctrine of new social defence, and it is no more accurate to present it as such than it would be to assert that those who advocate the neo-classical view of punishment wish to revive the rigidly preordained system of penalties provided—for instance—by the French Code of 1791. The new social defence movement is not trying to force the lawyer or criminal scientist to choose between criminal law and social defence: the aim, on the contrary, is to integrate the ideas of social defence in a new concept of criminal law. This conception remains a genuine system of criminal law which like any such system finds a place for the rule of law, for legislative action, for judicial intervention in the application of such law by due process, and finally for procedural safeguards which must be all the more effective in so far as the measure applied to the convicted person might be of lengthy duration or of an indeterminate character.[22]

Above all, the new doctrine of social defence involves, first, upholding the rule of law without lapsing into the legalism of former days; and secondly, envisaging the reaction to crime as governed by legislative and social policy, which is both above and beyond criminal law conceived as a merely technical instrument. In this respect, as may be repeated once again, social defence rejoins the views of Liszt on three counts: first, his emphasis on the need to circumscribe the power of the State to intervene; secondly, his pioneer opposition to a discretionary system of 'social hygiene'; thirdly, his claim that criminal law remains the impassable boundary of social policy.[23]

As was pointed out earlier, however, there were times when Liszt himself would not or could not resist the attractions of legalism or legal fiction. His views of criminal policy were ultimately imprisoned in a legal system that had as its prime object the protection of the legal order. The penal policy of social defence indeed wishes to protect the social order, which it

[22] See Marc Ancel, *Rapport sur les mesures de sûreté en matière criminelle*, Paris, 1950; cf. the discussions at the first *Journées franco-latino-américaines* organized by the French Society of Comparative Legislation in April 1948, which dealt with the place of preventive measures in existing criminal law, *Bull. de la Soc. de Législ. comp.*, 1948, pp. 617 ff.; pp. 629 ff.; see in particular the general report by Patin which will also be found in *Rev. de Science crim.*, 1948, pp. 415 ff.

[23] *Aufsätze*, II, 102.

recognizes as uniquely real; but such protection must first ensure that the individual is safeguarded, for the social order exists by man and for man.[24]

The doctrine of new social defence comes close to Montesquieu and to some extent to Bentham, in so far as according to both these writers the object of good legislation is not to safeguard an abstract legal order, but to lay down the best conditions for the happiness of the people for whom such legislation is designed.

II

We have just seen that the primary characteristic of the new social defence movement from a positive standpoint is less an attitude hostile to the law—as has sometimes been asserted—than a so-called 'de-legalization' of certain concepts or certain aspects of criminal science. It will be seen that in the same way or by analogy the social defence movement produces what certain criminologists, particularly in America, have described as a 'de-criminalization' of certain fields which were at one time considered as exclusively within the province of repressive law: modern methods of dealing with delinquent juveniles are probably the most striking example of this change. Another positive and undoubtedly constructive aspect of the social defence movement, however, must be mentioned here: namely, the fact that the movement finds expression in a penal policy founded on a new attitude towards the offender, exemplified in realistic and effective social action which is far removed from the traditional punitive reaction against crime.

It is evident that this second aspect is the direct result of the first, or more precisely its corollary. The social reaction against crime always took the form of the authoritarian execution of public vengeance, whether in the earliest theocratic phase, the political phase with its notion of expiation, or the legal phase of repression. In all cases the offender was brought before a court which, if it found him guilty, punished him in the name of society by means designed by the latter for its own preservation and as retribution for the crime. This is the old Roman formula accord-

[24] See A. Besson, 'A propos de la Défense sociale nouvelle', in *Rev. int. de droit pénal*, 1954, pp. 321 ff.

ing to which punishment amounted to the infliction of harm in return for wrongdoing.[25]

The characteristic feature of social defence, on the contrary, from the beginning of this century and more especially in its most modern form, is the new attitude adopted with regard to the offender. He is no longer delivered up to criminal justice for the purposes of expiation, vengeance, or retribution: in this respect, provided certain explicit reservations made in the foregoing chapters are borne in mind, it may indeed be claimed that social defence is a non-repressive movement. Moreover, we ought also to avoid another source of confusion and not equate social defence doctrine with the positivist view which held that the offender, being irresponsible, could not be the object of a criminal sanction. It has been pointed out earlier that this conception led, not to the genuine doctrine of social defence, in the true sense of the term, but to a kind of passive protection of society that could result in a serious disregard of individual rights. Carnevale has very properly criticized Ferri's maxim to the effect 'Protect yourselves and do not judge'.[26]

But the starting point of Carnevale's criticism remained a legalism which has been left behind by the modern doctrine of social defence. These new conceptions endeavour to ensure the effective protection of the community through an assessment of the conditions in which the offence was committed, the offender's personal circumstances, the likelihood of his rehabilitation, and such moral and psychological resources as may be developed in him with a view to applying to him a true treatment of social readaptation.[27]

This is not a mere form of words or *desideratum*, but a firm directive that the new social defence movement wishes to impose on penal policy. The latter, indeed, ought henceforth to be wholly directed towards the treatment of delinquents; but this treatment is itself part of a generalized form of social protection which is a fundamental element in the struggle against crime. The work of a man such as Karl Schlyter, naturally steeped in the ideas and

[25] *Malum passionis propter malum actionis*: but with this formula may be contrasted that of Paulus: *poena constituitur in emendationem hominum*.

[26] *Diritto criminale*, vol. I, p. 312.

[27] See Marc Ancel, 'Évolution sociale et criminalité: le point de vue de la Défense sociale nouvelle', in *Rev. de l'Institut de Sociologie*, Brussels, 1963, p. 234.

especially the ideals of the modern social defence movement, was particularly influential in this field in substituting the word 'protection'[28] for the older expression 'criminal law'. Schlyter's views are in no way to be confused with some of the extreme theses dealt with in the preceding section. And when Stephan Hurwitz, for instance, argues that an essential reform might involve doing away with the classification of punishments, he hastens to add that in certain cases it is no less essential to deprive certain persons of their liberty or subject them to fines.[29] The essential point is that the notion of punishment should no longer be interpreted in its former sense: in particular, the concept should not confine itself to the idea of guilt nor simply refer to the incidence of moral responsibility; instead the idea of the prevention of criminal activity should be resolutely adopted as the positive and specific object of social action. As Hurwitz puts it, such a terminological change may have technical advantages and likewise give expression to a sound programme of penal policy. But the eminent Danish criminal scientist hastens to take issue with the advocates of the struggle against punishment who would assimilate all offenders to sick persons, and as such solely liable to remedial treatment.[30]

The meetings of Scandinavian criminal scientists, always of great interest, have shown how a system of sanctions unaffected by the old controversies might be worked out in a resolutely modern spirit.[31] The preliminary papers for the Swedish Criminal Code of 1962 are equally interesting in this respect.[32] Although the new

[28] In Swedish, *skydd*: see in particular, in what has been called the 'political testament' of Karl Schlyter, the following passage, cited by Thore Engströmer in the symposium in honour of the great Swedish criminal scientist (*Festskrift tillägnad Karl Schlyter*, Stockholm, 1949, p. 10): 'If in our various dealings with offenders we aim at the better protection of society and succeed in restraining the instinctive temptation to render evil for evil, if we earnestly try to apply to adults the lessons learnt in the treatment of young offenders, and if we pay close attention to the principle now written into the law that regard should be had to the convicted offender's dignity as a human being, then indeed there is hope that repressive ideas will gradually be replaced in a new era by a more humane and rational method of treatment.'

[29] See the conclusions of the record of the Social Defence Congress at San Remo; *Respekt for Mennesket*, Copenhagen, 1951, pp. 217 ff.

[30] *Den danske Kriminalret*, Copenhagen, 1950, pp. 111 and 112.

[31] See *Nordisk Kriminalistik Årsbok*, in particular for the years 1957, 1958, 1959, 1960, and 1961. See *Rev. de Science crim.*, (1955), p. 150; (1956), p. 251; (1957), p. 938.

[32] On the Swedish draft for a code of protection see also *Nordisk Kriminalistik Årsbok*, 1957, summary in English, pp. xx-xxviii, and cf. Thorsten Sellin, *The Protective Code, a Swedish Proposal*, Stockholm, 1957.

code finally retained the term 'punishment', it makes wide use of the expression 'consequence of the offence' (*brottspåföljd*).[33] The expression encompasses both punishment in the traditional sense and the modern notion of preventive measures. This type of compromise solution, more up to date than the intermediate or eclectic codes of the nineteen-thirties, is resolutely turned towards the new penal policy.[34] Moreover, it should not be forgotten that the criminal statute enacted for Greenland on 5 March 1954 constitutes a bold legislative venture which not only reconciles the principles of Danish criminal law with Greenland local custom, but also introduces certain innovations inspired in part by Ferri's draft of 1921.[35]

It is felt that this Scandinavian approach, at once subtle, progressive, and realistic, admirably exemplifies one of the essential characteristics of the new social defence doctrine. Treatment of a preventive nature has to be applied to the offender, but this does not necessarily mean that he will avoid all measures of a disagreeable kind, even those involving afflictive punishment. Nor will the offender's rights or his personality remain unaffected. But it must be clearly understood that the action of social defence is no longer concerned with symbolic retribution nor is seeking to achieve a kind of absolute criminal justice. The problem is one of reaction against crime envisaged both as an individual and a social phenomenon. Such an attitude should be guided by ideas of protection, so called to mark the contrast with those ideas of repression which dominated criminal law throughout its previous history.[36] That is what is meant by such criminologists as Glueck when they point to what they describe as the 'de-criminalization' of certain aspects of penal activity.[37]

[33] This does not involve the reappearance of the traditional retributive notion which equated the offence with the punishment imposed by law. On the contrary, the word 'punishment' is rejected as a generic term and the sanction is envisaged as the material consequence of the offence without any moral connotation.

[34] On this code, see *Rev. de Science crim.*, 1963, p. 417.

[35] See the text of this statute in *Les Codes pénaux européens*, published by the *Centre français de droit comparé*, vol. I, Paris, 1956, pp. 391 ff.

[36] See in particular the article already referred to of Thorsten Sellin, *The Protective Code, A Swedish Proposal*, 1957. Cf. Sutherland and Cressey, *Principles of Criminology*, 6th ed., 1960, pp. 314 ff. The same attitude is also to be found in the Home Office White Paper issued in 1959 under the title, *Penal Practice in a Changing Society*.

[37] *After-Conduct of Discharged Offenders*, London, 1949, p. 99.

The tendency is analogous to the movement of 'de-legalization' which social defence doctrine seeks to accomplish, and should be understood in the same way. This is not a matter of 'de-legalizing' criminal law, as some lawyers have facetiously pretended to think. Were this the case, social defence would be an absurd doctrine. It is not a question of so changing legal rules as to give them an 'anti-legal' character, but of reacting against legalistic excess and of bringing home to the lawyers themselves the fact that criminal law applies to irreducible concrete situations that are disregarded at one's peril. Similarly, criminologists who are concerned with the evolution of the sociology of crime can observe that the struggle against crime is no longer today necessarily repressive or retributive, and that for an increasing number of categories of offenders this reaction takes the form of methods which are non-punitive in character. Émile Garçon himself, writing of the system introduced for juvenile delinquents by the French statute of 1912, explained the transformation of the law concerning juvenile delinquency by the fact that, 'by unanimous consent', the scope of criminal law had ceased to be made applicable to children.[38] What would he have thought of the decree of 6 February 1945 and of the reforms which have established the new system in respect of juvenile delinquency, reforms that are universally accepted today and are already in process of being extended to young adults?[39]

Shortly after the enactment of the Belgian social defence statute of 1930, an experienced criminal scientist observed that the effect of the statute was to exclude punishment of a repressive kind from the measures applied to mentally abnormal and habitual offenders, thus adopting the same approach which the Belgian statute of 1912, a bolder and more effective version of its French counterpart of the same year, had applied to juvenile delinquents.[40]

Furthermore, a new element made its appearance in criminal legislation, from the Stooss draft of 1893 and the Norwegian

[38] *Le Droit pénal*, 1922, p. 154.

[39] On this latter category of offenders see in particular: *Seuils d'âge et législation pénale—Contribution à l'étude du problème des jeunes adultes délinquants*, published by the *Centre d'études de défence sociale* of the Institute of Comparative Law, University of Paris, 1961.

[40] N. Gunzburg, *Les Transformations récentes du droit pénal*, Brussels, 1935.

Criminal Code of 1902 to the compromise solutions embodied in the codifications of the nineteen-thirties: this was the introduction of preventive measures or, if a less debatable expression be preferred, of non-punitive methods of dealing with crime. Here already was a limitation of the former sphere of retributive punishment. The twofold approach of 1930 questioned the primacy of purely repressive methods in their traditional sphere. The special feature of the new system was that it required of the criminal judge, when considering the offence, something more than purely legal analysis of its components and the evaluation of the penalty according to legal criteria, even though these were tempered by concern to individualize the penalty in the neo-classical sense of the word.[41] The direct result of the introduction of these 'preventive measures' was a breach in the formerly monolithic character of the repressive system. This change is still more apparent when we move from the so-called 'double track' (that is to say, the cumulative or mixed system of punishments and non-punitive measures) to the alternative system where the court no longer applies both types of sanctions, punitive and non-punitive, but chooses one or the other. In England, where preventive measures as such are said not to exist, there is a marked change between the Prevention of Crimes Act (1908) and the Criminal Justice Act (1948).[42] Only one further step is needed to emerge from the province of criminal law altogether, a process that Émile Garçon considered had already taken place at the beginning of the century with regard to juveniles. This change may be said to hinge on the methods applied to sexual psychopaths. The non-punitive methods epitomized by the concept of preventive measures are sometimes clumsily improvised.[43] In other cases such measures are seriously studied, giving rise to fruitful encounters amongst specialists, carefully prepared projects and valuable

[41] Compare the well-known work of R. Saleilles, *L'Individualisation de la peine*, 1898, and *L'Individualisation des mesures prises à l'égard du délinquant*. (Published by the Comparative Law Institute, University of Paris), 1954.

[42] The Mental Health Act (1959), especially sections 26 and 60, must also be cited. See also R. S. Taylor, 'The Habitual Criminal', in *British Journ. of Criminology*, vol. I, No. 1, July 1960, pp. 21 ff. Likewise in Sweden there was a progression from the cumulative or 'double track' approach embodied in the 1927 statute to the alternative system embodied in the 1937 statute (penalty *or* preventive measures).

[43] In particular in the United States in the laws on sexual psychopaths: see E. H. Sutherland, 'The Sexual Psychopath Laws', in *Journ. of Crim. Law and Criminology*, Jan.-Feb. 1950, pp. 534 ff.

experiments.[44] This tendency towards 'de-criminalization' goes further than at first appears. The inadequacy of traditional methods of repression as a means of dealing with economic offences leads certain countries (where punishment for such crimes does not involve social opprobrium) to consider a more complex and variegated system in this respect. So the traditional sanctions of crime and imprisonment are supplemented or even replaced by new sanctions of a preventive or even sometimes para-disciplinary nature.[45] This new initiative in criminal law is often hesitant and sometimes frustrated by movements in the opposite direction.[46] But this trend at least serves to illustrate that one aspect of the reaction against crime is now stated in terms that are no longer those of traditional criminal law. We are thus brought face to face with the changed objectives of modern penal policy.

Some may argue that this is an independent tendency that exists apart from the social defence movement. The question arises, however, whether such a trend may not be primarily explicable by the widespread influence of social defence ideas even on those who claim to be unaffected by them. This question may be

[44] Cf. the Colloquium organized in Copenhagen in 1957 by the World Health Organization, the theme of which was the psychiatric treatment of offenders. See *Rev. de Science crim.*, 1958, pp. 679 ff.; cf. 'L'Établissement pour psychopathes de Herstedvester', by Dr G. K. Stürup, same *Revue*, 1958, pp. 593 ff.; see also T. C. N. Gibbens, 'Les Problèmes posés par le traitement psychiatrique des délinquants', same *Revue*, 1958, pp. 576 ff.

[45] See Marc Ancel, General Report on *Les Sanctions en matière de droit pénal économique*, in *Rapports généraux au Cinquième Congrès international de droit comparé*, published by the *Centre interuniversitaire de droit comparé* of Brussels, 1960, pp. 851 ff.; cf. Aftalion, *Derecho penal económico*, 1959.

[46] On the hesitation shown by French law, see the report by J. Hémard in the *Rev. de Science crim.*, 1958, No. 2, suppl., p. 53. In the U.S.S.R. the penal reform of the period 1958-1960, generally characterized by a humanization of repressive legislation, was followed in 1961 and 1962 by a revival of ruthlessly severe penalties for some economic offences. See Marc Ancel, *Introduction au Système de droit pénal soviétique*, Paris, 1962, pp. 65 ff.; cf. *Rev. de Science crim.*, 1959, p. 83; 1961, p. 854; 1962, p. 387. At the same time, however, a desire is apparent to avoid repressive punishment in the case of the trivial offender by affording him the help of social organizations on which he depends (see J. Bellon, *Droit pénal soviétique et droit pénal occidental*, 1961, pp. 153 ff.,) or by making him subject to a non-criminal jurisdiction of a social or disciplinary character applied by the comrades' tribunal. See Marc Ancel, *Introduction* (cited above), p. 53; cf. M. Fridieff, 'L'Organisation judiciaire soviétique', in *Rev. int. de droit comp.*, 1962, pp. 725 ff., (especially p. 738); T. Napolitano, *Il nuovo codice penale sovietico, I principi e le innovazioni*, Milan, 1963, pp. 180 ff.; see also in the same *Revue* (1962, p. 77), 'Les Tribunaux de camarades en Bulgarie' (Law of 22 June 1961).

answered by pointing to the fact that in this field the position taken up by the social defence movement is new in three respects, namely: first, its desire to take account of the existence, the strength, and the ultimate goal of this reformist trend; secondly, the wish to organize and co-ordinate the various scattered efforts that can only result in sporadic and makeshift innovation; thirdly, its concern to treat these efforts of renewal from the standpoint of penal policy, that is to say, from that of the rational organization of the social reaction against crime.

Here, no doubt, is the most significant contribution of social defence, which must be emphasized once again. The *via media* contained in the legislation of the nineteen-thirties tried to fit these non-criminal measures into the categories or even into the philosophy of the law. This indeed was one of the tasks assumed, sometimes surreptitiously, by the so-called 'pure law school', and explains the success enjoyed by its exponents among numerous lawyers whom these views served to reassure; this also explains the failure of such an approach from the standpoint of penal policy, for the 'pure lawyers' misunderstood the true scientific significance of that policy, which they thought of merely as a transient one. It is no exaggeration to assert that in this respect the contribution of the social defence movement involves an undeniable renewal and a liberation from slavish adherence to certain forms of thought.

'De-legalization' and 'de-criminalization', so-called, spring from the same idea that the purely repressive measures formerly applied are incapable of dealing with the true nature of the criminal act and of the criminal human being. In the light of comparative experience on the one hand, and of the lessons to be drawn from the social sciences on the other, it appears at least inadequate, if not absurdly oversimple, to treat the offence—the criminal act committed in a concrete situation by a particular human being—as the formal violation of a rule of law and as corresponding precisely with a legal definition. In the first place, no doubt, the criminal offence is an act classified as such by the law; such classification is essential, and is a necessary preliminary to all other steps involved in the reaction against crime. On this point the doctrine of new social defence has no wish to depart from certain traditional positions: the legal basis of crimes and punishments is too precious a possession to be abandoned by a system which claims to be based on the idea of protection. The definition of the criminal offence and the recognition in law of its existence are essential requirements of social defence doctrine, and in this respect that doctrine differs once again from the notion of anti-social behaviour (*antisocialità*) advocated by Gramatica, for whom the rule of law is accepted only as a necessary evil. In our view, on the contrary, it is the indispensable guiding principle for the organization as well as for the understanding of the system.[47]

Once this rule is accepted, however, the new social defence doctrine tries to make it clear that such classification in law does not suffice to define the offence as a concrete social and individual reality, nor does it enable its consequences to be effectively neutralized. While declaring that legal analysis of the offence is indispensable, the social defence movement expressly denies that this is enough, for the problem of crime cannot be resolved simply by placing an offence in its legal category and imposing an abstract penalty. On close inspection it becomes clear that the new social defence movement does not reject the traditional view of the offence, but simply maintains that this view is inadequate and fails in the end to meet the essential problem. The argument is that the crime cannot be isolated from the social environment in which it took place, or divorced from the human being who committed it. It is a vain task to attempt to judge an offence in isolation according to purely legal criteria. Social defence doctrine criticizes the neo-classical system for its failure or refusal to understand this profound and inescapable truth. It criticizes that system, too, for having reduced a living reality to the level of a mathematical equation. Finally, neo-classicism is criticized for having sought to avoid the difficulties and complexities of a concrete human problem through reliance on abstract solutions. Thus the social defence movement considers that the classical approach, however justified it may have been in its own sphere, made the great mistake of refusing to go beyond that sphere or to recognize its limits. The penal policy of social reaction against crime, if it is to be modern, well thought out, rational, and enlightened, must therefore be constructed on a broader base. Of course, penal law will be retained, and will even be strengthened;

[47] See P. Nuvolone, 'Le Principe de la légalité et les principes de la défense sociale', *Rev. de Science crim.*, 1956, pp. 231 ff.

but it will be no more than criminal law: it will not be criminal science, for it must henceforth reckon with the existence of criminology.[48]

III

There is hardly any need to point out that this new attitude to the phenomenon of crime is above all, perhaps, a new approach to the offender himself, seen as the author of the criminal act. The essential features of this approach must now be indicated as precisely as possible. It may be said straight away that this conception, in which the offence is so to speak removed from the purely legal sphere, is dominated by the desire to relate the act to its author and to make the one inseparable from the other, so that the offence is treated as a projection of its author's personality into the social context. This new approach on the part of criminal science, and especially of penal policy based on the findings of the criminological sciences, could be greatly extended. For the moment it is essential to stress three particular points.

In the first place, the attitude which social defence doctrine wishes to take up with regard to the offender imperatively requires that his personality should be taken into consideration and systematically studied by scientific methods. Secondly, and in so far as this fundamental attitude is designed to reform and improve the existing system, a general reorganization of existing penal sanctions inevitably becomes necessary. Thirdly and finally, in so far as this effort of renewal is conceived in the context of a penal policy which is concerned to be effective, it finds expression in the organization of a social action directed against crime and conceived in a realistic spirit. These three points must now be investigated, for they are fundamental for anyone who wishes to understand the constructive side of the doctrines of new social defence.

[48] The best proof of this is the reform in France which, sometimes in a rather unsatisfactory manner, introduced criminology into the syllabus of law studies. See S. Stefani and G. Levasseur, *Droit pénal général et criminologie*, 2nd ed., 1961, No. 48; Vouin and Léauté, *Droit pénal et criminologie*, 1956, p. 39; cf. on the question of the relation between criminal science and comparative law, discussed at the colloquium held to mark the twenty-fifth anniversary of the *Rev. de Science criminelle et de droit pénal comparé*, the introductory paper by Jiménez de Asúa (same *Revue*, 1962, pp. 225 ff.) and the discussion (pp. 296 ff.). See also Jean-Marie Aussel, 'L'Enseignement de la criminologie en France', in *Rev. de Science crim.*, 1962, pp. 649 ff.

A

The first element in this new attitude towards the offender, which remains the essential feature of modern social defence, is the attention given to his personality. In this way, the new social defence movement is related to positivism, but also to the broader trend which thrust the personality of the offender into the forefront of criminal law problems, as was recalled by Paul Cornil at the opening session of the seminar held in December 1951 under the auspices of the United Nations and devoted to the scientific study of offenders.[49] The attention thus paid to the personality of the criminal was gradually differentiated from the biological approach of Lombroso, not only because the new attitude purported to consider the individual in society and to understand him together with all the influences and blemishes resulting from his environment,[50] but also because the individual, instead of being treated simply as a biological or even social being, an object of scientific study, is envisaged as a person who partakes of legal rights and duties. Indeed, the study of man in this sociological perspective presupposed a deliberate reference to moral values on which social defence doctrine placed growing emphasis as the increasingly firm basis of the policy of social readaptation.

What then is the significance for penal policy of the attention thus paid to the criminal's personality? It should be pointed out immediately, and with emphasis, that for modern criminologists this problem tends to take pride of place and is presented in a form quite different from that favoured by the positivists.[51] So as to

[49] The technical papers of the Seminar were published in a special issue of the *International Review of Criminal Policy* (published by the United Nations Secretariat), No. 3, January 1953. Particular mention may be made of the remarkable opening address by Paul Cornil (translated from the French), 'General Observations on the medico-psychological and social examination of offenders', pp. 3 ff. See also the report on the French Social Defence Congress held at Strasbourg (1957), in *Rev. de Science crim.*, 1957, pp. 835 ff.

[50] See F. Exner, *Kriminologie*, Berlin, 1949, pp. 221 ff.

[51] See the papers of the eighth *Journées françaises de défense sociale*, and in particular the report by Levasseur, *Rev. de Science crim.*, 1960, pp. 621 ff. See also *Bull. de Soc. int. de Criminologie*, 1958, pp. 153 and 187; cf. the papers of the first French Criminological Congress, held at Lyons in October 1960, *Annales de l'Université de Lyon*, vols. I and II (*Examen de personnalité et criminologie*), Paris, 1961; Cf. Bouzat et Pinatel, *Traité de droit pénal et de criminologie*, vol. III (*Criminologie*, by J. Pinatel, Paris, 1963, pp. 419 ff.).

treat this question schematically and avoid facile digressions, it is proposed simply to enumerate the ways in which the new penal policy takes the criminal's personality into consideration, as follows:

1. The offender as an individual will be integrated into the criminal trial, which hitherto was exclusively the judgement of a particular act. This aspect need not be dwelt on further, but it should at least be carefully understood that it is not or is no longer asserted—as some of the earliest positivist writers tried to do—that where the criminal trial is considered as a form of social defence, the criminal act will not be taken into account or will be treated as no more than a fortuitous or even negligible sign of a dangerousness which alone will be examined by the court. The court will indeed judge the act which the law considers an offence, but it will do so according to the subjective elements of the offender's personality and not according to objective legal criteria. Modern discussions of the ways in which the criminal courts may work out satisfactory methods of sentencing, illustrate the increasing importance of the offender's personality in the final judicial analysis of the question. These discussions also show how the problem is made even more complex by the normal background and training of judges.[52] The remarkable extension of studies on sentencing, in the Common Law countries, indicates the universal character of the problem, quite apart from the methods of any particular system of law or procedure.[53]

2. An investigation of the particular offender is therefore required of the criminal judge, but such investigation is no longer a merely judicial examination of the kind advocated by the nineteenth-century movement in favour of individualized punishment. It is not simply the external circumstances of the act or the exclusively legal antecedents of the accused that are taken into

[52] See the preparatory papers of the Eighth International Congress on Criminal Law held at Lisbon in 1961, and the discussions of the Congress, concerning the methods employed by the criminal judge in working out the sentence to be imposed, *Rev. int. de droit pénal*, 1960, pp. 7 ff.; cf. Giuseppe Sabatani, *L'Uomo nel sistema penale*, *Giustizia penale*, 1955, col. 129. Cf. Emilio Mira y Lopez, *Manuel de psychologie juridiqne* (French transl.), 1959, pp. 123 ff. Cf. Ernst Seelig, *Lehrbuch der Kriminologie*, 2nd ed., Graz, 1951, (in the French translation, *Traité de criminologie*, Paris, 1956, pp. 334 ff.).

[53] On the problem of sentencing, see the special number of *Law and Contemporary Problems* (Summer, 1958): cf. E. Green, *Judicial Attitudes in Sentencing* (Cambridge, *Studies in Criminology*, vol. XV, 1961).

consideration, but the offender's physical characteristics, psychological reactions, and social situation: so it is that in the view of the social defence movement, the criminal trial necessarily involves a scientific examination of the criminal. It is significant that this fundamental point successively preoccupied the Twelfth Penal and Penitentiary Congress at The Hague in 1950, the United Nations Seminar held at Brussels in 1951, the international courses on Criminology held in 1952 and 1955 (especially the latter)[54] as well as a number of other gatherings already mentioned. The work accomplished by these meetings cannot be discussed at this point, but the correlation between them needs to be stressed. There is indeed a striking and almost inevitable convergence of purpose between all those who are interested in the development of criminal law, criminal justice, and penological practice: whatever may be their particular reactions or the difference in approach between one gathering of specialists and another, all are led to study the same problem. Equally significant is the fact that the need for a social investigation, no longer challenged in the field of juvenile delinquency, should be increasingly felt as regards adult offenders. In Belgium, especially, a movement of considerable interest, which was mainly of judicial origin, urged that in every case a 'personality file' should be opened.[55] In France, since a remarkable judgement of the *Tribunal de la Seine* of 6 March 1956,[56] the Courts have recognized that in certain situations it would be feasible to arrange for experts to examine the offender's personality before the court gives its decision, and to give an opinion on his dangerousness and his prospects of social readaptation. This would be the case particularly when a question

[54] See especially the results of the first of these international courses: *L'Examen medico-psychologique et social des délinquants*, lectures published by G. Heuyer and J. Pinatel, Paris, 1953; cf. the results of the course held in 1955 under the supervision of Grispigni and published under the title *Delitto e personnalità*, Milan, 1955.

[55] On the personality file see Versele, 'Le Dossier de personnalité', *Rev. de droit pénal et de criminologie*, 1949, pp. 309 ff. Cf. in the same *Revue* the articles by R. Screvens and P. de Cant, 1951, pp. 265 ff.

[56] See the report of this decision, given under the presidency of J. Chazal, at *J.C.P.* 1956, 9338, and the note by G. Levasseur; cf. the remarks of Légal in *Rev. Science crim.*, 1956, p. 837. This decision was followed by many others. Along the same lines should be mentioned the examination of personality undertaken by the prison administration at Poitiers (see the study by Perdriau, *Rev. Science crim.*, 1955, p. 277) and by the prosecutor's department (*Pariquet*) of Lyons; see the remarks by the *Procureur* Gaultier, same *Revue*, 1958, p. 470.

arose as to whether the offender should be subjected to *relégation* or, on the contrary, receive a suspended sentence. At Strasbourg, in 1957, the series of discussions entitled *Cinquièmes Journées françaises de Défense Sociale* dealt in their turn with the question of the 'personality file'.[57] Again, in 1959, the International Penal and Penitentiary Foundation devoted an important group of studies to the observation of offenders.[58] All these endeavours share a common awareness that scientific investigation of the offender has become a necessity which modern criminal law and the penal policy of new social defence make a point of emphasizing.

A glance at the way in which modern penal legislation has developed is enough to indicate that this basic approach has achieved explicit recognition. Here is a legislative trend of an international character and significance, one of those trends in penal policy that may be identified and defined throughout the study of comparative law.[59]

In twentieth-century systems of criminal law individualization of punishment has become a statutory obligation and is no longer —as was the case in the nineteenth century—something which the court might apply at its discretion according to the circumstances of the case. Therefore it is not only the external features of the act, but the offender's motives both before and after the offence was committed, as well as his personal situation, that have to be considered. This is a principle which is now universally applied in the field of juvenile delinquency, and is also increasingly relied upon as regards adult offenders. The codes of the nineteen-thirties had already pointed the way in this connexion and gave expression in almost identical terms to a new conception of penal policy.[60]

[57] On the reports by Professor Kammerer of the medical faculty and by Judge Vassogne, together with the general report by Professor Léauté of the Faculty of Law, see *Revue de Science crim.*, 1957, pp. 835 ff.

[58] See the work of the *Cycle d'études de Strasbourg* (Berne, 2 vol., 1959); cf. the *Synthèse des travaux du Cycle d'études de Strasbourg: Trois aspects de l'action pénitentiaire*, by Marc Ancel and J.-B. Herzog (Berne, 1961).

[59] See the article by Marc Ancel in the symposium published in honour of Dean Julliot de la Morandière under the title 'Réflexions sur l'utilisation de la recherche comparative en droit pénal, (*Etudes juridiques*, Paris, 1964, pp. 9 ff.).

[60] See in particular: Italian Penal Code (1930) art. 133; Polish Penal Code (1932), art. 54; Rumanian Penal Code (1937), art. 21; Swiss Penal Code (1937), art. 63; Colombian Penal Code (1936), art. 36; Cuban Code of Social Defence (1936); Uruguayan Penal Code (1934); Brazilian Penal Code (1940), art. 42.

The movement thus initiated became increasingly influential after the second World War[61] and its effects were felt even in the Socialist countries, at a time when these were returning to a legalistic neo-classical approach.[62]

The systematic introduction of preventive measures reinforced this tendency, for what was desirable with regard to the traditional penal sanctions became necessary and even indispensable when the problem was to find a measure which should prevent a recurrence of the offence. Legal dogma itself founds the concept of 'preventive measures' on the dangerousness of the offender. Whence the need either to find a legal definition of dangerousness or, at any rate, to impose on the criminal judge the duty of ascertaining whether such dangerousness exists in any particular case and evaluating the prospects of curative, re-educative, or purely preventive measures.[63] The Italian Penal Code of 1930 clearly showed how the application of preventive measures is a more exacting process than the mere individualization of punishment, even when this is understood in its modern sense.[64] Thus in practice the court will be led to find as a fact that there is dangerousness and to forecast the probable course of social readaptation. In any event the wide range of modern penal sanctions necessarily depends on this evaluation of the individual causes of the offence and of the personality of the offender.[65]

It is enough to take this process one step further in order to realize the logical consequences of this new penal policy. The criminal judge cannot simply rely on his own intuitive assessment of the case or on the information he may gather from the examining magistrate's file (in countries where the office of *juge d'instruction* exists) or again from such indications as may be supplied in the course of the hearing.[66] The new system, especially where

[61] See the Greek Penal Code (1950), art. 79; Greenland Criminal statute of 1954 (the individualization of punishment based on the appreciation of the personality is the foundation of the system of sanctions, arts. 86 ff.; see even the Korean Penal Code of 1953, art. 51; cf. Ethiopian Penal Code, 1957, arts. 86 and 134.

[62] Bulgarian Penal Code, 1951 (art. 35); Penal Code of the Russian F.S.S.R. (1960), art. 37; Yugoslav Penal Code of 1950, revised in 1959, art. 38.

[63] See Cuban Code of 1936, art. 48.

[64] See Italian Penal Code of 1930, art. 204.

[65] The Swiss Criminal Code of 1937, articles 42 ff., foreshadows the wide discretionary power contained in the Greenland statute of 1954.

[66] E. Seelig, *Lehrbuch der Kriminologie*, 2nd ed., Graz, 1951 (in the French translation thereof, *Traité de criminologie*, Paris, 1956, see esp. pp. 334 ff.)

non-punitive measures of a preventive character are concerned, requires a preliminary scientific investigation of the accused. The evolution here has been analogous to that which took place as regards individualized punishment, from discretion to obligation. Until relatively recently the criminal judge might, if he thought fit, resort to expert evidence (*expertise*): today an expert's report is in certain cases obligatory. It is curious to note that the Anglo-American systems, while professing to ignore the notion of preventive measures, are particularly wide awake as regards this new trend in penal policy. The statute known as *Briggs' Law*, enacted in 1921 in the State of Massachusetts, requires that any person who is accused of a capital crime or has already been convicted of a criminal offence should be subjected to a mental examination.[67] In California since 1947, and in Michigan and Colorado since 1949, a personality investigation is required in all cases of felony. A similar enquiry is in fact carried out in New York, New Jersey, and, generally speaking, in the majority of the states of the U.S.A., as well as in Federal criminal procedure.[68] The new idea underlying this trend is that neither an indeterminate or long-term sentence, nor an order for probation, nor even a prison term can hope to be effective unless the judge who imposes them is thoroughly acquainted with the particular individual concerned.[69] In England, following the important reforms carried into effect by the Criminal Justice Act (1948), the Prison Commissioners pointed out that the new measures, such as corrective training,[70] should only be applied to those who needed them and for whom such measures were appropriate.[71] This explains the sustained effort undertaken in Great Britain to create remand centres and observation or

[67] See Weihofen, *Mental Disorder as a Criminal Defence*, Buffalo, New York, 1954, pp. 340 ff.

[68] See Will C. Turnbladh, 'Substitutes for Imprisonment', in *The Annals of the American Academy of Political and Social Science*, May 1954, special number entitled *Prisons in Transformation*, p. 113.

[69] See Norman Fenton, same *Review*, issue cited above, p. 51.

[70] Measure of re-education provided for by the Act of 1948 in respect of persons over 21, who already have a certain number of convictions. On this subject, see Sir Lionel Fox, *Introduction au droit criminel de l'Angleterre*, published by the Comparative Law Institute, Paris, 1959, pp. 269 and 284.

[71] 'If the corrective training is to succeed, it is important that those who receive the sentence should be persons who both need this form of training and are reasonably likely to profit by it' (1950 report, cited in the *Howard Journal*, vol. VIII, 1952, p. 135).

classification centres for the methodical investigation of adult offenders.[72]

3. It is not enough, however, simply to assert the necessity for a scientific and comprehensive knowledge of the offender or to provide for the organization of an enquiry into his case. The further question arises how the study of the offender's personality can be integrated into the record of the criminal trial. So it is that all systems concerned with implementing the requirements of modern penal policy have had to consider the legal status of a pre-trial investigation of the accused. In the Civil Law systems of the Continent, largely based on Roman law, and attached both to their codes and, in general, to the office of examining magistrate or *juge d'instruction*, the necessary changes were carried out by amendment of the rules of criminal procedure. In Switzerland, a federal statute of 15 June 1939 provided that the judge in criminal cases should determine 'all the facts concerning the person of the accused'.[73] More specifically, the Code of criminal procedure of the Canton of Neuchâtel, enacted in 1945, laid down as a general rule that the preliminary investigation of crime should throw light on those personal circumstances which would decisively affect the application of the criminal statute.[74] Article 81 of the French Code of criminal procedure of 1958, which provides that the examining magistrate shall enquire into the personality of the accused and also into his material, family, or social situation,[75] is part of the same legislative trend. The codification of 1958 expressly defines the result of the investigation envisaged—which is indeed a medical, psychological, and social enquiry as this is understood by modern writers—as a

[72] See the Home Office White Paper *Penal Practice in a Changing Society* 1959, (translated into French in the *Revue int. de Droit pénal*, 1959), Nos. 27 ff. Cf. Hugh Klare, *Anatomy of Prison*, London, 1960, p. 117.

[73] Art. 40. Cf. F. Clerc, *Le Procès pénal en Suisse romande*, Paris, 1955.

[74] Article 112; and see to the same effect article 57 of the Genevese Code of criminal procedure, 1940.

[75] Article 81 § 5 of the 1958 Code provides that the enquiry, which is compulsory for the more serious offences (*crimes*) and optional for *délits*, may include a 'medical and psychological examination'. Under article 16 the object of the enquiry is to provide the court with 'necessary information concerning the past and present way of life of the accused'. The Code adds that the 'personality file' cannot deal with the question of the proof of guilt. On the restrictive way in which the Cour de Cassation interpreted this new provision, see Cass. crim. 1 December 1960, Dalloz, 1961, 385, note M.R.M.P., and G. Levasseur, 'De la minimisation de l'enquête de personnalité à la généralisation du pouvoir discrétionnaire', *Rev. de Science crim.*, 1961, pp. 83 ff.

'personality file' (*dossier de personnalité*).[76] This official recognition is significant. The value, from the legislative standpoint, of the reforms introduced in France by article 81 of the 1958 Code of criminal procedure has frequently been stressed. The French example has attracted attention even in Japan, where certain authorities urged that it should be followed in a reform of the Japanese Code of criminal procedure of 1948, which provides for the examination of personality only in the case of juvenile offenders.[77] This shows that we are here concerned with a dynamic trend in modern criminal procedure.

Yet a considerable innovation is involved, which upsets many well-entrenched traditional attitudes and still perturbs some lawyers preoccupied with the notion that a criminal trial should involve no more than the objective judgement of the act prohibited by law, leaving out of account the offender as an individual. It is in this connexion that social defence doctrines play a vital rôle, teaching that here is a necessary evolution which must be accepted, understood, and organized in a rational manner.

We should not, however, disregard the difficulties inherent in the process of incorporating a scientific investigation of the offender's personality into the criminal trial. This thorny question has provoked a considerable literature and numerous meetings of specialists from the time that the problem of the medical, psychological, and social examination of offenders was clearly raised at the series of seminars organized in Brussels by the United Nations in 1951.[78] It may be noted in this regard that, in the course of the discussions just mentioned, those who—openly or otherwise—oppose any changes in criminal justice try to defend the legislative or judicial *status quo* in the name of current practice and alleged common sense.

[76] See F. J. Doll, *Le Dossier de personnalité*, *J.C.P.*, 1961, I. 1631.

[77] Makino, *Interrelation of a Code of Criminal Procedure and Criminal Policy. Keisei*, Tokio, 1960, p. 223.

[78] See the papers of this series of seminars, reported in the issue already cited of the *International Review of Criminal Policy*, published by the United Nations, No. 3, January 1953; see also the First International Course on Criminology (Paris, 1962); the eighth French *Journées de défense sociale* (Paris, 1960), in *Rev. de Science crim.*, 1960, pp. 595 ff.; the First French Criminological Congress (Lyons, 1960), and the preparatory session for the Eighth International Congress of Criminal Law (Lisbon, 1961), held in Paris in 1960 (*Rev. int. de droit pénal*, 1960, p. 350). On this same question see also in particular the articles published in the *Bulletin de la Société int. de Criminologie* (1959, pp. 187 ff.), and R. Vouin, 'L'Individualisation de la répression dans le Code de procédure pénale', in *Rev. de Science crim.*, 1959, pp. 291 ff.

4. One of the main arguments used by this reactionary group lies in the assertion that scientific investigation of all criminals is not possible. Furthermore, it is argued, if everyone who commits an offence, even of a trivial character, should be subjected to systematic investigation, the logical course would be to extend the operation as a precautionary measure to all those who are or might be considered as potential offenders, but who have not yet committed an act punishable by law. Thus the population as a whole would be exposed to the ordeal of such an enquiry. The short answer to this kind of argument is that no thesis is effectively refuted simply by being carried to the point of absurdity. The social defence movement does not wish to give the psychiatrist or psychoanalyst an untrammelled right to peer into the activities of the average law-abiding citizen. Moreover, those who rely on such arguments as a weapon against the generalized use of scientific methods in the treatment of crime—an evolution which they feel is inevitable—forget, sometimes deliberately, that the doctrine of new social defence, emphasizing individual rights and the importance of the rule *nulla poena sine lege*, always insists that a criminal offence—an act defined as such by law—must have been committed before a person can be brought before a criminal court.[79]

In order to combine the scientific approach with the criminal trial, however, traditional criminal procedure has to be changed.[80] Some criminal scientists in the Scandinavian countries, Belgium, and France strongly urge that the criminal trial should be divided into two stages.[81] This might perhaps be likened to the system long established in England, whereby the stage of conviction is separated from that of sentence: these writers consider that in the modern criminal trial the judge should first decide the facts at issue, the law applicable thereto, and whether they can be imputed

[79] See in particular J. Chazal, 'Où en est la défense sociale nouvelle?' (Chronique de défense sociale) in *Rev. de Science crim.*, 1961, p. 169.

[80] See Marc Ancel, *Le Procès pénal et l'examen scientifique des délinquants*, 1952; P. Nuvolone, 'L'esame biopsichico preventivo del delinquente come problema penale e processuale', in *Studi Parmensi*, 1950.

[81] Paul Cornil, 'La Césure entre le prononcé et l'exécution de la peine, '*Journ. des trib.*, Brussels, 1948, p. 406; see on the same question, Simon, *Revue de droit pénal et de crim.*, 1948, p. 687; J. Constant, same *Revue*, 1948, p. 203, and M. P. Vrij, *ibid.*, 1951, p. 236. For the Scandinavian countries, see in the *Nordisk Kriminalistik Årsbok*, the striking intervention by I. Strahl, 1949-1950, p. 81; see also Versele, report to the Colloquium on social defence held at San Marino in September 1951, *Riv. di difesa sociale*, 1951, pp. 66 ff.

to the accused. Should the accused be found guilty, the second phase would involve the choice of a penal sanction appropriate to his personal situation and his characteristics as an individual. Such a division of the criminal trial is by no means inconceivable in the Continental systems, more particularly in the Franco-Belgian system. On the contrary, for in France such a system lay at the root of the classical procedure applied in courts of assize (*cour d'assises*) where the jury, under the code of 1808, were the sole judges of fact, whereas the court imposed the statutory penalty. Classical notions of law meant that once it had been found as a fact that the offence had been committed, the sentence provided by law was imposed as a matter of course. This led, during the nineteenth century, to the gradual obliteration of the distinction between the two phases in the criminal trial. One of the clearest results of the attention paid to the offender's personality, however, is precisely the re-emergence of this distinction. In particular, thanks to this technical device it is possible to carry out such an investigation even in the case of an offender who has been brought before the *tribunal correctionel* as the result of a summary complaint or arrested *flagrante delicto* and is acknowledged as the undoubted author of the offence, before an individualized sanction is applied. As has been pointed out, the Common Law system, which appeared archaic in this respect, is now in the forefront of this renovating procedural trend,[82] whereas the problem is still a live one for those trained in other systems.

Besides, this is not the only procedural change involved in the process of taking the offender's personality into account during the criminal trial. Only a few other examples will be cited here. If a thorough acquaintance with the offender is essential, it would be absurd to retain the traditional rule which rigidly separates the preliminary investigation of a case from the hearing in court, the examining magistrate (*juge d'instruction*) taking no part whatever in the trial itself. This rule remains applicable to adult offenders but has been abandoned or even reversed in criminal law as applied to juveniles, which constitutes a 'law of social defence' applied by magistrates in juvenile courts (*juge des enfants*). In the continental system the magistrate concerned with juvenile matters is the first to investigate the particular case and acts very much as

[82] See J.-M. Canals, 'Classicism, Positivism and Social Defence', in *Journ. of Crim. Law, Criminology and Police Science*, vol. 59, No. 6, pp. 541 ff., especially p. 549.

an examining magistrate. Nevertheless, and indeed because of the sustained knowledge of the offender's personality which he thus acquires, the same magistrate will sit as chairman in the juvenile court which ultimately deals with the case.[83] So it is that in the context of social defence a procedure which formerly seemed inconceivable or illogical now appears not merely conceivable or tolerable, but necessary. This argument may even be taken a step further: the rule which was once considered as a safeguard for the rights of the person charged may now appear, on the contrary, inconvenient or even dangerous, so that the protection now afforded to the juvenile offender is the direct result of the deliberate disregard of the rule formerly applied.

According to another traditional rule, fully justified in principle, the accused should have access to all the documents produced and hear all the evidence given in court. However, it is clear that nothing is more harmful psychologically for an accused person than that he should become acquainted with certain psychiatrists' reports or with the results of certain tests. Here again the law as applied to juvenile offenders is conceived in a reformist spirit. In the more advanced systems, at any rate, the court may order that the offender be excluded from the hearing while some kinds of evidence are given concerning him or his family, or again while medical witnesses are heard. The very modern code of criminal procedure enacted in the Canton of Neuchâtel (Switzerland) in 1945 extends these rules even to the adult offender.[84]

Some lawyers of a conservative bent are doubtless opposed to this disregard of traditional safeguards in criminal procedure. They forget that even if the accused himself be excluded from certain parts of the hearing and prevented from seeing certain documents, his counsel will necessarily have access to the whole file and hear all the evidence. Above all, they forget that in criminal procedure as this is now applied to juvenile delinquents, it is not so much a case of shielding the accused from the attacks

[83] See J. Chazal, *Le Juge des enfants, pratique judiciaire et action sociale*, Paris, 1948.

[84] Code of criminal procedure of the Canton of Neuchâtel, art. 199, § 2. The report of the special commission of the *Conseil d'État* of the Canton on the draft code (Neuchâtel, 1945) defends this innovation on the grounds of 'humanity and charity' (p. 85). Article 304 of the Netherlands Code of criminal procedure laid down a similar rule. See also, on this problem as a whole, S. C. Versele, 'De la contradiction et de la publicité dans une procédure de défense sociale', *Rev. de Science crim.*, 1952, pp. 567 ff.

of the prosecution as of seeking, with the co-operation of the juvenile court and of the social services which are inseparable therefrom, to work out, in an impartial manner, the measure of protection that would be most appropriate in the particular case. An important article by Graven has rightly pointed out that a characteristic feature of criminal procedure conceived as a means of social defence is precisely the wish to avoid making the judgement of the case depend on the traditional 'legal duel' between prosecution and defence.[85]

When criminal procedure is guided by this new approach the old antithesis between inquisitorial and accusatorial procedure tends to become meaningless. This is more particularly the case where a distinction is made between conviction and sentence. The first phase necessarily retains an accusatorial flavour and continues to rely on traditional procedural safeguards. Social defence does not take issue with the legalism of the law of evidence in the Anglo-American systems.[86] During this first phase the question is whether the accused is guilty or innocent. It may indeed be said, as in a recent article, that classical criminal law seems 'to be aimed not so much against the offender as against the process of criminal prosecution itself'.[87] In this sense the code of criminal procedure, like the old *Code d'instruction criminelle* which was in force in France before 1958, is a 'code for law-abiding people'. Strict interpretation and respect for procedural forms are therefore the principal safeguards of the citizen. But it would be a mistake to believe that once the legal question has been disposed of, criminal justice has no further problem to face. On the contrary, a new and exceedingly complex problem now arises: during the second phase, that of the sentence, it is no longer a case of protecting a possibly innocent person against unjustified criminal proceedings, but of determining—by scientific as well as merely legal means—the best method of dealing with the offender in question, with a view to carrying out a genuine and effective processs of social readaptation.

5. In such a context it is likewise inaccurate—or at any rate insufficient—to repeat the traditional distinction between pre-trial,

[85] J. Graven, 'Introduction à une procédure pénale rationnelle de prévention et de défense sociale', *Rev. pénale suisse*, 1950, pp. 170 ff.

[86] See W. P. J. Pompe, 'La Preuve en procédure pénale', *Rev. de Science crim.*, 1961, p. 269.

[87] Statement on the occasion of the twenty-fifth anniversary of the *Revue de Science criminelle*, in that *Revue*, 1962, p. 308.

trial, and, post-trial phases of procedure. It is clear from the work of American penologists on the problem of classification (as this term is understood in the United States)[88] that the offender should be under close observation in all phases of the criminal proceedings: modern penologists consider that such observation is a continuous process parallel to that of social readaptation, which is the object of the 'penitentiary action'.

The emergence of the notion of 'treatment of offenders' also makes it clear that the criminal trial should henceforth be envisaged no longer simply as the judgement in law of an act which is classified as an offence, but as a continuous process which begins with the charge initially brought against a person after the offence was committed and ends only with the conclusion of the last measure taken against the offender. As early as 1889 the first manifesto of the International Union of Criminal Law had taken issue with the arbitrary separation between the trial and the penitentiary or post-trial phase, which was concerned with carrying the sentence into effect. Certain modern legislative trends may be noted in this connexion, and first of all the movement towards the appointment of magistrates responsible for supervising the post-trial phase in which the sentence of the court is carried into effect. In France such a magistrate is called *le juge d'exécution des peines* or *le juge de l'application des peines*.[90] Also to be noted in this

[88] On the question of classification, see Barnes and Teeters, *New Horizons in Criminology*, chapter xxxi, p. 756; see also *Handbook on Classification in Correctional Institutions*, New York, 1947; see also H. Mannheim and J. C. Spencer, *Problems of Classification in the English Penal and Reformatory System*, London, 1951; cf. Sutherland and Cressey, *Principles of Criminology*, 6th ed., 1960, p. 462; R. M. Coe and A. J. Shafter, 'Survey of Classification Systems in the United States', in *Journ. of Crim. Law, Criminology and Police Science*, November 1958, pp. 316 ff.; Howard Jones, *Prison Reforms Now*, 1959.

[89] See in particular the papers of the seminars organized by the International Penal and Penitentiary Foundation at Strasbourg. An account of the work accomplished has been published under the title: *Trois aspects de l'action pénitentiaire*, Berne, 1961.

[90] See J. Beleza dos Santos, 'Le juge d'exécution des peines au Portugal', in *Rev. int. de dr. comp.*, 1952, pp. 401 ff.; cf. also the first *Journées franco-belgo-luxembourgeoises de science pénale* (November 1951), 'Le rôle du magistrat dans l'exécution des peines', Paris, 1952, pp. 81 ff. See also the resolutions of the Third International Social Defence Congress in 1954, *Actes du Troisième Congrès international de défense sociale*, Antwerp, 1955, p. 312. See also 'Les Dixièmes Journées de défense sociale, Lyon, 7-8 juin 1962', in *Rev. de Science crim.*, 1963, pp. 574 ff.; cf. C. Germain, *Eléments de science pénitentiaire*, 1959, p. 78, and Cuello Calón, *La moderna penologia*, t. I, Barcelona, 1958, pp. 268 ff.

regard is the movement towards making 'conditional discharge' (release on parole, *libération conditionnelle*) a measure that should depend at least in part on the decision of a magistrate.[91] In the U.S.A. the emergence of the system of indeterminate sentences has resulted in the organization of a real tribunal concerned with the prolongation or cessation of the measure which applied to the offender, and the former system of conditional discharge or even release on parole, as it was first envisaged by Americans, tends to be replaced by a more complicated process designed as a careful preparation for the discharged person's return to freedom.[92] Related phenomena are the appearance of institutions such as the 'prison tribunal' in Finland or the endeavours of some criminologists to encourage the establishment of a 'treatment tribunal'.[93] All these innovations may be seen as spontaneous expressions of concern—in the interests of social defence—that the judgement of the criminal and his treatment after trial should henceforth be intimately related.

Furthermore, it may be recalled that in the mid-twentieth century, reforms of the prison system have often enough made a greater contribution to the acceptance of social defence ideas than have reforms of criminal legislation itself.[94] The fact that in the more advanced countries there has been a spontaneous movement in prison administration away from the automatic and merely

[91] Giuliano Vassalli, *La riforma della liberazione condizionale, Rassegna di Studi penitenziari*, 1951, pp. 997 ff. On the French reform effectuated by the statute of January 5, 1951, the decree of April 1, 1952 and the directive of June 25, 1953, see *Rev. de Science crim.*, 1953, 'Chronique pénitentiaire', pp. 117 and 689, 'Chronique législative', p. 324. See also G. Simson, 'Aperçu comparatif de la législation sur la libération conditionelle', in *Rev. de Science crim.*, 1955, p. 257.

[92] See Marc Ancel's report to the United Nations on *Indeterminate Sentences*, 1954, and compare Howard Jones, *Crime and the Penal System*, 1962, pp. 181 ff.

[93] The Finnish statute of 1932 allows the criminal judge in certain cases to send the delinquent to an institution for persistent offenders, where he will undergo an indeterminate sentence. The length and terms of the period of detention are fixed by the 'prison tribunal', an administrative body which nonetheless has a settled procedure and is careful to safeguard the rights of the detained person. See Norval Morris, *The Habitual Delinquent*, pp. 198-99. On the treatment tribunals, see also S. and E. Glueck, *After Conduct of Discharged Offenders* (English Studies in Criminal Science, vol. V, London, 1949, chap. viii); cf. S. Glueck, *Law and Psychiatry, Cold War or Entente Cordiale?*, 1962.

[94] See in particular, in France, the reports to the Ministry of Justice on Prison Administration, 1952 and 1953; see also C. Germain, *Le Traitement des récidivistes en France*, 1953, and *Éléments de science pénitentiaire*, 1959, for Belgium see J. Dupréel, *Aspects de l'action pénitentiaire en Belgique*, 1962.

passive application of the penalty fixed by law, explains why attention has been drawn to the notion of treatment of offenders and to the need for arousing the interest of the criminal courts in a whole range of criminological problems which will determine the efficacy of the treatment ordered by the court. Criminal lawyers, even the most conservative-minded, who have examined judicial methods of sentencing,[95] have been squarely confronted with this new aspect of a classic problem. They were no longer concerned with the traditional 'dosage' of punishment, but with the establishment of rules having a penological as well as a legal basis and specifically designed to prepare and facilitate the 'treatment' of the offender. The French Code of criminal procedure of 1958, which in devoting an important group of articles to procedures relating to the execution of sentences,[96] is surely the most radical expression of this legislative trend, emphasizes certain broader aspects of modern criminal law and lays the foundation for individual treatment based on consideration of the offender's personality. The French reform of 1958 is only part of a widespread and international trend in penal policy, which is evidenced by other reforms as various as those recently enacted in the Netherlands[97] and Venezuela,[98] and which—as some of the most reputable criminologists have observed—throws into relief the close relationship between the criminological and penological sciences.[99]

[95] It will be recalled that this was the theme of the Eighth International Congress of Criminal Law at Lisbon; see *Revue int. de droit pénal*, 1960, p. 5; and in particular the general report by Marc Ancel, pp. 350 ff. In this field there was a broad convergence of views between criminal scientists brought up in the Romanist and continental tradition on the one hand, and the ideas of Anglo-American specialists on the problem of sentencing.

[96] On this group of articles in Book V of the Code of 1958, see the study by Marc Ancel, entitled 'Les Réformes apportées par le Code de procédure pénale de 1958 au régime d'exécution des peines', in *Annales de la Faculté de Droit de Liège*, 1961, pp. 157 ff.

[97] Lamers, 'Les Bases de l'exécution des peines aux Pays-Bas', in *Rev. de Science crim.*, 1961, p. 743.

[98] See *Rev. de Science crim.*, 1962, p. 614.

[99] J. Pinatel, 'Criminologie et droit pénal', *Rev. de Science crim.*, 1953, pp. 595 ff. 'Les Diverses Conceptions de la science pénitentiaire', same *Revue*, 1949, pp. 705 ff.; 'Les Nouveaux Horizons de la réforme pénitentiaire', *Rev. int. de droit pénal*, pp. 215 ff.; 'La Criminologie: ses problèmes fondamentaux', same *Revue* 1951, p. 101; Levasseur, 'Sociologie criminelle et défense sociale', *Rev. de Science crim.*, 1957, p. 301.

B

From the standpoint of the penal policy of new social defence, this concept of 'treatment' of the offender had one notable consequence that requires particular emphasis, since it led to the reorganization of the existing system of criminal sanctions. The logical consequence of establishing a rational and scientific system for the treatment of offenders is the integration of both punishment and measures of prevention in a unitary system of social defence, thereby resolving the difficult and hitherto insoluble problem of the difference between a 'measure' and a 'punishment'. This is an essential point in social defence doctrine, and one of those which has been most subject to misinterpretation. The question is straightforward enough, however, so long as we are willing to approach it without preconceived ideas.

Pure classical law held that the crime was the wilful act of a man responsible for his actions, leading necessarily to the imposition of a penalty which would serve both to punish the criminal's moral fault and to restore the legal order that had been disturbed by the criminal act.

In a purely positivist system, on the other hand, squarely based on deterministic principles laid down *a priori*, punishment is strictly speaking inconceivable, for the criminal sanction is regarded either as an anachronistic survival of the former repressive system or as the result of scientifically inadequate analysis of the reaction to crime. Since no one can be held 'responsible' for his acts, it is merely a case of enacting 'preventive measures' for the purpose of securing society against the dangerousness of the offender. It is in this sense that the positivists sometimes spoke of 'objective' or 'social' responsibility: the act that has been committed entitles society to intervene for the purpose of neutralizing the offender, but it is no longer a case of applying sanctions for his fault. The term 'guilt' is thus emptied of meaning, just as the social reaction no longer connotes any element of moral censure. The classical and positivist doctrines are thus completely antithetical.

There was indeed an attempt to reconcile the two extreme positions. A balance between them was achieved, in appearance at any rate, in the eclectic system evolved in the first half of this century, which found expression in criminal codes enacted between the two World Wars. A person to whom a crime was 'imputable' was subject to the rules of moral responsibility and would therefore incur punishment, which would thus fulfil its normal function. Where the offence was not 'imputable' to the person in question, he could not be accountable for a fault for which he was not responsible, and would simply be subjected to a preventive measure.[100]

The system would be perfectly satisfactory if those persons to whom a crime might be 'imputed' could always be distinguished from those to whom it could not be thus 'imputed'. But enacted law, which must come to grips with social realities, has to accept the fact that in many cases the author of a criminal offence will fall into both categories, or again that the case is a marginal one, lying on the boundary between imputability and non-imputability. So it is that in many countries the legislator, anxious to reconcile the two tendencies, while avoiding the drawbacks of the system of diminished responsibility, laid down that one and the same person could incur a penal sanction in respect of his fault and also be subjected to a measure of prevention designed to guard against his dangerousness. It was claimed that this mixed solution met different needs and reconciled opposite doctrines, by taking over the useful and effective elements in both of them. The practical value of this ingenious compromise is, however, doubtful, for its basis is purely intellectual.

Although the cumulative imposition of punishment and prevention was the prevalent trend in criminal law at the beginning of the twentieth century,[101] this system is being progressively

[100] See Léon Cornil (Speech on the occasion of the *rentrée* of the Court of Appeal in Brussels on 16 September 1929, that is, at the ceremonial opening of the legal year): 'The insane person, who is irresponsible, should not be punished but subjected to preventive measures. The abnormal offender, who is partly responsible, should incur punishment in proportion to his degree of responsibility for his action, and preventive measures to the extent that he is irresponsible. But some punishment should always be applied, because the offender always enjoys a certain measure of freedom and hence should be punished for having misused that measure of freedom'.

[101] See the resolution passed by the Tenth International Penal and Penitentiary Congress held at Prague in 1930: 'It is essential that the system of punishments should be completed by a system of preventive measures so as to ensure the defence of society when punishment is inapplicable or inadequate.' (*Actes* of the Congress, I, p. 45). In England, the Prevention of Crimes Act (1908), adopted the cumulative system, the punishment being carried out before the preventive measure; the Criminal Justice Act (1948), prefers the alternative system and empowers the

abandoned today for a number of reasons. The first is that even on the theoretical level, where the *rapprochement* between the two extremes appeared most stable, it was impossible to find a firm and conclusive answer to the question whether, punishment and prevention being applicable to the same offenders, the punishment should precede the measure of prevention or *vice versa*. This difficulty is sufficiently illustrated by the tergiversations of the legislative systems which adopted this so-called 'double track', such as the Italian (Rocco) Code of 1930, the Swiss Code of 1937, and the Greek Code of 1950. Another reason for the rejection of this system was the gradual emergence in judicial and penitentiary practice, as well as in penal doctrine, of the idea that a choice should be made between the two types of sanctions, only one of which could logically be applied in any single case. Therefore the cumulative system was gradually replaced by an alternative system; in other words, a different conception of the 'double track' was preferred.[102]

According to this new approach the judge, following certain principles laid down by statute, would be entitled to choose between a penal solution and a solution based on considerations of social defence. This is a change really important in itself and even more so in its consequences. But the fact is still ignored in some circles, and the very term 'double track' contributes to the confusion. The idea that the judge should choose between a retributive and a preventive approach to crime supposes that the two are fundamentally different, which serves to stress the alleged antithesis between punishment on the one hand, and preventive measures on the other. One view, largely derived from nineteenth-century German and Italian dogmatic theories, as these were interpreted under the influence of von Liszt's reformist approach,

---

judge to choose between punishment and prevention. See on this topic Fox, *The English Prison and Borstal Systems*, 1951, p. 302. A similar evolution took place in Sweden between 1927 and 1937: see G. Simson, 'Le Traitement des délinquants d'habitude en Suède', *Rev. de Science crim.*, 1949, pp. 693 ff. On the modern trend from one system to another, see Marc Ancel's report to the I.P.P.C. on the theme, *Les Mesures de sûreté en matière criminelle*, 1951, p. 41.

[102] See the general report by Grispigni at the Sixth International Congress for Criminal Law, held at Rome in September 1953, *Rev. int. de droit pénal*, 1953, pp. 757 ff.; cf. on the advantages of the so-called 'double track', Mezger, *Deutsches Strafrecht*, 2nd ed., 1941, pp. 150-52.

goes so far as to assert that the distinction must necessarily be preserved: the core of the argument is that the notion of punishment should be retained undiminished, since punishment, being the appropriate sanction for the offence seen as a legal concept, is alone able to restore the legal order which was destroyed or jeopardized by the crime.

This dogmatic and legalistic attitude is still ardently defended by some eminent criminal lawyers, who maintain in sound logic that punishment and preventive measures should be applied in completely different spheres.[103] The latter, it is argued, are based not on the responsibility but on the dangerousness of the offender: they are in no sense retributive and are designed exclusively to protect society against crime irrespective of moral considerations, so that on intellectual and even ethical grounds such measures must be clearly separated from the idea of punishment.

Other writers, while aware of these problems, are careful to point out that in fact—and certainly from the historical standpoint—this view of the rôle of preventive measures amounts to an attempted compromise between the classical system defended by Binding and the more modern trends advocated by the International Union of Criminal Law. Thus Stooss, in his draft Swiss Criminal Code of 1893, tried to reconcile the neo-classicists to the notion of preventive measures, treating these as a supplementary or additional method of reaction against crime, but preserving the theoretical purity of the notion of punishment. Initially, therefore, this was just an intellectual exercise without any analysis of sociological realities.[104] It is noteworthy that the measures which had already found legislative expression—*relégation* in France (1885), *manicome* in Italy (1889), the Belgian statute of 1891 (which in its provisions for *la mise à la disposition du Gouvernement* gave the administration a tutelary rôle in relation to vagrants), preventive detention in England (1908)—took no account of fine distinctions and were boldly classed as punishments, to which a new dimension was thus

[103] See L. Jiménez de Asúa, 'La Mesure de sûreté, sa nature et ses rapports avec la peine', in *Rev. de Science crim.*, 1954, p. 21; cf. also, on the Colloquium held at Buenos Aires in 1960, *Jornadas de derecho penal*, Buenos Aires, 1962, 2nd section, 'Penas y medidas de seguridad', pp. 93 ff.

[104] See W. P. J. Pompe, 'Les Rapports entre la peine et la mesure de sûreté in *Rev. de Science crim.*, 1963, p. 529; cf. the discussions in the course of the colloquium above mentioned, held at Buenos Aires, and in particular the remarks of Graven.

assigned. Carl Stooss's theory was an ingenious utilization of pure law; but it dealt in an abstract and technical way with the practical problem of penal policy and social efficacy, encouraging lawyers to impose this intellectual structure on a legislative phenomenon that should have been approached in quite a different way, as is evidenced by the endless discussions which the question has aroused.[105] By way of contrast, we may note the instinctive wisdom of Anglo-American criminal lawyers and penologists who, in practice, have succeeded in building up a highly flexible system of non-punitive methods of dealing with crime without getting bogged down in the academic controversies of their Romanist continental brethren.

It is precisely here that social defence doctrines seek to shed new light on the problem, though not by substituting a new theory for those already in existence. Here again the social defence movement merely seeks to introduce an element of realism and a critical spirit. As Plato, Aristotle, and Montesquieu were all fully aware, legislation is not purely a matter of intellectual speculation, even when it purports to engage in political philosophy: the spirit of the laws can only be derived from their actual provisions. The doctrines of new social defence require that criminal scientists should step outside the narrow bounds of an unnecessary dogmatism and make a serious effort to clarify the issues.[106] Now when we examine the relationship between punishment and preventive measures from this standpoint, we observe that the discussion has been complicated in the first place by the fact that the conflicting protagonists did not really approach the problem from the same angle. For the lawyer, concerned to preserve the theory that protection of the legal order is the purpose of criminal law, and that punishment is the necessary sanction of the offence, 'punishment' and 'preventive measures' are defined in purely abstract

[105] See in particular the results of the Sixth International Congress of Criminal Law, Rome 1953, on the *Problème de l'unification des peines et des mesures de sûreté* (The problem of the assimilation of punishment and preventive measures) dealt with in the general report by Grispigni (*Revue int. de droit pénal*, 1953, p. 757; special reports in the same *Revue*, 1953, p. 475; 1954, p. 307; summary records of the discussions, 1954, pp. 257 ff. See also the *Convegno* at Como-Bellagio-Milan (24-27 April 1958), published by the *Centro Nazionale di prevenzione e difesa sociale*, Milan, 1961, pp. 47 ff.; cf. *Pene e misure di securezza* (*Convegno di studio Enrico di Nicola*), Milan 1962, pp. 5 ff.

[106] This point of view was thoroughly grasped by Roberto Lyra, in particular in *Novissimas Escolas penais*, 1956, p. 85; this work deals precisely with the relationship between punishment and preventive measures.

terms: so in a purely legal sense there are two distinct and clearly irreconcilable notions. From their theoretical and absolute point of view, therefore, these lawyers are right in asserting that the assimilation of punishment and preventive measures is, strictly speaking, inconceivable.

Other writers, on the contrary, approach the problem from the penitentiary standpoint. Among others, Sir Lionel Fox, Cornil, Norval Morris, and Grünhut have all remarked that in fact there is no difference—nor indeed any possibility of differentiating—between the respective means of carrying out punishment and a preventive measure involving deprivation of liberty, i.e. institutional treatment. The purely legal content of the two notions seems irrelevant, the more so as a widespread and almost irresistible tendency can be observed at present in various legislative and penitentiary systems in favour of a single penalty (or measure) involving institutional treatment.[107] Everywhere, indeed, it is sought to apply the treatment which is most appropriate for the individual detained in a penitentiary institution, whether he is serving a prison term or is confined on preventive grounds. If a satisfactory penitentiary system can be discovered which is indeed calculated to improve the offender, it is clear that such a system should be applied to all who are confined in penal institutions. Consequently, from the standpoint of penitentiary practice, the distinction between punishment and preventive measures becomes a mere fiction or at any rate a purely academic problem of no practical importance.

The attitude of these criminal scientists or penologists is as fully justified from their point of view as is the attitude of the pure lawyers from *their* standpoint. Must we then simply take note of this disagreement, or else, adopting a sceptical and relativist approach, leave to either side its share of the truth? No, for there

[107] On this movement see the papers of the International Penal and Penitentiary Commission and the resolution adopted at the last meeting (July 1951), *Recueil de Doc. en matière pén. et pénit.* (vol. XV, November 1951), p. 480; cf. A. Luisier, 'Vers la peine unique', *Rev. de crim. et de police technique*, 1952, pp. 315 ff.; also Germain, *Eléments de science pénitentiaire*, 1959, pp. 26 ff.; Dupréel, General report to the I.P.P.F. discussion groups at Strasbourg (*Travaux*, Berne, 1959, pp. 441 ff.; as regards Switzerland, see François Clerc, 'Les Travaux de révision du Code pénal suisse', in *Rev. de Science crim.*, 1956, pp. 277 ff.; and for the Scandinavian countries, Norway in particular, see *Nordisk Kriminalistisk Årsbok*, 1956, with a summary in English, p. xxi.

is a third approach, inspired by considerations that are neither wholly legal nor wholly penitentiary, but are based on penal policy. As regards the treatment of offenders, the first concern of a penal policy designed to cope effectively with crime is to prevent recidivism.[108] In this respect, such a penal policy seeks to control crime effectively on three fronts—legislative, judicial, and penitentiary. It would be absurd to pay tribute in the legislative sphere to legal concepts that would be inapplicable in the penitentiary sphere. Moreover, such a method would thwart the operation of the judicial system which is responsible for applying the criminal statute in question, in order that the penitentiary action may take place. Consequently the problem is neither that of making an abstract choice among different theories, nor simply of perfecting the practical measures applied in fact in institutions for the confinement of offenders. The essential problem is to grasp all the methods by which the control of crime can be effectively organized, in the interests of society, without disregarding the interests of the individual. In this context, as we have already observed, punishment and preventive measures may both have their part to play.

Indeed, the modern evolution of criminal law favours the use both of retributive sanctions and of non-punitive methods with a preventive purpose. There is therefore no question of doing away with punishment altogether and substituting measures of an exclusively curative or remedial kind, as was urged by the positivists and is still advocated by Gramatica. On the contrary, in the new system of penal policy, the judge should be able, if need be, to resort to a repressive penalty, and we have emphasized that even the most modern forms of legislation on juvenile delinquency have not wholly given up the possibility in certain circumstances of having recourse to such a penal sanction. On the other hand, there are many situations in which preventive measures of a remedial, educative, or neutralizing kind will be more appropriate. But the rational penal policy of 'prevention of crime and treatment of offenders', as these words are understood by the United Nations and the movement encouraged by the international

[108] S. and E. Glueck have admirably demonstrated how, from the point of view of practical social action, there should be taken into account not the anonymous mass of merely potential offenders, but first of all those who are or have been at odds with criminal justice: *After Conduct of Discharged Offenders*, London, 1949, pp. 95 ff.

Organization, wants its action against crime to be guided mainly by the effectiveness of its sanctions with regard to the individual concerned, and to the group to which he belongs. So it is that punishment will be replaced by preventive measures, not on grounds of legal theory or administrative convenience, but for biological, medical, psychological, or sociological reasons, in short because the offender's personality is taken into consideration.

Punishment and preventive measures are thus no longer antithetical. If the 'pure lawyers' wish to continue comparing and contrasting these two concepts, for reasons of intellectual scruple, the social defence movement will raise no objection, but will simply consider the point as an academic and ideological factor which has strictly nothing to do with the social action directed against the phenomenon of crime, which is the purpose and *raison d'être* of the new penal policy. According to this penal policy either method could be used indifferently, for what matters is not its classification as 'punishment' or 'preventive measure' but the content and, so to speak, the flavour of the sanction, much more than its classification in legal terms. This is true to such an extent that the penal policy of social defence, apparently turning its back on one aspect of the modern evolution of criminal law, could even envisage linking up an educative measure with a repressive measure on the ground, for example, that placing an offender on probation could well be accompanied by the imposition of a fine. The harmonious development of penal sanctions in the spirit and against the background of this new penal policy really depends on creating a state of affairs in which, thanks to the abandonment of the rigid categories of punishment and preventive measures, either type of sanction may be freely and scientifically applied in accordance with the individual and social requirements of the particular case. Such individualized application of these sanctions will transform them into genuine tools of that social readaptation which remains the principal object of the penal policy of social defence.

It is in this sense that one can—and indeed should—say that what is involved in this doctrine is not the assimilation of punishment to preventive measures or vice versa, but the integration of all kinds of sanctions into a unitary system based on physical, social, and moral criteria, and which depends for its organization on a penal policy where criminal law fulfils its normal but essential vocation as a necessary safeguard of individual freedom.

However, the integration of the notion of 'preventive measure' into a general penal policy of social defence raises one last problem which must also be faced. Indeed, if preventive measures are envisaged not simply in legal terms as something that must be clearly distinguished from punishment, but as the instrument of a rational social reaction against crime, then the question arises whether it would not be logical to accept the application of preventive measures *ante delictum*, before the offence. It is a fact that the dangerousness of a particular individual, the delinquent tendencies of his personality, may find expression before any legal offence as such has been committed. Do not such measures of a 'pre-delictual' kind almost necessarily follow from the acceptance as the foundation of penal policy of ideas of prevention and protection coupled with the thorough investigation of the personality of the individual?

The question has already arisen more than once in the course of the foregoing chapters, where it was stressed that the new doctrines of social defence do not result—as some authors have too readily asserted—in the rejection of all systems of law and their replacement by a discretionary system of prevention or an unlimited power of the State to intervene in the case of potential offenders. It should be emphasized once again that the general principles or 'common core' of the new doctrine of social defence preserve the system of the rule of law and expressly uphold the rule *nulla poena sine lege*, which itself excludes the possibility of criminal proceedings against someone who has not committed an offence punishable under the then existing law.

If, however, we observe sociological realities, we soon notice that all systems have long since made provision for preventive measures designed to anticipate possible criminal acts. This is the case at least as regards the insane, for in all countries such persons may be confined even before they have committed any offence. But the point may be taken further: a striking characteristic of the existing systems of law is the existence of exceptional situations where criminal justice is entitled to intervene before an offence has actually been committed. So in some member States of the British Commonwealth, the judge may, as a preventive measure, require a person to find sureties for good behaviour or to be bound over to keep the peace.[109] Moreover, for reasons of penal policy, the old institution of the bail-bond or surety has acquired a new importance in modern criminal law, especially in Switzerland.[110] Again, it may be noted that certain forms of dangerousness have long been regarded by the legislator as justifying a protective intervention. This was so in the 'ancien droit', before 1789, as regards vagrants and persons of disreputable life. In the classical law the solution was felt to lie in the creation of specific offences covering these particular kinds of dangerousness, and this course was followed more particularly in nineteenth-century legislation on vagrancy and mendicity. Such legislation has, however, clearly failed, not only because in this field preventive measures should evidently be substituted for punishment, but also because vagrancy is not something which the criminal law can deal with in the same way as with any other offence, but is a situation or condition peculiar to the individual in question.[111] So it was that, from the Belgian statute of 1891 (which gave the Government tutelary powers in respect of certain vagrants) to the Spanish *ley de vagos y maleantes* of 1933, there was a marked legislative trend in this field away from the punishment of specific offences and towards the prevention of a certain form of dangerousness.[112]

In Italy, a statute of 27 December 1956, of great importance from the standpoint of penal policy, introduced a comprehensive system of supervision and measures of prevention for the idle,

[109] On the power of the English judge to insist on sureties or binding over, see J. W. C. Turner, *Kenny's Outlines of Criminal Law*, 18th ed., 1962, No. 768, p. 608.

[110] See F. Clerc, 'Le Cautionnement préventif en droit pénal suisse', *Rev. de droit pén. et de criminologie*, 1957/58, pp. 782 ff.; P. Graven, 'Une mesure méconnue; le cautionnement préventif', *Rev. de Science crim.*, 1962, pp. 9 ff.; and, by the same author, *Le Cautionnement préventif. Die Friedensbürgschaft*, Bâle, 1963.

[111] In the present systems of law, vagrancy, mendicity, and prostitution are 'crimes of personal condition'; on the character *sui generis* of these offences, the blatant inadequacy of existing legislation and the growing conviction that in this field punitive measures are useless, see Forrest W. Lacey, 'Vagrancy and Other Crimes of Personal Condition', *Harvard Law Review*, vol. 66, May 1953, pp. 1203ff. See also the *Journées franco-belgo-luxembourgeoises de droit pénal*, session held at Luxemburg in May 1960, where the problem of vagrancy was studied. See the General Report by Yvonne Marx to the Third French Criminological Congress on the subject, 'Les Aspects juridiques des problèmes posés par l'état dangereux prédélictuel', in *Annales int. de criminologie*, 1962, pp. 416 ff.

[112] See the 'Chroniques de Défense sociale' in the *Rev. de Science crim.*, by J. B. Herzog, 1953, No. 2, p. 354, and No. 4, p. 711.

vagrants, or persons whose behaviour raises a presumption that they have delinquent tendencies.[113] In the United Kingdom, the Mental Health Act (1959) provides for the compulsory hospitalization of certain persons who are considered dangerous even though they are not guilty of any offence.[114]

The question is whether, in a genuine policy of social defence, such enactments should remain exceptional or should, on the contrary, be multiplied. Jiménez de Asúa, who long advocated legislative action as the means of dealing with dangerousness, has since recognized the danger for individual freedom inherent in such a legislative policy.[115] The problem is that of reconciling the rule of law or rather the legal framework with the notion of preventive measures.[116] Another and still larger group of authorities shares the view expressed by Vienne when he wrote: 'If the test of dangerousness as proposed by the criminal sciences and diagnosed in practice by institutions for applied criminology were absolutely reliable, the lawyer, who would thus know that the individual concerned would inevitably commit a crime, could and ought to take the appropriate steps to prevent the crime. But neither criminal science nor criminological practice has yet reached this stage of perfection.'[117]

So it is that both on scientific and on social grounds generalization of such 'pre-delictual' measures of prevention would seem undesirable.

Here again, however, it may be claimed that social defence doctrines lead to a greater awareness of realities. It is submitted that vagrancy, mendicity, and prostitution should receive separate

[113] See on this statute the study by Nuvolone in *Revue de droit pénal et de crim.*, 1959, pp. 855 ff.

[114] *Mental Health Act*, Section 26; cf. Glanville Williams, *Criminal Law, The general Part*, London, 1961, pp. 428 ff.

[115] L'État dangereux dans les législations ibéro-américaines', *Rev. pén. suisse*, 1952, pp. 424 ff.

[116] See the *Convegno di diritto penale*, held at Bressanone in 1961, under the title *Stato di diritto e misure di sicurezza*, Padua, 1962, and in particular the reports by P. Bouzat, p. 77, G. Zuccalà, p. 131, and P. Nuvolone, p. 161 and esp. p. 169.

[117] R. Vienne, 'L'État dangereux', in *Rev. int. de droit pénal*, 1951, p. 495. Cf. *Le Problème de l'état dangereux* (Second International Criminological Course held at Paris in 1954, especially the third part), pp. 467 ff. See also the report by Guy Houchon to the third French Criminological Congress, 'Définition et éléments constitutifs de l'état dangereux pré-délictuel', in *Annales int. de criminologie*, 1962, pp. 369 ff. Cf. in *Stato di diritto e misure de sicurezza*, cited above, the report by P. J. Da Costa, p. 153.

legislative treatment: in addition to general measures of a social character—which Ferri used to call 'substitutes for punishment'—a system of preventive measures should be introduced to deal with these forms of dangerousness and potential delinquency. A similar approach should be adopted with regard to alcoholics and drug addicts: in this connexion, two French statutes of 24 December 1953 and 15 April 1954, concerned respectively with alcoholics and drug addicts, may be considered as good examples of 'social defence statutes'.[118] It may be noted that it was in this 1954 statute that the idea of dangerousness first received explicit legislative recognition in France.[119]

A proper balance between the principle of the rule of law, which applies to preventive measures as well as to punishment, and the establishment of a system of social prevention in what may be called the 'pre-criminal' stage, can be maintained fairly easily, provided that the following conditions are observed: first, a special kind of dangerousness needs to be clearly distinguished and carefully defined. Secondly, the boundaries of this socially dangerous condition must be delimited by means of a legal formula which should be worked out with the greatest possible precision. Thirdly, there ought to be statutory recognition of the State's right to intervene for purposes of prevention, such right to be exercised only within narrow limits strictly defined by statute. Fourthly, the specific conditions in which the State may exercise its right to intervene should form part of a system of judicial and procedural safeguards which ought, in principle, to be those laid down by the general law. With these reservations and within these limits, legislation inspired by modern penal policy may include a system of pre-criminal measures of prevention in certain particular cases. In connexion with the so-called offence or rather the condition of idleness, a disturbing social problem, J. A. Roux and Graven have shown how a solution of social defence might

[118] See the *Journées de Défense sociale* held at Montpellier in 1955, reported in *Rev. de Science crim.*, 1955, pp. 578 and 724; 1956, p. 162. See also in the publication by the Comparative Law Institute, Paris, under the title *La Prévention des infractions contre la vie humaine et l'intégrité de la personne*, 1956, the articles by A. Légal, vol. I, p. 129; Lebret, vol. I, p. 153; Dublineau, vol. II, p. 333; G. Heuyer, vol. II, p. 371. Cf. Germain, *Éléments de science pénitentiaire*, 1959, p. 175.

[119] See the article by Marc Ancel, 'Deux aspects nouveaux de la législation pénale française', in *Rev. de Criminologie et de police technique*, 1954, p. 243; cf. Larguier, 'Alcoolisme et mesures de sûreté', *Juriscl. périodique*, 1954, I. 1181.

be applied, which would safeguard the rights of the State as well as those of the individual.[120]

The importance of a realistic approach has already been stressed more than once in the previous chapters, and we have pointed out how the new social defence movement has maintained a realistic attitude towards the facts of life in society. This fundamental aspect of the social defence movement will not be further emphasized, save to underline the fact that the primary aim of this realism is to carry out in an effective manner the social readaption of the offender.

The essential purpose is thus to restore the author of the criminal act to a free and conscious social life. In this sense we may say that the penal policy of social defence is conceived in a non-repressive spirit, since punishment is not employed for its own sake or for the sole purpose of making the offender suffer, and is not seen in terms of an abstract and theoretical satisfaction, supposedly designed to cancel the criminal act. Moreover, in so far as such a penal policy is, or is concerned to be, realistic, it will take account of the relevant social environment. Those who support the doctrines of social defence are not unaware that the positivist theory never succeeded in becoming part and parcel of enacted legislation, nor that a large section of public opinion, confronted with the news of a particular crime, still clamours for truly repressive action on the part of the State. Although the success of the penal policy of social defence depends on educating public opinion as a whole, it should be remembered that such a process is difficult, that it is inevitably gradual, and that there is little advantage in relying on sudden and spectacular changes which all too frequently provoke negative reactions of equal force. So it is that criminal law, like civil law, should give

[120] In the *Rev. de crim. et de police technique*, 1951, pp. 83 ff., J. A. Roux had advocated the establishment of a 'crime of idleness' (*délit de fainéantise*) primarily characterized by the fact of not engaging in any regular work, coupled with the absence of means of subsistence; Graven ('Le Délit de fainéantise, une solution de Défense sociale', same *Revue*, 1951, pp. 163 ff.), notes the progress accomplished by penal policy and legislative technique in so far as it is the principle of anti-social idleness itself and no longer its effects or consequences that are taken to task. After having insisted on the substantial legal and procedural safeguards required, Graven adds that one is here confronted with a *délit de mise en danger*, a creation of a form of dangerousness, for which a criminal code concerned with the requirements of social life ought to provide 'side by side with crimes involving harm in the strict sense of the word' (p. 174).

expression to social behaviour and not endeavour to reform this single-handed.[121]

C

The point of view having been clearly stated, two final observations may be made regarding the realistic approach favoured by the new penal policy with which we are concerned.

In the first place, the new doctrines of social defence pay particular attention to the history of penal institutions and to comparative criminal law. Penal reformers have too frequently neglected the lessons to be drawn from history and from foreign legislation. Furthermore, those who look back to the history of institutions or draw analogies with the existing institutions of other countries are too often concerned simply to discover historical or comparative examples which favour their particular thesis, rather as was done by Montesquieu. Since the positivist period, however, scientific methods have also encroached upon the sphere of criminal science. It is high time that the considerable contribution of comparative law to the development of a realistic and effective penal policy should be acknowledged, as it has too often been disregarded.[122] It is time also to understand that, if a doctrine of penal policy is to possess the qualities of certainty and effectiveness, those responsible for its definition should be well informed concerning the earlier forms of that penal policy, whether in the past history of the same legislative system or in contemporary foreign systems. Furthermore, it is time to realize that penal policy, although normally standing above the enacted rules of criminal law, which it should guide and inspire, is never-

[121] In this respect the example of Latin-American legislative systems, directly influenced by positivism, is characteristic: thus the Mexican Criminal Code of 1929, based on the principle of responsibility before the law and on the comprehensive notion of dangerousness, was replaced by the 'pure law' code of 1931 which had decided to 'base itself on the modern social defence school by adapting the necessary changes to the principles of the constitution'. (La Vega, *Réforme des lois pénales au Mexique*, 1931, p. 22). Cf. also, for other Latin-American States, particularly Colombia, where the positivist draft of 1925 was replaced by the 'pure law' code of 1936, Jiménez de Asúa, *Codigos penales ibero-americanos, estudio de legislación comparada*, Caracas, 1946, vol. I, pp. 137 ff.; cf. *Jornadas de derecho penal*, Buenos Aires, 1962, S. I, 'Orientaciones sobre la reforma de los codigos penales', in particular pp. 46 ff.

[122] See Marc Ancel, 'Politique criminelle et droit comparé', in *Les Principaux Aspects de la politique criminelle moderne*, Paris, 1960 (Collected Essays in memory of Henri Donnedieu de Vabres), pp. 61 ff.

theless dependent on comparative law, envisaged principally as a social science concerned to observe legislative facts; for it is through the comparative approach that the reaction against the phenomenon of crime in the various legislative systems can be understood and assessed, thus constituting a legal sociology which may prove extremely fruitful.[123] Close study of this sociology of law, and the analysis of foreign systems of criminal law, makes it possible to evaluate the main legislative currents in the modern world and to disclose their origin, their characteristic features, their ebb and flow, and their general tendencies. Such a comparative study leads to awareness of the dynamic force of certain reforms and also throws light on their success or failure in one country or another. Too frequently, disregard of the strength and direction of certain currents in legislation has gravely handicapped some lawyers whose training and practical experience had been exclusively bounded by their national law. Like any other policy, penal policy involves the art of anticipating and guiding; it cannot afford to ignore the conscious use of the comparative method which serves as an instrument of prediction.[124]

It is from this standpoint and in the light of the evolution of penal institutions that the adherents of social defence, and criminologists of the widest theoretical and practical experience such, for instance, as Pinatel, have taken the view that the existing rules of law regarding delinquent juveniles foreshadow what will tomorrow be a feature of criminal law as a whole. This assertion is made more and more generally, which causes some anxiety to those who, for doctrinal reasons, wish to leave intact many of the repressive and retributive features of criminal law. Such persons claim that it would be a mistake to try to apply to adult offenders a system which is almost wholly based—for juvenile offenders—on consideration of the offender's personality, for the result would be to dissociate the criminal sanction from the criminal act, which would be contrary to legal principles.

In fact, however, those who seek to introduce into criminal law as a whole the principles which are today applied to juvenile delinquents are not trying to dissociate the sanction from the act:

[123] See Marc Ancel, 'Réflexions sur l'utilisation de la recherche comparative en droit pénal', article published in the symposium in honour of Dean Julliot de la Morandière, *Etudes juridiques*, Paris, 1964, pp. 9ff.

[124] H. C. Gutteridge showed acute awareness of this point in his all too brief treatment of comparative criminal law: see *Comparative Law*, 2nd ed., 1949.

quite the reverse, for their aim, from the social point of view, is in a practical way to bring the act and its sanction closer together, so as to make the author of the offence realize that his act will necessarily result in the imposition of a sanction. Neither, however, will be regarded as a legal entity, and it will no longer be stated as a general rule that the sanction should take the form of punishment in the classical sense of the word. The true inspiration of the movement in favour of extending to adult offenders the law at present applied to juveniles lies in that new attitude towards the offender, which, as we have repeatedly emphasized, is in many respects the essential feature of the penal policy of social defence.[125]

The law currently applied to juveniles has got rid of the notion—indeed the fiction—of discernment, and is conceived mainly as a process of re-education for life in society.[126] We have pointed out that intimidation remains an important ingredient in this process, which may even in certain cases involve an element of retribution. The process frequently combines the features of punishment and social welfare, as is indicated by the term 'prison-schools', and as is revealed by study of the English Borstal system. It is highly significant that the system of prison-schools in France or the Scandinavian countries, and the Borstal system in England, now deal with offenders who in most cases, at any rate, are no longer juveniles in the technical sense. The important contemporary legislative trend towards the application of a special system to 'young adults' has a value which should not be confined within the limits of the legal notion of 'minority' (in England, 'children or young persons'). The essential feature of the system applied to young adults, as of the rules applied to juvenile offenders proper, is to provide for the young offender not only a professional training, but also a moral training which will restore his sense of responsibility: such a training may take the form either of non-institutional treatment, as in the case of probation and educational supervision, or in a specially designed institution. The term used in the United Kingdom and the United States

[125] Cf. Sol Rubin, *Crime and Juvenile Delinquency—A Rational Approach to Penal Problems*, 2nd ed., New York, 1962.

[126] See J. Chazal, *Le Juge des enfants, pratique judiciaire et action sociale*, Paris, 1948; *Études de criminologie juvénile*, Paris, 1952; cf. H. and F. Joubrel, *L'Enfance dite 'coupable'*, 2nd ed., 1950; M. Dubois, *Ces enfants qui ont failli*, Brussels, 1952; M. and H. Veillard-Cybulsky, *Les Jeunes Délinquants dans le monde: ce qu'ils sont, ce qu'on fait pour eux*, Neuchâtel, 1963; J. Chazal, *Déconcertante jeunesse*, Paris, 1962.

is 'institutional treatment', and international gatherings have shown the wide contemporary influence of this idea.

Moreover, the social defence movement is naturally concerned to take up a realistic attitude, and when it maintains that the treatment today applied to juveniles should serve as a guide to the treatment which it would be desirable to apply to adult offenders, it is not intended to produce a complete identification of the two systems. Such a result would be contrary to the scientific attitude favoured by the social defence movement, and also to that classification (*sériation*) of offenders, illustrated in the first place by the distinction made between adult and juvenile delinquents. Social defence doctrine in no way wishes to treat the adult as an *infans*, not responsible for his actions, for this would be ridiculous and would abolish the very notion of majority in the criminal sense.[127]

Still for the sake of clarity and realism, these doctrines maintain that penal policy should dispense with the legal and metaphysical fictions which paralyze the development of criminal law in the name of notions that can only be justified on purely legal grounds. Furthermore, a realistic approach makes apparent the inherent absurdity of requiring all the rules to be changed as soon as the offender attains his majority in the eyes of the criminal law, whether this be fixed at sixteen or eighteen years of age. The policy of social defence here seeks to establish distinctions based not so much on clearly segregated legal categories as on age groups considered from a criminological standpoint: these new categories would be flexible enough to ensure that the information revealed by the offender's birth certificate would not necessarily prevail in all cases over the physiological and psychological data available.[128]

Such a policy, as applied to adult offenders, is in fact inspired by contemporary attitudes in the field of juvenile crime, where the law takes the form of a social action designed to protect both society and the individual offender. There remains a place for punishment in this modern doctrine, and it is clear that the use of

[127] Here again reference may be made to the reports, discussions and resolutions of the International Social Defence Congresses at Stockholm, 1958, and Belgrade, 1961. Cf. also the remarks by J. Graven on 'L'Activité du groupe médico-psycho-juridique de Genève' (Colloquium on criminal responsibility), in *Rev. de Science crim.*, 1961, pp. 325 ff., esp. pp. 329-30.

[128] *Seuils d'âge et législation pénale* (published by the *Centre d'Études de Défense sociale*, Comparative Law Institute of the University of Paris), 1961.

punishment will be much more frequent and much more usual as regards adults than as regards juveniles. But punishment is integrated into a new system of sanctions, where it co-exists naturally with measures of an educative, curative, or disciplinary nature. To urge that the rules applied to juveniles and to adults should be brought closer together, or even to advocate in the long run a certain degree of unification between them, is simply to anticipate an inevitable evolution towards a general system, unitary and coherent, of social defence.

IV

At this stage of the discussion it appears necessary to return for a moment to the question of responsibility as this is envisaged by the doctrine of social defence. In view of the pages already devoted to this question in the present and the previous chapters, we may now deal quite briefly with the problem, which ought logically to be discussed at very considerable length.

As a movement of penal policy which claims to be both realistic and humanist, the new doctrine emphatically proclaims the irreducible nature of criminal responsibility from the human, social, and moral points of view.[129] Similarly, the movement is led to consider both the classical and positivist approaches to this problem as equally out of date. As Gabriel Tarde wrote over sixty years ago, the problem cannot be solved either in terms of free will or by an intransigent determinism.[130] There are, of course, several concepts of responsibility, some of which are of merely historical interest and have been superseded,[131] while others still produce controversy between different intellectual disciplines.[132]

[129] See Marc Ancel, 'Responsabilité et défense sociale', in *Rev. de Science crim.*, 1959, p. 179, and the same author's contribution to the Geneva Colloquium, 1960–61. Cf. *La Responsabilité pénale*, (Papers of the Strasbourg Colloquium), Paris, 1961.

[130] Preface to *L'Individualisation de la peine* by R. Saleilles, 1898, pp. ix ff.

[131] See Graven, 'L'Activité du groupe médico-psycho-juridique de Genève', (Colloquium on criminal responsibility), in *Rev. de Science crim.*, 1961, pp. 325 ff.; P. Cornil, 'L'Impasse de la responsabilité pénale', in *Rev. de droit pén. et de crim.*, 1961-1962, pp. 637 ff.

[132] *Une Nouvelle École de science criminelle, l'école d'Utrecht*, edited and introduced by J. Léauté, Paris, 1959, part 3: 'La Nouvelle Théorie de la responsabilité pénale', which deals especially with the points of view of the criminal scientist, the criminologist, and the psychiatrist, pp. 97 ff.

The concept of intention as expounded by the Continental classicists, or the Anglo-American notion of *mens rea*, remain as obscure as in the days of Cicero.[133] Classical law, which was mistrustful of any analysis of culpability, tried to distinguish intention from motive and to establish a close relation between the offender's fault and his crime. But as Pinatel has pointed out, the edifice is a flimsy one and is not in keeping with criminal theories as a whole.[134] Both the eclectic school of the beginning of this century and the agnostics, so-called, who are still with us, try to get rid of the very idea of responsibility.[135] However, the supporters of determinism are no longer content simply to deny the existence of free will, whereas Christian criminologists no longer take refuge in an equally erroneous denial of the value of the social sciences. The result is a curious meeting of opposites, half-way, so to speak, between the former absolutist theories. Thus criminal scientists of materialistic outlook from the Eastern European countries are today seeking to build up an almost neo-classical system of responsibility, whereas Catholic psychologists are careful to take into account the various methods that may explain the dynamic of crime,[136] and these same Christian psychologists may indeed be brought to criticize traditionalists who persist in defending 'traditions that have become untenable from the scientific point of view'.[137]

These criminologists urge us, in the first place, to go behind the abstractions of pure classical doctrine in order to grasp the concrete realities. It is even necessary to step outside the biological and psychological criteria, which still form the basis of the most carefully-worked-out criminal statute law such as that of Switzerland.[138] We are similarly urged to reject the notion of diminished responsibility as this was envisaged by the neo-classicists of the late nineteenth and early twentieth centuries, namely as a mathematical apportionment of guilt on the basis

[133] *Nihil obscurius voluntate humanum* (*Pro Murena*, 17, 36).

[134] *Traité de droit pénal et de criminologie*, vol. III, *Criminologie*, 1963, No. 178.

[135] See P. Cornil, *L'Impasse de la responsabilité pénale*, cited above.

[136] See Marc Ancel, paper read at the Geneva Colloquium, cited *supra*, p. 331.

[137] The expression is Pinatel's, and was applied to de Greeff's effort to 'incorporate scientific progress into the body of Catholic doctrine' (La Théorie des instincts d'Étienne de Greeff', in *Rev. de Science crim.*, 1961, p. 827). Cf. 'La concezione dinamica della personalità nello studio dei delinquenti', by Father Gemelli, *Riv. di diritto penale*, 1955, pp. 8 ff. in particular p. 29.

[138] Graven, *op. cit.*, concerning the Geneva Colloquium, p. 328.

of evidence provided by experts.[139] Of course, as was stressed by Sebastian Soler, diminished responsibility is indeed, in certain respects, 'a psychological reality which cannot be ignored by the criminal law'[140] and modern statutes have often made good use of the notion for reasons of penal policy.[141] But the point is that this psychic reality should be thoroughly understood and not simply presumed to exist without further enquiry into its content.

What should be thoroughly grasped is the reality of an intimately felt and natural sense of personal responsibility. Modern psychiatrists, psychologists, and criminologists stress this individual sense of responsibility which normally exists in every human being and which, as de Greeff used to say, gives a man 'the certainty of inner freedom' and so constitutes 'his own experience of free will'.[142] Even psychoanalysts pay some attention to culpability and to the reality of the feeling of responsibility.[143] This feeling, in its psychological reality, relates man to his activity and to his prospects of growth as a person. The experience of freedom means that our acts 'emanate from and express our whole personality'.[144] Thus it is that in the new doctrine of social defence the

[139] See Dr Grasset, 'Demi-fous et demi-responsables', in *Revue des Deux Mondes*, 1906, p. 887; and the same author's *La Responsabilité des criminels*, 1908. Cf. the discussions within the *Société des Prisons*, *Revue pénitentiaire*, 1922, pp. 699 and 745; see also Garçon, *Code pénal annoté*, art. 64, No. 31.

[140] *Proyecto de código penal*, Esposición de motivos, and note under article 25, Buenos Aires, 1960.

[141] Strahl, 'Les Délinquants anormaux mentaux en Suède', in *Rev. de Science crim.*, 1955, pp. 19 ff. Moreover, in the United Kingdom, the acceptance of certain cases of diminished responsibility was one of the main innovations of the Homicide Act (1957).

[142] *Notre destinée et nos instincts*, Paris, 1945, p. 58. Cf. *Les Instincts de défense et de sympathie*, Paris, 1947, p. 37, where de Greeff declares that this sense of responsibility is equally and vigorously present in the normal individual, the imbecile, and the insane person. See also de Greeff, 'Sur le sentiment de responsabilité', *Rev. int. de déf. soc.*, 1956, pp. 1 ff. Cf. Pinatel, *Criminologie*, No. 178.

[143] See E. Glover, *The Roots of Crime*, 1960, pp. 302 ff.; Melitta Schmideberg, 'A Major Task for Therapy: Developing Volition and Purpose', in *Amer. Journ. of Psychotherapy*; cf. H. H. Jescheck, *Das Menschenbild unserer Zeit und die Strafrechtsreform*, 1957, pp. 17 ff.

[144] Bergson has written: 'We are free when our acts emanate from our whole personality and are its expression, in other words when there exists between personality and action that likeness which defies description but is sometimes to be found between an artist and his work. It is pointless to suggest that this involves a surrender to the all-powerful influence of the character; for the character and the person are inseparable: if, by a process of intellectual abstraction, we have distinguished the reflective self from the active self so as to consider them each in turn, it would be somewhat childish to draw the conclusion that one aspect of the person is decisively

notion of responsibility appears as the individual's awareness of his own personality, in so far as this finds expression in his acts. Individual man does not, however, feel that he alone is responsible: because he has the feeling of responsibility, he considers others to be responsible also. This collective sense of responsibility, this right to ask everyone to account for his actions, as well as the individual's own obligation to account for his acts—an obligation which is accepted or undergone but is in any case felt—are directly related to that psychological and social reality which we call the feeling of responsibility. The penal policy of social defence must itself take this into consideration as a factor in the rational organization of the reaction against crime. If an individual's personality finds expression in the sense of responsibility, this is also the test of his capacity from the criminal standpoint.[145] This suggests several specific consequences in the sphere of criminal justice.

(a) Intention can no more be separated from motive[146] than man from his actions. Consideration of the dynamic of crime leads in many ways to a renewed emphasis on the importance of the act committed, an importance which had been overlooked by the positivist and neo-positivist theories which sought to detach the criminal from his crime in order to consider him in isolation.

---

influenced by the other . . . In short, if we agree to describe as free everything that emanates from the self and the self alone, my personal act is truly free, for it springs from myself alone. The argument would thus be vindicated if it were agreed that this quality of freedom should be sought only in the particular nature of the decision taken, in other words, in a free action.' (*Essai sur les données immédiates de la conscience*, 78th ed., 1948), p. 129.

[145] We are not unaware that a distinction has often been made, not only between *dolus* and *culpa*, but between culpability, imputability, criminal capacity, and dangerousness. See in particular S. Ranieri, *Manuale di diritto penale*, vol. I, 1956, pp. 251 ff., pp. 468 ff.; cf. Jiménez de Asúa, *Tratado de derecho penal*, vol. V, pp. 20 ff.

[146] See J. Dabin, *Théorie générale du droit*, 2nd ed., Brussels, 1953, 'Since external acts emanate from man, an intelligent and free being, they cannot be considered—even by the lawyer—solely in their material aspect and apart from any question of intention. Society being made up of individual persons, it is only in the light of its intention (*mobile*) that an act takes on true moral and even social significance. Society cannot therefore remain indifferent to the question whether the intentions behind the act were innocent or evil, social or anti-social; this explains the need to treat acts according to their intentions and so to diversify and vary the legal provisions which apply.'

(b) There is no room for doubt that, for the social defence movement, the act committed is the legal offence with which the accused is charged, and this demonstrates once again how inaccurate are the allegations according to which this movement would reject the legal definition of the crime. The only difference between this approach and the traditional view is that the offence is not envisaged in itself, but as the projection into the social sphere of the offender's personality. The crime is thus not only the *occasion* for the offender's appearance before the criminal court but the *reason* for that appearance: here is the practical social expression of the obligation to account for one's acts, an obligation which is itself the tangible expression in the social context of the idea of individual responsibility.[147]

(c) In this perspective it is clear that there is no longer any irreducible conflict between responsibility and dangerousness; for they are both expressions—social expressions—of personality. The context of social and human reality, the distinction made by the neo-classicists between culpability and dangerousness, is as artificial as the parallel distinction between punishment and safety measures. Responsibility and dangerousness must both be taken into account by the criminal judge, who may employ one type of sanction or the other in deciding how to deal in practice with the cases before him.[148]

(d) Social defence cannot dispense with deterrence any more that it can dispense with responsibility, for the latter is to some extent the reflexion of the former. Modern criminologists have drawn attention to the over-simple character of the theory derived from the neo-positivist tradition,[149] and frequently expounded at the beginning of this century, according to which deterrence has

[147] Jerome Hall writes that '... to be responsible means to be accountable for voluntary conduct', 'Psychiatry and Criminal Responsibility', *Yale Law Journal*, 1956, pp. 761 ff., at p. 765. It may be mentioned that the reservations made in this respect by Roger Merle ('L'Évolution du droit pénal moderne', *Annales de la Faculté de droit de Toulouse*, vol. VI, fasc. 1, 1958, pp. 133 ff.) are aimed at those whom he describes as the extremists of social defence (p. 141), but not at the new social defence movement (which indeed is quite in agreement with him: see in particular p. 143).

[148] See the comments by Pinatel on the occasion of the 'round table discussions' organized by the Comparative Law Institute in Paris on the theme 'Les Rapports entre la peine et la mesure de sûreté', in *Rev. de Science crim.*, 1963, p. 532; cf. Bouzat and Pinatel, *Traité*, vol. III, (*Criminologie*, by J. Pinatel, No. 313 ff.).

[149] G. F. Kirchwey, 'Crime and Punishment', in *Journ. of Crim. Law*, vol. I, 1910-1911, pp. 71 ff.

no effect on any category of offenders: the fact is that the modern sciences of behaviour have made the classical theory of deterrence out of date.[150] What evidently remains, at any rate, is the fear of having to account for one's actions, fear of criminal proceedings and fear of the judge, who will take cognizance of the positive manifestations of anti-social behaviour. The realistic and humane doctrine of social defence would be the last to disregard this essential element in social psychology.

(e) Thus considered from a twofold standpoint, individual and social, the concept of responsibility undoubtedly lays an additional burden on the court. On the basis of the concrete elements pointing to the offender's responsibility in the actual case, and having regard to the degree of dangerousness of the individual in question, the judge will have to produce a veritable criminal prognosis.[151] Gemelli has said that in the modern view the criminal judge 'is no longer imprisoned in the ivory tower of the offence envisaged simply as the infringement of a predetermined legal rule' and that he handles the case 'on the firm foundation of psychological realities provided as the result of a clinical examination'.[152] It should be noted in passing that his new task presupposes a revision of the traditional rôle of the expert witness and a genuine collaboration between the medical profession and criminal judges.[153] The trial, conviction, and sentence are all orientated towards the determination of the treatment most appropriate in the circumstances. But this notion of treatment is inseparably bound up with the examination of the offender's personality and with the notion of individual responsibility. After being the first factor that was taken into account in evaluating the personal and social behaviour of the offender, responsibility thus becomes the essential motive force in the process of social readaptation. The

[150] See Paul W. Tappan, *Crime, Justice and Correction*, New York, 1960, pp. 241 ff.; cf. J. C. Ball, 'The Deterrence Concept in Criminology and Law', *Journ. of Crim. Law, Crimin. and Pol. Science*, 1954-1955, p. 347.

[151] H. Schultz, 'Strafrechtliche Bewertung und kriminologische Prognose', in *Stellung und Aufgabe des Richters im modernen Strafrecht, Mélanges Oscar Adolf Germann*, Berne, 1959, pp. 245 ff.

[152] 'La concezione dinamica della personalità nello studio dei delinquenti', cited *supra*, p. 30.

[153] See Graven on the Geneva Colloquium on criminal responsibility, *Colloque sur la responsabilité pénale*, cited above, p. 330. See also the *Onzièmes Journées françaises de défense sociale* held at Rennes in June 1963, *Rev. de Science crim.*, 1963, pp. 751 ff., 774 ff., 779ff., 855 ff.

primary aim of the treatment is to 'make the offender aware of social imperatives and to give him a new attitude towards the sanction'.[154] The sense of responsibility can thus be usefully employed as a means of reintegrating the offender in the social group.[155] In this connexion, Pinatel observes that 'the experience of culpability' should be 'remodelled in terms of the age and *temps intérieur* of the offender'.[156]

These consequences of the doctrine of new social defence on responsibility suggest the following conclusions: the new social defence movement does not wish to eliminate the notion of responsibility, but, on the contrary, by thinking out this concept anew, to 'revalue' it, so to speak. The notion of diminished responsibility might itself acquire a new importance and a new rôle by being applied to the qualitative problem of social readaptation instead of being used quantitatively to determine the degree of retribution. The social defence movement proposes to replace the classical formula (criminal offence = punishment) by a new formula consisting of three terms (criminal offence—personality—treatment). The classical notion of responsibility, which was an unspoken part of the old equation, now becomes an active element in the new trinomial formula. In the classical system, responsibility was no more than a postulate transformed into a presumption of law and was relied on only once, at the time of sentence,

[154] J. Graven, *op. cit.*, p. 329, remarks that more than any other type of criminal, the offender whose responsibility is limited should be treated as responsible. Similarly, Cornil remarks that it is observed in penitentiary practice that certain criminals become consciously aware of their crime, and of certain social prohibitions, only after several years of treatment. (*L'Impasse de la responsabilitié pénale*, p. 637, cited above); Cornil however, draws a conclusion which to our way of thinking is rather exaggerated, concerning the exclusion of criminal responsibility in such cases; in our view this observation is an excellent argument in favour of a treatment of social readaptation based on the individual's awareness of his responsibility.

[155] See Zilborg, *The Psychology of the Criminal Act and Punishment*, London, 1955, particularly pp. 112 ff., 128; Melitta Schmideberg, 'The Offender's Attitude towards Punishment', *Journ. of Crim. Law, Crimin. and Pol. Science*, Sept.-Oct. 1960, pp. 328 ff., esp. p. 334.

[156] P. Bouzat and J. Pinatel, *Traité*, t. III (*Criminologie*, by J. Pinatel), p. 468, with the very interesting quotation from Debuyst, *Criminels et valeurs vécues*, p. 328; the expression *temps intérieur* might be translated, very roughly, as the individual's subjective sense of the passing of time. On the use of the sense of responsibility for the social readaptation of the convicted offender, see also Franchimont, 'Notules sur l'imputabilité', *Rev. de droit pénal et de crim.*, 1961-1962, pp. 342 ff., esp. p. 358, and J. Ley, *Les Fondements psychologiques et sociaux d'une réforme de la politique criminelle*, Paris, 1961, pp. 113 ff.

as a kind of working hypothesis. Where criminal law is inspired by considerations of social defence, the notion of responsibility is a concrete reality which is referred to at all times and thereby remains the rational basis of criminal justice, called upon to exercise a decisive influence on the anti-social act or behaviour of the citizen and so to determine the appropriate sanction, which can only be just in so far as it is individualized in terms not only of the particular offence and the offender's personality, but also of his responsibility considered *in concreto*. The internal or personal sense of responsibility, strengthened by the collective sense of responsibility, is indeed the essential foundation for criminal justice.

There is no point in maintaining—as does Cornil in a subtle and authoritative fashion—that this 'universal' concept of penal responsibility would lead to a dilemma and that the traditional idea of criminal responsibility[157] should be replaced by a social responsibility—a sort of renewal of Ferri's theories: society would defend its interests by means of the criminal law, disregarding the question of responsibility while reserving the possibility of applying such methods to persons other than the criminal, and to other factors, so as to avoid all 'harmful influences'.[158] This neo-positivism, whose limits are not clearly defined, may seem rather disquieting. In particular, it would seem that for the sake of immediate efficacy—which is praiseworthy as far as it goes—such a theory might eventually forget its point of departure, which was the individual human being.[159] The sense of responsibility is not an obstacle but a motor, or a driving force. It is not present to the same extent—nor even, in utilitarian terms, to a sufficient extent—in all criminals, even when they do have this feeling in a confused sort of way. The problem is therefore to develop the sense of responsibility in each offender, to make him aware of the social realities which impose limits on his behaviour and constitute the remedy for his 'anti-sociality'. The sense of responsibility can be inculcated by means of an education which seeks to transform the innate idea of freedom not only into the experience of freedom but also into a consciousness of freedom as of something fully

[157] *L'Impasse de la responsabilité pénale, op. cit.* [158] *Ibid*, p. 650.

[159] See P. Cornil, 'Une Politique criminelle réaliste', in *Les Principaux Aspects de la Politique criminelle moderne* (published by the Comparative Law Institute, Paris, 1960), pp. 29 ff.

accepted with its necessary limits.[160] What finer vocation can be imagined for a penal policy of social defence?[161]

V

The purpose of the social action undertaken by modern criminal justice, as illustrated in particular by the new rules applied to juvenile offenders, is primarily practical and utilitarian. So this approach contrasts with the absolute element in the traditional criminal law which was centred on the idea of retribution. Seen in terms of social defence, criminal justice is always relative and always subject to revision and amendment, since it is engaged in a work of human justice and social prevention. However, what has been said earlier, especially concerning responsibility, enables us to understand why the task of criminal law in the eyes of the social defence movement is above all a work of justice. The modern law applied to juveniles and young adults, and the methods of treatment designed to achieve the social readaptation of adult offenders, should not therefore be seen merely in curative or therapeutical terms. It is worth repeating that a system of criminal justice based on social defence, prevention, and the treatment of offenders, is intended to focus the attention of the offender himself on those notions of social morality which he disregarded and to restore his sense of duty towards the community, while ensuring that the State fulfils its own obligations towards the individual.[162] As opposed to the abstract legal order envisaged by the classical law, a legal order that punishment was intended to preserve or restore, the new social defence movement sets up the notion of a social order that exists and has its being only through the conscious and active participation of all in the collective task.

[160] See J. Serano, *La Culpabilité*, Paris, 1957, where the author distinguishes between the *feeling of responsibility*, which may be childish or pathological, and the *sense of responsibility*, which is capable of development and re-education. The conscious sense of guilt of an adult person, integrated into his total personality and into the community, will be shaped, so to speak, and related to a doctrine or even a faith: in this sense, says the author, culpability is a transcendence.

[161] It is pleasing to note that this conclusion is in many respects similar to that of Pompe, especially in his 'La Responsabilité en droit pénal', *Rev. int. de droit pénal*, 1952, p. 303, and in his paper on the criminal scientist's viewpoint in *Une Nouvelle École de Science criminelle, l'École d'Utrecht*, Paris, 1959, pp. 97 ff. Cf. also the ideas expounded by Dean Richard in his book *La Mission méconnue de la justice pénale*, Paris, 1957.

[162] See E. Mira y Lopez, *Manual de psicologia juridica*, Buenos Aires, 1954 (see, in French trans., *Manuel de psychologie juridique*, Paris, 1959, pp. 105 ff.).

Thus the doctrine of social defence in its positive aspects means the recognition of certain moral values, the affirmation of a social ideal, which the movement seeks to respect and indeed promote. The offender is no longer regarded as a sinner called upon to expiate his fault, as in the old theological or theocratic doctrine, which was very largely taken over by the classical theories of law, nor is he an irresponsible being whom nature or inevitable extraneous factors have condemned to a criminal way of life: he is a member of society, whom society should study and understand, in order to discern the reasons for his anti-social behaviour and then apply the appropriate treatment, since in many cases society itself is in part responsible for these manifestations of 'anti-sociality'. In the moral sphere, social defence is the antithesis of positivism, whereas in the social sphere the movement contrasts with the classical system which was interested in the crime considered as an objective entity and not in the criminal as an individual, who was left to fend for himself once he had paid the penalty for his offence.[163]

This approach clearly stresses the individual offender's right to a treatment of social readaptation,[164] but likewise focuses attention on the idea of a social order which would replace the abstract concept of a legal order dear to the theorists of classical law. The State, of course, is the guardian of this social order, responsible for its establishment and safe-keeping. But the individual also must contribute to that order and participate in it; he is doubtless entitled to require that everything should be done to restore his place in the social framework, but it is a place which he has to deserve. A kind of balance—social, political and moral—is thus introduced between the rights of the individual and those of the State. Above all, it is in this way that there emerges the fruitful concept of a social community in which the individual has his

[163] Roger Merle has written very truly that 'the perfectionist ambitions of classical law have remained a dead letter' and that the French statutory reforms concerning *relégation* and prohibition of residence (*interdiction de séjour*) 'which are very strongly influenced by ideas of social defence' are none the less compatible with the general principles of criminal liability (*op. cit.* in *Annales de la Faculté de droit de Toulouse*, 1958, p. 144).

[164] See the general report by Lamers to the Colloquium of the International Penal and Penitentiary Foundation, Brussels, September 1959, on *La Réadaptation du détenu à la vie libre*, *Travaux préparatoires*, Section II, pp. 492 ff.; cf. H. Klare, *Anatomy of Prison*, London, 1960.

place, a community which, indeed, exists by and for individual persons, but which also places natural emphasis on the idea of moral obligation where a personal fault and a personal effort of social readaptation will necessarily be taken into account.[165]

So it is clear that a policy of social defence does not simply amount to a kind of sentimental humanitarianism, as has sometimes been alleged, but aims at promoting a system of criminal law which should be both universal in expression and humanist in inspiration. The system is, or should be, universal precisely to the extent that the penal policy in question goes beyond the technical particularism of various legal systems. No doubt it is not a case of imposing a general unification of criminal law from without, and each national system retains its own value, significance, and methods: the study of comparative law not only teaches us to look beyond apparent differences so as to rediscover and single out certain 'constants' in legal thinking, or certain common factors in legislative practice, but also—when practised as a descriptive social science—teaches us to understand that each system carries within itself certain autonomous, independent elements which we must learn to identify. The universal character of social defence ideas has therefore nothing in common with the material unification of the actual provisions of criminal legislation,[166] but relates solely to the necessary awareness of the social needs that are common to different countries which have reached the same level of civilization. This universal character also involves the encouragement of mutual exchanges of views and experience between different countries and different systems, and the constitution of a common body of ideas and tendencies which might nourish and stimulate the development of a universal penal policy based on human requirements and human values. The social defence movement here rejoins the main stream of ideas represented in France by René David and more recently by André Tunc, when he urges lawyers to 'grow out of the neolithic age',[167]

[165] It has become a commonplace to maintain that probation and (broadly speaking) conditional discharge are of use only to the extent that the individual concerned actively co-operates in his reintegration in society.

[166] See Marc Ancel, 'La Tendance universaliste dans la doctrine comparative française au début du XXe siècle', *Festschrift für Ernst Rabel*, Tübingen, 1954, pp. 17 ff.

[167] A. Tunc, 'Sortir du néolithique (Recherche et enseignement dans les Facultés de droit)', *Dalloz*, 1957, Chron., p. 71.

or by Savatier, when he tries to make his fellow lawyers pay greater attention to changes in the law.[168]

An emphasis on the universal and permanent character of human values quite naturally brings to mind the humanist ideal, and we have already observed, in passing, the historical and spiritual links between social defence ideas and the humanist tradition.[169] It is no accident that there should be a new and systematic development of such ideas at the present time, when the concept of humanism is increasingly influential in most spheres.[170] Indeed, it is arguable that the term 'humanism' is perhaps too freely used today, just as in a more restricted sphere there is a tendency to overdo the use of the term 'social defence'. In both cases, however, this terminological emphasis reveals a state of mind that it would be improper to disregard and which, on the whole, is reassuring.

In so far as the doctrine of social defence reacts against certain fictions, or tries to shake off certain ways of thinking which conceal the realities of human existence, or consciously seeks emancipation from subservience to purely technical legal concepts—in these cases the movement does no more than give practical effect to traditional humanist aims.[171] More especially, however, the doctrine in its latest form clearly gives expression to those modern humanist ideas which contemporary thinking seeks to work out among the chaos of institutions and events. Faced with a world that seems manifestly absurd, modern man is moved to revolt, but he thereby acquires a new awareness of his work as a human being, the misery and the grandeur of the human condition providing the twofold foundation for a system of thought and of action which will give meaning to man's existence on this earth. Perhaps, as has been said by Teilhard de Chardin, man may thus become aware of the magnitude of his rôle, in the course of an evolution of which he himself is the ultimate expression. In that case the *socialization* of man will not take place at the expense of the

[168] R. Savatier, *Les Métamorphoses économiques et sociales du droit privé d'aujourd'hui*, Troisième série, Paris, 1959.

[169] 'Le droit comparé, science humaniste', in *Rev. de droit int. et de droit comparé*, Bruxelles, 1949, pp. 27 ff.; 'La Fonction judiciaire et le droit comparé', in *Rev. int. de droit comparé*, Paris, 1949, pp. 57 ff.

[170] See in particular Bichara Tabbah, *Droit politique et humanisme*, Paris, 1955.

[171] See the comments of Nuvolone in *Riv. di diritto penale*, 1956, p. 782.

individual.[172] We cannot here examine this body of ideas, which goes far beyond the sphere of law and even of penal policy, finding certain philosophical or literary forms of expression that have become prominent in our day. But it is worth noting the connexion between the new social defence movement and this trend of thought, from which the movement derives part at least of its present dynamism.[173]

It would be inaccurate, however, simply to equate social defence with the revolt of modern man, and all the more with a kind of existentialism, for we should not forget that among the moral values and traditions of thought from which the new social defence movement derives its inspiration, there are at least two main trends, which come together on this occasion, whereas for too long it was sought—quite arbitrarily—to separate them. The movement seeks to proclaim and to safeguard the rights of man as these were understood by the French Revolution, and is constantly concerned to preserve the liberty of the individual. Social defence gives a new form to the assertion of individual rights in the face of society, and firmly proclaims that the individual has a right to social readaptation, just as in earlier times it was declared that the individual had a right to liberty, security, and property, and the right to work. However, since the movement is fully aware of the realities and exigencies of the modern world, the individual is considered as an element in the social community in which he will exercise his activity as a free human being.

At the same time, the new social defence movement is very closely related to the Christian tradition. From the first, the movement has been able to quote the authority of some of the Fathers of the Church, and the earliest ideas of social defence served to introduce the Christian concept of charity into a repressive system dedicated to expiatory punishment. Nor is there any need to repeat what has already been said in these pages concerning the canonical conception of punishment as a healing process (*la peine médicale*). Moreover, in what is now the field of action of

[172] 'The social phenomenon is the culmination and not the attenuation of the biological phenomenon', writes Teilhard de Chardin in *Le Phénomène humain*, p. 247; cf. *L'Avenir de l'homme*, p. 57: 'It seems that the hour has struck for the socialization of humanity, but for the World this means not the end, but much rather the beginning, of the time when the person will come into his own.'

[173] See again R. Legros, 'Pour une défense sociale élargie', *Rev. de l'Université de Bruxelles*, June-July, 1960.

social defence, it was the Christian tradition which introduced and developed the idea of redemption for the fault committed, and the notion of a personal effort by the sinner (or criminal) to blot out that fault by trying to rehabilitate himself and reform his life. This idea of personal effort and of awareness, both of the material consequences and of the moral significance of the harm caused, is maintained by the new social defence movement, in contrast with the views of the positivists.

While the 'minimum programme' of the International Society for Social Defence was in course of preparation, an explicit reference to the Christian tradition was envisaged, but during the final discussion the idea was allowed to lapse, for fear that the insertion of such a statement in the text of the programme itself would give a confessional flavour to the doctrine of social defence.[174] This seems a regrettable omission, in our view, inasmuch as such excessive prudence will tend to conceal one of the undoubted sources of the movement. The point ought in fact to be stressed. The precise meaning, the moral significance and—we might add—the almost emotional aspect of the new social defence movement will not be understood unless we bear in mind these different factors which are naturally joined together in the movement. For the doctrine of social defence, both in the demands which it makes in the field of criminal policy and in the penal philosophy in which it necessarily and naturally finds expression, provides a bridge which serves to conciliate the doctrine of the rights of man, as this was understood by the revolutionaries of 1789, with the Christian tradition of charity and redemption. It is this tradition which inspires the notion of a renovated criminal law with the social readaptation of the offender as its ultimate target.[175]

[174] See Marc Ancel, 'Un Programme minimum de défense sociale', *Rev. de Science crim.*, 1955, p. 564.

[175] The social defence movement can appropriate as its own the words of Pope John XXIII on the occasion of an audience granted to Professor Di Tullio, honorary president of the International Society of Criminology; see on this point the note by Father Vernet, in *Rev. de Science crim.*, 1962, p. 157.

Chapter Seven

ANSWERS TO SOME CRITICISMS

IN THE FOREGOING CHAPTERS we have sought to describe the remote origins of social defence ideas, their emergence in the late nineteenth and early twentieth centuries, and the principal stages in the modern movement of social defence. We have then tried to place the new doctrine in perspective by explaining in turn what it *is not* and what it *is*. The main objections that are levied against these doctrines have thus been anticipated or answered along the way. More particularly, it has already been shown how very unfounded are the allegations that ideas of social defence lead to the abolition of criminal law, that they give the State a totalitarian control over the individual, that they constitute either a kind of latter-day positivism or a para-medical theory according to which all criminals would be treated as invalids or diseased persons. Moreover, we have pointed out that the new social defence movement, far from abandoning the moral values that underlie any genuine system of criminal law, is in fact concerned to reintroduce these moral values into the penal policy of social readaptation of the offender and social prevention, which it purports to establish.

There would probably be no point in going back to this question, were it not for the fact that the doctrines of social defence have recently been the object of a series of new attacks,[1] which deserve attention because of their unusual character and their curious origin. Certain critics appear to have lost all sense of proportion, and indeed all intellectual balance, where social defence is in issue, some going so far as to substitute journalistic polemic for rational discussion and to rely on vituperation instead of argument. Others systematically distort the theories of social defence, producing an outrageous caricature of these doctrines which they

[1] The French Minister of Justice has even thought it appropriate to take issue with these doctrines in the course of a lecture on *La Doctrine de la Ve République en matière de répression*, summarized in *Rev. pénitentiaire*, 1963, pp. 281 ff.

then have the easy satisfaction of demolishing, allegedly in the name of common sense. Such exaggerated hostility may indeed appear absurd, but also does more even than certain tributes to underline the importance and the widespread character of the social defence movement. The supporters of the *status quo* and the enemies of all progress towards a better criminal law have understood the extent to which their approach is imperilled by the existence of a doctrine which maintains a critical attitude towards the present and remains steadfastly turned towards the future. The present writer has no intention of adopting a polemical tone, and this chapter will be concerned first to examine, from a strictly scientific standpoint, the confusion of mind which lies at the root of most of these objections, and then to show briefly the extent to which they are unfounded.

I

Criticism of the social defence doctrine comes from two main sources which are mutually contradictory.

A first group of critics are the followers of the neo-classical tradition who wish to retain retributive punishment, to preserve the purely legal character of the criminal offence, and to restrict the judge's rôle to an automatic application of the law. This fundamental approach is sometimes coloured by metaphysical considerations or by an appeal to the Christian tradition.[2] In other cases, certain writers who were initially opposed to this kind of approach, believe that by taking up an attitude hostile to the social defence movement they are preserving the supremacy of what German and Italian theorists refer to as legal dogmatics.[3]

[2] See, on the questions of the death penalty and of the Italian concept of *ergastolo*, Bettiol: *Riv. italiana di diritto penale*, 1956, pp. 555 ff.; 'Orientamenti generali nel diritto penale', *Jus*, 1951, pp. 451 ff.; 'Punti fermi in tema di pena retributiva', *Scritti giuridici in onore di Alfredo de Marsico*, 1960, vol. I, pp. 53 ff. Cf. various comments on the occasion of the colloquium on criminal law held at Buenos Aires in 1960 (Proceedings: *Jornadas de derecho penal*, Buenos Aires, 1962). See also the much more subtle approach of R. Merle, which reveals a more accurate understanding of social defence doctrines, 'L'évolution du droit pénal moderne', in *Annales de la Fac. de droit de Toulouse*, 1951, pp. 135 ff.; J. Larguier, *Le droit pénal* (in the Series *Que sais-je?*), 1962 pp. 12 ff. Nuvolone has been quick to retort that criticism of social defence on the basis of expiatory punishment in fact involves making the Old Testament prevail over the Gospels (*Riv. italiana di diritto penale*, 1956, p. 782).

[3] See in particular L. Jiménez de Asúa, 'La nueva defensa social', *La Ley*, 29 August, 1957, and *Tratado de derecho penal*, vol. II, 2nd ed., No. 533; Quintano Ripolles, 'La evolución del derecho penal moderno (contra corrientes)', *Anuario de derecho penal y ciencias penales*, 1957, pp. 283 ff.

The more extreme supporters of these various tendencies are then led to consider social defence as the incarnation of a subversive approach or even—as certain Western opponents of the new doctrines appear to believe—as a more or less surreptitious form of communism.[4]

Another source of criticism, curiously enough, is to be found in the theories advanced by criminal scientists from the Eastern countries or the 'people's democracies'. They take the view that social defence doctrine is inspired both by considerations of religious propaganda instigated by the Vatican and by the desire to impose the institutions of American capitalism, typified—it seems—by the indeterminate sentence.[5] This approach, complacently developed during the Stalinist period, does not seem to have been revised since, although such a revision is very necessary.[6] Writers on criminal law in the so-called socialist countries still make the doctrine of social defence appear as a product of capitalist conceptions which tends to establish an illegal and arbitrary system designed to maintain the exploitation of man by man.

It is rather piquant to find that those Catholic lawyers who, in France, became indignant over the fact that social defence should assign such an important place to the rehabilitation of the criminal or pay greater attention to the daily fare of convicted offenders than to the technique of repression, are manifestly at variance with the attitude and the words of Pope John XXIII, who, very early in his reign, made a long visit to a prison to bring comfort to the prisoners, and who adopted as his own the expression 'social reintegration' which is criticized by some doctrinaire Catholic

[4] Bettiol and Frey have no hesitation in making such an allegation. Nuvolone replies that the concept of 'poena medicinalis' (treatment) is not derived from Hegel and Marx, as Bettiol would have us believe, but from the Canon Lawyers (*Riv. int. di diritto penale*, 1959, p. 148).

[5] See Jerzy Sawicki, 'O Nowej Ochronie Spolecznej', reprinted from *Panstwo i Prawo*, Warsaw, 1955; see the critical comments by Y. Marx in *Rev. de Science crim.*, 1955, pp. 588 ff.

[6] See Tioutkovski and Tadevosian, report on the Fifth International Congress for Social Defence, in the review *Soviet State and Law* (in Russian, March 1959); cf. the remarks by Piontkowsky at the Round Table Discussions on the Reform of Soviet Criminal Law held in May 1963 at the Comparative Law Institute of the University of Paris, reported in *Rev. de Science crim.*, 1964, No. 1, (January-March); Miklos Kadar, 'Quelques remarques au sujet d'un article sur les aspects juridiques de la situation actuelle en Hongrie', *Rev. de droit hongrois*, 1961, p. 42 ff., esp. p. 47.

writers in this field.[7] Equally odd is the fact that lawyers faithful to the Soviet party line were very slow in becoming aware of the imperative requirements of the rule of law, unceasingly advocated by the new social defence movement.[8] And again, it is curious that the process of 'liberalization' and the tentative movement towards the protection of individual rights, in the criminal law of the Eastern European countries, is still a far cry from the active protection of the individual which social defence seeks to ensure. There is no point in further stressing this twofold contradiction save to observe that many of those who oppose the ideas of social defence, in the West as in the East, are at heart really supporters of an authoritarian system of repression, which they merely wish to camouflage under the phraseology of the neo-classical tradition and under the outward appearance of a purely formal adherence to the concept of the rule of law.

These uncertainties and contradictions, moreover, are derived from a double confusion of thought, of which those who examine social defence doctrine superficially are too often guilty.

First there is the persistent confusion between the penal policy of social defence and the theories of the positivist school. The critics of the former rely on arguments which constitute a refutation of the latter, but without realizing that social defence is itself a very clear reaction against the determinist assumptions and the 'scientism' of the Italian school at the end of last century.[9] Among some lawyers this approach finds expression in a resolutely hostile attitude towards criminology and the lessons to be drawn from the social sciences.[10] Besides, there is here a confusion between pure law on the one hand—which on its own level can indeed

[7] See *Rev. de Science crim.*, 1962, p. 157.

[8] As we know, the Soviet Codes of 1922 and 1926 had accepted the principle of guilt by analogy (art. 16 of the 1926 Code) which the criminal law of Hitler's Germany was to affirm in a still more totalitarian context. From 1937 onwards, the social defence movement has proclaimed its adherence to the rule of law (see Marc Ancel, General Report to the International Congress for Criminal Law, in *Rev. int. de droit pén.*, 1937, pp. 240-65; cf. Marc Ancel, General Report to the Fourth International Congress for Comparative Law, 1954, 'L'Analogie en droit pénal', *Rev. int. de droit pén.*, 1955, pp. 227 ff.

[9] This is partly true of Jerome Hall (see in particular *General Principles of Criminal Law*, 2nd ed., 1960) and also to some extent of the group of criminal scientists who have been called the 'Utrecht School'. See *Une Nouvelle École de science criminelle, l'École d'Utrecht*, edited and introduced by J. Léauté, Paris, 1959.

[10] See Clarence Ray Jeffrey, 'The Historical Development of Criminology', *Pioneers in Criminology*, London, 1960, pp. 364 ff.

dispense with criminological studies, provided it does not deny their existence—and penal policy on the other, which in this second half of the twentieth century is doomed to remain ineffective if it seeks to disregard the information supplied by the social sciences. Fortunately, the better-informed criminal lawyers are beginning to avoid such mistakes.[11]

Another source of confusion results from an over-simple and outdated analysis which treats the doctrines of social defence as a single theory which is most fully represented by its more extreme spokesmen, and so criticizes some of the views expounded by Gramatica. We have been careful to point out as clearly as possible in an earlier chapter, however, just how the doctrine of *new* social defence outlined in the present work differs from Gramatica's theory. There is no need to go over the same ground again: it is enough to make the point that in our view there is a fundamental contrast between the new social defence movement and this kind of extreme interpretation. An illustration of this contrast is provided by the *minimum programme* of the Society for Social Defence, the importance of which has already been discussed in the appropriate context. Here again, these indispensable distinctions are now widely accepted by well-informed critics.

There is no need, therefore, to recapitulate our arguments to show that the new social defence movement does not reject either criminal law or the concept of the rule of law, does not abolish responsibility or punishment, and does not aim at establishing an arbitrary system of prevention in which every individual is envisaged *a priori* as a potential criminal. It only remains to discuss certain more weighty objections which do not disregard the significance of the genuine doctrines of new social defence.[12]

[11] Apart from the writers already referred to, we may note that on the occasion of the criminal law colloquium held at Buenos Aires in 1960 (*Jornadas*, 1962, pp. 52 ff., 89 ff.), eminent specialists such as Professors Laplaza (Argentina) and Eduardo Novoa Monreal (Chile), expressed views which, though critical, showed a much less categorical approach.

[12] No attention need be paid here to a violently polemical article entitled 'La Crise de la politique criminelle de défense sociale', which appeared in *La Vie judiciaire* of 9 April 1962: the author's intemperate language and his regular use of incomplete or truncated quotations deprives the pamphlet of any scientific value. See moreover the excellent replies of R. Gaudefroy-Demombynes ('Le Succès du mouvement de défense sociale', *La Vie judiciaire*, 7 May 1962) and of S. C. Versele, 'À propos d'un improbable "chant du cygne" de la Défense sociale nouvelle', *Revue de criminologie et de police technique*, 1962, pp. 117 ff.

II

Our enquiry will be limited to three main objections.

A. The first often takes the form of a doubt rather than a criticism proper. The argument runs as follows: it is a good thing, no doubt, to want to treat the convicted offender and rehabilitate the criminal, but will this not tend to weaken the system of repression and lead to disregarding the need for general prevention?[13] Whatever we may do or say, assert the critics of social defence, the idea of retribution still remains very much alive in the public opinion of all countries, and this public opinion requires that the commission of a criminal offence should be followed by the infliction of a sentence of retributive punishment. Furthermore, such a retributive penalty is itself a means of general prevention and could not be got rid of without abandoning one of the essential safeguards of the social order.

We have already discussed this theory of general prevention and of retribution, inasmuch as it would purport to restore, in law, a legal order which has been disturbed by the commission of a crime, and we have shown that from the point of view of penal policy, if not from the point of view of criminal law or the philosophy of criminal law, it is pointless to invoke this purely abstract function of punishment. We have likewise shown that it is equally pointless to adopt a position based on a metaphysical or purely abstract concept of the criminal, whose superego, ideally free to act as he chose, would always be able to make an absolute choice between good and evil,[14] a choice which in theory would be

[13] The late Maurice Patin, former President of the Criminal Division of the Court of Cassation, expressed his misgivings in this form, but at the same time gave his approval to the moderate doctrine of social defence: see his statements at the *Quatrièmes Journées de Défense sociale* at Bordeaux (*Rev. de Science crim.*, 1956, p. 650) and also on the occasion of the twenty-fifth anniversary of the *Revue de Science criminelle et de droit pénal comparé*, the same *Revue*, 1962, p. 251. See also R. Merle, *Droit pénal général complémentaire*, 1957, pp. vi ff., and the study, cited earlier, in the *Annales de la Faculté de droit de Toulouse*, 1958, pp. 133 ff.; L. Jiménez de Asúa, *Tratado de derecho penal*, vol. II, 2nd ed., 1959, No. 533.

[14] On the 'metaphysical' nature of this conception, see Olof Kinberg, 'La Psychiatrie criminelle sans métaphysique', *Rev. de Science crim.*, 1949, pp. 513 ff. Cf. *Les Problèmes fondamentaux de la criminologie*, Paris, 1960, esp. pp. 36 ff., 75 ff. See also Paul Cornil, 'L'Impasse de la responsabilité pénale', *Rev. de droit pén. et de crim.*, 1961-1962, pp. 637 ff. Cf. Franchimont, 'Notules sur l'imputabilité', same *Revue*, pp. 342 ff.; Zilborg, *The Psychology of the Criminal Act and Punishment*, London, 1955; E. Glover, *The Roots of Crime*, London, 1960, p. 12.

decisively affected by the possibility of incurring punishment for commission of a crime. It is true that public opinion demands that criminals be punished and believes in general prevention, and this observation carries greater weight from the point of view of the realistic penal policy on which we have taken our stand. Several answers suggest themselves, and may be rapidly enumerated:

1. As has already been shown, the doctrine of social defence in its new form does not necessarily reject all punishment of a retributive kind: thus punishment is retained more particularly for a number of *délits artificiels*, the disappearance of which in the near future is hardly likely, at a time of increasing intervention by the State and in view both of the considerable modern development of a 'social and economic criminal law'[15] and of the persistence of what has on the Continent come to be called *la criminalité astucieuse*,[16] a general term intended to cover such offences as obtaining by false pretences, embezzlement, and so forth.

2. It matters little whether or not the measure applied to the offender is classified by the law as punishment. All, save those who cling to an outdated ideology, are taught by experience that the deterrent value of preventive measures is at least as great as, if not greater than, that of punishments in the true sense of the term. Committal to an institution for an indefinite period—*relégation*—is a much more daunting prospect for the relapsed criminal than is a fixed prison term. In England, juvenile delinquents are more afraid of being sent to Borstal than of short-term imprisonment or even corporal punishment.[17] All those who have studied the way

[15] See on this topic the papers of the Sixth International Congress on Criminal Law held at Rome in September 1953, Third Section, general report by M. P. Vrij (*Rev. de Science crim.*, 1954, No. 1, pp. 202 ff.). Cf. E. R. Aftalion, *Derecho penal económico*, Buenos Aires, 1960.

[16] J. Larguier has pointed out, very properly (*Le Droit pénal*, in the series *Que sais-je?*, 1962, p. 13) that 'a singularly broad conception of what constitutes "illness" is needed in order to consider as pathological the act of the trader who cooks the accounts, or that of the industrialist who mixes noxious substances with the products which he offers for sale for human consumption'.

[17] On this question of deterrent effect, Norval Morris writes that reforming techniques, with their corollary of individualized punishment and the abandonment of the statutory scale of penalties (which enables the offender to make a reasonably accurate estimate of the penalty he is likely to incur if he is found guilty) will ultimately strengthen the deterrent value of punishment on society and the criminal: *frequently* it is the unpredictable quality of punishment that conditions its deterrent force' (*The Habitual Delinquent*, London, 1951, p. 12).

in which indeterminate sentences are applied and work in practice, are aware that the indefinite nature of the measure is itself a more formidable menace than a fixed penalty, and the Belgian experience shows us that committal to an institution of social defence such as a detention centre, for instance, is no less feared than the infliction of a prison term. If any doubt exists on the point, it certainly exists neither in the minds of potential criminals nor for public opinion as a whole,[18] being valid only for the 'pure lawyers' who are alone in making a theoretical distinction between retributive punishment and preventive measures which are the instrument for the treatment of the offender.

3. From the point of view of the potential criminal, moreover, which is the only viewpoint from which the question of general prevention should be envisaged, it is necessary to recall once again that the deterrent effect of punishment is never more than a mere assumption. Potential criminals are said to be held back by the fact that there exists, written into the law, a penalty that they may incur if they commit the offence to which they are tempted. But all modern criminologists agree that in reality—as distinct from theory—this deterrent force has been greatly overestimated.[19] In a strikingly original chapter of her book on 'arms of the law', Margery Fry analysed the value of the supposedly deterrent effect of punishment with a lucidity shorn of all theoretical considerations: this 'digression on fear' led her to the conclusion that the deterrent factor ultimately affected only a very small number of individuals.[20] Furthermore, it is well known that in many cases, the reduction of the penalty initially imposed for certain crimes has not in fact resulted in any recrudescence of these offences, and

[18] See Gresham M. Sykes, 'The Dilemmas of Penal Reform—An American View', *Howard Journal*, vol. 8, No. 3, 1960, pp. 194 ff., esp. p. 199 (concerning dangerous and incurable individuals): 'It makes little difference if we call their place of confinement a maximum security unit, an isolation ward or a hospital, or something else.'

[19] See Sutherland, *Principles of Criminology*, 3rd ed., chap. IX, pp. 355 ff.; cf. G. Rusche and O. Kirchheimer, *Punishment and Social Structure*, New York, 1939, pp. 141 ff.; Thorsten Sellin, *Culture Conflict and Crime*, New York, 1938, and *Étude sociologique de la criminalité* (General report to the Criminological Congress held in Paris in 1950), *Proceedings* of the Congress, vol. IV, pp. 109 ff.; Lionel W. Fox, *The English Prison and Borstal Systems*, pp. 11 and 71 ff.; O. Kinberg, *Les Problèmes fondamentaux de la criminologie*, Paris, 1960, pp. 51 ff., which discusses von Liszt's assertion that the threat of punishment serves as a 'warning' and a 'means of terror'.

[20] *Arms of the Law*, London, 1951, pp. 73 ff.

this is one of the traditional arguments of those who advocate the abolition of capital punishment.[21]

4. A completely objective analysis of social realities leads to the conclusion that the genuinely deterrent factor lies not in the sanction finally applied by the judge, but in the intervention of the authorities of the State, which takes place as soon as it is found that an offence has been committed. Besides, popular good sense openly acknowledges this, in speaking not of the criminal's fear of punishment or the judge, but of his 'fear of the policeman'. What is capable of deterring most potential criminals is in fact the setting in motion—automatically if possible—of the process of prosecution which forces such potential criminals to account for their acts and their conduct in a court of law. It could even be said that appearance in court constitutes for public opinion the immediate atonement demanded, to such an extent that this same public opinion will often be moved to pity the particular criminal in the course of the hearing, as is often the case with the trial jury. It very often happens in the end, therefore, that the offender, with universal consent as it were, will finally be sentenced to a penalty much less severe than the law allows. Here again it is the lawyers who focus attention on punishment, whereas public opinion, or the criminal himself, is primarily aware of the police, the prosecution, and the judge.[22]

[21] See Olof Kinberg, *op. cit.*, *Rev. de Science crim.*, 1949, pp. 527-29; also the remarkable issue of the *Annals of the American Academy of Political and Social Science* (November 1952) devoted to *Murder and the Penalty of Death*; see also the comments in the U.S.S.R. after the criminal law amendments which reduced the penalty for culpable homicide to a sentence of detention for a maximum of ten years (capital punishment being inflicted only for 'counter-revolutionary' crimes), *Le droit pénal soviétique, partie spéciale* (published by the Institute of Legal Sciences of the Ministry of Justice of the U.S.S.R., Moscow, 1951), report in the *Rev. de Science crim.*, 1953, pp. 751 ff.; cf. Thorsten Sellin, *The Death Penalty*, Philadelphia, 1959, p. 21; see also the two reports by Marc Ancel, one to the Council of Europe, *The Death Penalty in European Countries*, Strasbourg, 1962, and the other to the United Nations, *Capital Punishment*, New York, 1962; see also Marc Ancel, 'Les Doctrines de la Défense sociale devant le problème de la peine de mort', *Rev. de Science crim.*, 1963, pp. 404 ff.

[22] At the same time, this intervention by the proper authorities has the effect of making perceptible the moral censure that attaches to any offence, at least in the category of *mala in se*. Some lawyers therefore conclude that 'the significance of a rule of criminal law lies in its very existence rather than in its actual application' (J. Larguier, *Le Droit pénal*, in the series *Que sais-je?*, Paris, 1962, p. 14). Does it therefore follow that if the statutory rule is accompanied by a sanction which is not strictly punishment in the legal sense, such a sanction thereby lacks all social efficacy and practical importance?

5. Furthermore, this attitude is strengthened by modern, penitentiary practice. We are no longer in the age of Beccaria who as the apostle of the purely 'legalistic' approach, urged not only that the penalty for each crime should be fixed, but also that reprieve should be prohibited. It is well known not only that the sentence remains uncertain until the end of the judicial proceedings, but that the way in which that sentence will be carried out is equally uncertain. The method of its execution, as we know, changes the real character of the sentence imposed by the court, and individual penitentiary treatment has made such progress that it now possesses a margin of discretion which goes much farther than the power of individualized sentences that is at the disposal of the court.[23] We are no longer concerned, therefore, with the system in which punishment, in the classical sense of the term, was imposed once and for all: it is a fiction or indeed an illusion, not to say a sign of hypocrisy, to envisage punishment simply in terms of the penalty laid down by statute or imposed by the judge, while paying no attention to the measure actually applied. Criminal offenders, like the public, are beginning to be aware of the varied forms of sentence which may be applied, and are also aware that an amnesty or a reprieve may be subsequently granted: these are measures that the condemned man frequently applies for, which indicates a further disintegration of the theoretical value of deterrent punishments.[24]

6. Finally, we have already stated, and at this stage can but repeat, that a penal policy of social defence can be genuinely established only in a climate of social morality by which such a policy is understood, justified, and developed.[25] In so far as the ideas outlined above are not yet completely accepted by an insufficiently enlightened public opinion, we should strive to make them progressively accepted. This change of climate, so to speak, is no more inconceivable than that which led to the eradication—in

[23] See C. Germain, *Éléments de science pénitentiaire*, 1959, p. 28. It has been claimed that in England the principle of individualized treatment was laid down by the Gladstone Committee as early as 1895. See Howard Jones, *Crime and the Penal System*, 2nd ed., 1962, p. 160.

[24] See Hugh Klare, *Anatomy of Prison*, London, 1960, pp. 14 ff.; cf. Melitta Schmideberg, 'The Offender's Attitude towards Punishment', in *Journ. of Crim. Law, Criminology and Police Science*, Sept.-Oct. 1960, pp. 328 ff.; see also W. F. Roper, 'The Attitude to the Prisoner', *Howard Journal*, vol. VIII, No. 3, 1952, pp. 158 ff.

[25] See J. D. Morton, 'The Function of Criminal Law in 1962', *Five Talks for Radio*, Toronto, 1962, esp. pp. 3 ff., 34 ff.

principle at least—of the old notions of expiatory vengeance. Nobody today maintains that even a heinous crime should simply be punished out of hand, according to the *lex talionis*. This is what a considerable section of public opinion seems to demand, no doubt, if we are to judge by the attitude of the public when the popular Press, always eager for sensation, features certain criminal cases. But no modern criminal scientist would support public opinion on this point, and in this respect the effect of the new social defence movement is simply to bring home both to criminal lawyers themselves and to the man in the street that mere retribution is not enough: society can be effectively protected only by social action of the kind we have endeavoured to describe in the preceding chapters.[26]

B. A second group of objections attacks what we have termed 'de-legalization' (*dé-juridicisation*). This expression has naturally troubled the lawyers, but it was chosen intentionally. We will not concern ourselves with certain extreme critics who focus attention on this term as a pretext to accuse social defence doctrine of using a jargon which is incomprehensible to the average man,[27] or of rejecting all systems of law. We have never denied having deliberately coined a dreadful neologism, but our purpose is to make an impact on people's minds, and the success of the expression—even among its critics—is a sufficient justification of our attitude. As for the allegation that the doctrine of *new* social defence tends to abolish law and the rule of law, such an argument can be invoked only by those who fail to understand the doctrine.

However, many criminal scientists make it clear that they wish to preserve a 'legal law', to use Roger Merle's intentionally vivid pleonasm.[28] In any case, is it not dangerous to sever the penal

[26] This agrees to a large extent with the approach of the 'Utrecht School' (see *Une Nouvelle École de science criminelle*, presented by J. Léauté, Paris, 1959). See also A. Besson, 'A propos de la Défense sociale nouvelle', *Rev. int. de droit pénal*, 1954, pp. 321ff. Cf. Barbara Wootton, 'Crime and the Criminal Law', *Hamlyn Lectures*, 15th series, London, 1963, esp. pp. 32 ff.

[27] Most of the writers who take up arms against this 'jargon' do not realize that they thereby reject the language of criminology, because they have failed to become accustomed to that language or even to understand it. If, according to the well-known formula, every intellectual discipline is in the first place well-constructed language, it is reasonable that in order to build itself up as a science, criminology should create its own particular language.

[28] *Droit pénal général complémentaire*, 1957, p. vii; cf. the study, already cited, in the *Annales de la Faculté de droit de Toulouse*, 1958, where Roger Merle gives expression to the misgivings of lawyers in the face of 'those who wish to take the legal element

system from legal methods? Would not such an approach create a split between criminal law and other branches of law, by introducing into the former an examination of the criminal's personality and an explanation of his individual conduct which are far removed from the rules concerning legal capacity in the law of contract or in what the Common Law systems call the law of torts?[29]

Here again, we should not be led astray. As has already been explained, the 'de-legalization' proposed by the doctrine of new social defence does not mean that criminal law should cease to be a juridical science or be deprived of the techniques which this involves. It only intends to point out the limits of that science, and especially to uphold the view that the phenomenon of crime can neither be understood nor evaluated in the social context simply by means of legal analysis. Again, social defence stresses the fact that side by side with the criminal law—undeniably important and increasingly asserted to be autonomous[30]—there exist other parallel disciplines that are not subordinate to the criminal law and which should be recognized, in their turn, as autonomous also. Above all, the 'de-legalization' advocated by the social defence movement involves a struggle against excessive legalism (*juridisme*) which, by relying on fictions and purely abstract forms of reasoning, often threatens to conceal the real nature of crime and the criminal. Finally—the criminal law being confined to its own sphere and to its necessary relationship with civil law—the notion of de-legalization involves assessing the need for, and the part to be played by, a rational penal policy which is logically half-way between criminology and penology on the one hand, and legal science on the other, but which exercises a decisive influence over the development of penal institutions. As Sheldon Glueck said about psychiatry, the question is whether

---

out of criminal science' (*dé-juridiciser la science criminelle*, p. 136). Jiménez de Asúa, Bettiol, and Quintano Ripolles have expressed their misgivings even more sharply (see passages already cited).

[29] This idea, put forward by Roger Merle, was taken up by Lautecaze in his preliminary report to the *Neuvièmes Journées francaises de Défense sociale, Toulouse*, 1961; see *Rev. de Science crim.*, 1961, p. 843.

[30] See the notable collection of studies published under the supervision of G. Stefani under the title *Quelques aspects de l'autonomie du droit pénal*, 1956; cf. Legros, 'Essai sur l'autonomie du droit pénal', *Rev. de droit pénal et de criminologie*, 1955-56, p. 143.

there shall be a 'cold war' or an 'entente cordiale' between criminal law and penal policy. This is recognized by some first-rate criminal lawyers when they themselves put forward a series of coherent reforms designed to humanize and socialize the criminal law.[31]

C. A third series of objections is aimed at these reforms, or at any rate at those among them which are advocated by the social defence movement. Here again the critics do not altogether avoid a certain confusion of thought. Many in fact attack Gramatica's extreme thesis, and some even take issue with an outdated positivism. These various objections, which are interrelated, may be summarized as follows.

It is said that the social defence movement is concerned with the person and not with the act. Classical criminal law, in punishing the criminal act, protected the person, since the reaction against crime was confined within specified legal limits. The notions of 'dangerousness' and 'anti-sociality' lead to a subjective system which leaves the widest discretion to the judge, and this arbitrary element is a threat to the individual. Worse still, if 'dangerousness' is the only criterion, this must be sought out and controlled before any offence has been committed: preventive measures *ante delictum* are another threat to freedom. Indeterminate sentences are yet another such threat, since a man will no longer know what penalty he may incur. Finally, even the concept of treatment and social readaptation is denounced as dangerous: if such treatment is aimed at the criminal's personality, will not this lead to a desire to change that personality and so to a form of 'brain-washing'? Certain theorists from Eastern Europe, strangely transformed into champions of liberalism, even go so far as to assert that social defence leads to the institution of a police state and to extermination camps.[32]

These reckless assertions can deceive only the gullible. As we have already said, the new social defence movement has no intention of substituting the notion of dangerousness for that of responsibility, or of replacing a legal sanction by the arbitrary and discretionary intervention of the judge. It was the totalitarian régimes imbued with ideas of repressive punishment which

[31] See in particular R. Merle, *op. cit.* in *Annales de la Faculté de droit de Toulouse*, 1958, especially pp. 143 ff.

[32] See the study by Sawicki, *O Nowej Ochronie Spolecznej*, already cited.

invented concentration camps, physical torture, and the medico-psychological alteration of the personality: in fact the modern social defence movement sprang initially from a revolt against totalitarianism and was primarily concerned to impose respect for the human personality. Besides, the movement takes good care to stress the principle of the rule of law, so that preventive measures *before* the commission of an offence normally play no part in its approach to the control of crime.[33]

There remains the charge—or the fear—that social defence would abandon the liberal tradition and the individualism that were characteristic of neo-classical criminal law. This assertion need not trouble us when it comes from the supporters of authoritarian regimes, for such people make it sufficiently clear, by word and deed, that they are in fact hostile to liberalism: in their view the word is no more than an alibi, and its use by certain theorists in countries of Eastern Europe is indeed curious. On the other hand, when a similar anxiety with regard to social defence is expressed by such men as de Asúa in Latin America and Merle in France, the question deserves serious thought.[34]

The answer, however, is not very difficult to find. In the first place, this type of criticism is not aimed at the actual content of social defence doctrine or at its 'platform', so to speak, but at what the doctrine might become. These traditionalist critics, who oppose the concept of 'dangerousness' or potential criminality, are condemning not the doctrine as such but its latent possibilities and the ways in which it might be extended. To dispose of this

[33] At most, it will be considered that certain forms of behaviour, before any offence has been committed, might be taken into consideration and given a legal definition, so that they can be controlled, if need be, by non-penal measures of a therapeutic nature, confined within strict limits. See on this point the papers of the Third French Criminological Congress, in particular the general report by Y. Marx on 'Les Aspects juridiques des problèmes posés par l'état dangereux pré-délictuel', *Annales int. de criminologie*, 1963, No. 2, and the synthesis by Lebret (*Actes* of the Congress, Paris, 1963, pp. 248 ff.; see also the remarks by Bouzat at the same Congress (*Actes*, p. 215). On the problem of preventive measures before an offence has been committed, see further P. Nuvolone, 'La prevenzione nella teoria generale del diritto penale', *Riv. italiana di diritto penale*, 1956, pp. 13 ff. Cf. on this subject the highly pertinent comments by Stefani and Levasseur, *Droit pénal général et criminologie*, 2nd ed., 1960, in particular No. 498.

[34] Jiménez de Asúa, 'La nueva defensa social', *La Ley*, 29 August, 1957; R. Merle, *op. cit.* in *Annales de la Fac. de droit de Toulouse*, 1958, pp. 133 ff. Cf. the comments of Gresham M. Sykes, 'The Dilemmas of Penal Reform', *Howard Journal*, vol. X, No. 3, 1960, pp. 194 ff.

objection based on the supposedly unacknowledged tendencies of the movement, it is enough to underline the contrast between Gramatica's extremist theory and the doctrine of new social defence.

We should also discuss the notions of individual and individualism, which the neo-classicists—as in the case of responsibility—were content to treat in abstract, *a priori* terms which had no connexion with human realities. Individualism, as understood by the neo-classical school, means no more than an illusory 'state of nature' and goes no further than the primitive conceptualism of Jean-Jacques Rousseau.[35] The citizen envisaged by the Declaration of the Rights of Man is deemed free to make a contract or to refrain from committing a crime, a point of view which becomes untenable in the face of modern planning, the standard-form contract and the dynamic of crime. The 'free man' of the eighteenth-century philosophers, who voluntarily submitted to the social contract but was fundamentally hostile to organized society, is the direct ancestor of those who, in our day, are his last descendants—the anarchist and the libertarian. That kind of individualist long appeared to be satisfied with—or at any rate kept in check by—the liberal State as keeper of the peace, until the emergence of the Welfare State transformed him into a kind of social atheist. The upsetting of the balance between State and individual showed up the danger of the opposition between them which the classical system had sought to preserve. A sound modern penal policy must start from the evident truth that the individual is not a political and social entity in himself, over against organized society. He only manifests himself socially, through contact with his fellows, and it is from this necessary encounter that the social group emerges in the first place. The individual should therefore be postulated or thought of as existing not *against* the State but *within* the social community. Similarly, his conflict with other individuals should be reduced, not by complete amalgamation in the totalitarian sense or by his political and economic absorption into the group, but through a new harmonization of social relationships. This approach has certain affinities with certain

[35] Strangely enough, Rousseau's categorical views are still found among some legal theorists today, even those inspired by the Christian tradition: see A. Richard, *La Mission méconnue de la justice pénale*, Paris, 1956, and the comments by Marc Ancel in *Rev. de Science crim.*, 1957, pp. 254 ff.

modern philosophical trends, such as the 'personalism' which Emmanuel Mounier contrasted with the classical doctrine of individualism[36] or the pages that Teilhard de Chardin devotes to 'hominization', a process of human development which in his view leads naturally to a necessary socialization.[37]

According to this conception, the rights and powers of the State should no longer be a menace to the individual, any more than individual rights menace those of the State, for the latter is no more than the social and legal expression of the organized human group envisaged as a kind of collective conscience:[38] man as an individual, the irreplaceable human entity, can neither be done away with nor persecuted by a State that only exists through him and for him. Thus understood, the notion of 'fraternity' ceases to be only a slogan and becomes both a reality and a duty: it is neither a threat to freedom—as was feared by Ripert and by jurists attached to traditional liberal notions[39]—nor to the social structure. Going farther than the outmoded 'solidarism' of the late nineteenth century,[40] the modern doctrines of penal policy seek to take as their starting-point a social structure that rightly understands this notion of fraternity and considers it as one of its essential foundations, so that the notion will ultimately find expression in the institutions of society.

So individualism as understood by the social defence movement, thought out anew, is more closely in touch with reality, and more fruitful, than the purely passive individualism of the neo-classicists. It is therefore fundamentally inaccurate to see social defence

[36] See E. Mounier, *Manifeste au service du personnalisme*, 1936, and *Le Personnalisme*, 1949. For Mounier, 'personalism' should be distinguished from individualism in as much as it 'stresses the collective and cosmic element in the person'.

[37] P. Teilhard de Chardin, *Le Phénomène humain*, *Œuvres*, vol. I, 1955, pp. 180 ff. André Tunc has taken up some of Teilhard de Chardin's ideas in a suggestive article entitled 'Le Juriste et la noosphère (La Fonction possible des études comparatives dans le monde contemporain)', in *Problèmes contemporains de droit comparé*, Tokyo, 1962, vol. II, pp. 493 ff.

[38] The word 'conscience' is here given the same meaning as by Teilhard de Chardin.

[39] See especially G. Ripert, *Le Régime démocratique et le droit civil moderne*, 2nd ed., 1949: *Le Déclin du droit*, 1949, and *Les Forces créatrices du droit*, 1955. See however Paul Roubier, *Théorie générale du droit*, 1st ed., 1946, pp. 189 ff., 230 ff.

[40] See *Léon Bourgeois*, *Esquisse d'une philosophie de la solidarité*, 1902. See also Duguit, *Le Droit social, le droit individuel et l'État*, 1908. It is also necessary to go beyond 'sociologism' as conceived by Durkheim, though without disregarding it altogether (See *Sociologie et philosophie*, 2nd ed., 1951).

as even a remote threat to individual freedom and the rights of the human person. The expression 'social readaptation' (*resocialisation*) has sometimes been turned into a reproach against the doctrine of social defence, but this expression should not be given a distorted meaning, any more than the term 'de-legalization', also favoured by the new doctrine, which was discussed earlier. For the social defence movement, the words 'social readaptation' do not imply the arbitrary and authoritarian alteration of the criminal's personality, but a treatment of re-education[41] which restores to the offender his awareness of the meaning of social life and its imperative demands.

It is indeed peculiar to see a certain form of neo-classicism appealing to liberalism and moderation, whereas the same doctrine loses all sense of proportion in its almost pathological antagonism towards new ideas, its self-styled protection of the individual leading to support of capital punishment, to demands for increased repression, and to the establishment of emergency courts. The penal policy of social defence rejects the bloodthirsty anachronism of capital punishment, not out of humanitarian sentimentality but because of an enlightened humanism.[42] The parallel rejection of methods that are merely primitive and solely intended as expiation for the past comes from the same confidence in man's nature and destiny. In fact, an active policy of social readaptation will provide the best protection for society and the best safeguard for its moral values. It is none the less strange to find that social defence is accused by its detractors not only of removing the deterrent element from the reaction against crime,

[41] On this dynamic conception of the treatment of social readaptation, seen in the context of a humanist prison policy, see the remarkable reports read at the series of discussions held under the auspices of the International Penal and Penitentiary Foundation at Strasbourg (September 1959) by Dupréel (*Travaux préparatoires*, fasc. II., pp. 443 ff.) and E. Lamers (*ibid.*, pp. 467 ff.); cf. H. E. Barnes and N. K. Teeters, *New Horizons in Criminology*, 2nd ed., pp. 632 ff.; R. Korn and L. W. McCorkle, *Criminology and Penology*, 1959, pp. 532 ff. As regards the United Kingdom, see 'L'Évolution du système pénitentiaire et les méthodes de traitement', by Sir Lionel Fox, in *Introduction au droit criminel de l'Angleterre* (in the series *Les Grands Systèmes de droit pénal contemporains*), vol. I, Paris, 1959, pp. 259 ff.; P. Bouzat and J. Pinatel, *Traité de droit pénal et de criminologie*, vol. III, *Criminologie*, by J. Pinatel, Paris, 1963, pp. 448 ff.

[42] On this aspect of social defence doctrines, which cannot be further discussed here, see Marc Ancel, 'Les Doctrines de la Défense sociale devant le problème de la peine de mort', *Rev. de Science crim.*, 1963, pp. 404 ff., and 'Le Problème de la peine de mort', *Rev. de droit pénal et de criminologie*, Feb. 1964, pp. 373 ff.

or promoting anarchy by disregard of the State in the interests of individuals, even guilty ones, but also of constituting a serious threat for each individual, wholly sacrificed to an all-powerful society.[43] These contradictions alone would be enough to expose the weakness of the objections usually advanced against the penal policy of social defence.

III

One last group of objections to the doctrine of social defence appears less as positive criticism than as a generally negative attitude, questioning the very usefulness of the concept as this has been defined in the foregoing chapters. These objections take various forms, from an over-simple and sometimes ingenuous disregard of the new doctrines (of which the critics are plainly ignorant) on the one hand, to the most astute glosses or insinuations on the other. Some critics have even gone so far as to assert that social defence is nothing but a kind of vague ideal, useful only in those cases where an insufficiently developed penal system still needs this kind of incentive.[44]

More weighty are the critical opinions based on considerations of a methodological kind, and these alone merit an answer. Thus Jiménez de Asúa disputes the proposition that social defence may constitute a distinct juridical discipline: it is a movement of penal policy, and penal policy as an autonomous intellectual discipline appears to have been abandoned even by the Germans, although it was they who once gave it so much importance.[45]

[43] The illogical nature of this contradiction among the opponents of the modern doctrines of penal policy—and criminology—has been well pointed out by H. Mannheim: see *Pioneers in Criminology*, London, 1960, Introd., p. 30.

[44] This curious assertion is found in the article by Frey, already referred to, in *Rev. pénale suisse*, 1953, p. 405. See Marc Ancel, *Rev. de Science crim.*, 1954, p. 222, and above all the decisive reply of Graven in *Rev. pénale suisse*, 1955, pp. 1 ff.

[45] 'La nueva defensa social', *La Ley*, vol. 88, 1957, pp. 693 ff., where Jiménez de Asúa notes that E. Mezger, having published a book which attracted attention under the title *Kriminalpolitik und ihre kriminologischen Grundlagen*, 3rd ed., 1944, agreed that the Spanish translation of this work should have the title *Criminologia*, and furthermore that the same author later published a small treatise on the same subject entitled *Kriminologie*, Munich, 1951. Moreover, Jiménez de Asúa's attention could be drawn to the fact that Franz Exner, who had published a well-known work entitled *Kriminalbiologie*, Hamburg, 1939, changed the title of the third edition to *Kriminologie*, Berlin, 1949, which he considered a better description of the contents of the treatise (see *Vorwort*, p. vi). It would be foolhardy to draw the conclusion that 'criminal biology', 'bio-criminology' does not exist as a scientific study. It may be added that Eberhard Schmidt, dealing with the problems raised by criminal law

This criticism is valid only if the expression 'penal policy' is given the narrow technical meaning assigned to it by von Liszt, namely the appropriate utilization of punishment, in relation to the offender's personality.[46] This is the sense in which some writers have been able to refer to legislation or a system inspired by considerations of penal policy. But Jiménez de Asúa himself is too well aware of the evolution of penal doctrine not to observe also that 'penal policy' may be given a much broader significance and that, from Beccaria and Romagnosi to Ferri, the term has been understood to mean the whole group of methods for the prevention and control of crime.[47] It was greatly to the credit of Henri Donnedieu de Vabres that he restored to this expression its normal meaning, i.e. the study of the methods by which 'the State controls crime'.[48] The present writer himself suggested that penal policy should be held to mean the rational organization of the control of crime by society, and this conception has been widely adopted.[49] Without taking the discussion any farther, we

---

reform in Germany, discusses them under the title 'Kriminalpolitische und strafrechtsdogmatische Probleme in der deutschen Strafrechtsreform', *Zeitschrift für die gesamte Strafrechtswissenschaft*, vol. LXIX, 1957, pp. 359 ff. No better demonstration is required of the respective positions of penal policy and of criminal law, and consequently of the autonomy of penal policy as a scientific discipline.

[46] Liszt, *Lehrbuch des deutschen Strafrechts* (in the French translation, *Traité de droit pénal allemand*, see vol. 1, § 13, p. 100; cf. § 15, p. 108). This idea is taken up both by Jiménez de Asúa (*La ley y el delito*, 2nd ed., 1954, p. 67), and by E. Cuello Calón (*Derecho penal*, 12th ed., 1956, vol. I, p. 40).

[47] *La ley y el delito*, p. 66. Finally, Jiménez de Asúa, recalling the work of Dorado Montero, sees penal policy as an intermediate school of thought which takes a dualist approach—both legal and experimental—(p. 68), leading to a 'strange pragmatism' that hardly deserves the name of science, yet thanks to which it has been possible to introduce numerous reforms into actual legislation, from the Norwegian Code of 1902 to the Brazilian Code of 1940 (p. 69). Cf. *Tratado de derecho penal*, 2nd ed., vol. II, pp. 89 ff. It was rather along these lines that Saleilles, more than half a century ago, contrasted penal policy with criminal law (see *L'Individualisation de la peine*, 2nd ed., 1909, pp. 189 and 193), although he attached much greater importance to penal policy.

[48] *La Politique criminelle des États autoritaires*, 1938, pp. 3-4. Cf. *Les Principaux Aspects de la politique criminelle moderne* (papers published by the Criminal Law Section of the Comparative Law Institute of the University of Paris, collection of studies in memory of Professor Henri Donnedieu de Vabres), Paris, 1960.

[49] See the meeting of Ministers of Justice of the European countries, sponsored by the Council of Europe's Committee on penal problems (Paris, 1961) and the comments by Marc Ancel, *Rev. de Science crim.*, 1961, p. 647. Cf. Paul Cornil, in *Rev. de droit pénal et de crim.*, 1962, p. 536, and J. Graven, in *Rev. de Science crim.*, 1961 (concerning the Geneva colloquium on criminal responsibility), p. 325.

should note that penal policy is both a science and an art, and that there may exist doctrines of penal policy just as, for example, there exist doctrines of criminal law and of the sociology of crime, or theories of medical therapy or educational practice (*pédagogie appliquée*). Particularly significant, in this regard, is the contemporary impact in the United Kingdom and the United States—where the term 'penal policy' is traditionally unknown—of new trends which aim at reorganizing the control of crime.[50] Social defence doctrine can no longer be criticized, therefore, merely on the pretext that the existence of penal policy is illusory.

Another objection of the same kind, frequently reiterated, is the assertion that social defence is no more than a kind of neo-positivism. Some, to simplify the argument, even go so far as to confuse the movement with positivism itself. We have already pointed out the radical differences between the doctrines of positivism and of social defence, and we may assert that the distinction is today generally accepted.

Finally, there is the kind of general criticism to the effect that the social defence movement as such is useless or superfluous because it contains nothing new. Some argue that only the extreme aspects of the doctrine could be justified: if it wishes to abolish criminal law and the existing system of legal procedure, then the doctrine is conceded to be 'new', but is rejected forthwith *en bloc*, in the name of the concept of 'due process of law'. If the doctrine simply advocates a moderate reform of criminal law based on the permanent character of the legal system, then it is not indispensable, since such reforms can perfectly well be accomplished without it.[51] It is claimed in some quarters that the social defence

[50] See A. J. Harns, 'Some Significant Developments in Criminal Law and Procedure in the Last Century', *Journ. of Crim. Law, Criminology and Police Science*, vol. 42, No. 4, Nov.-Dec. 1951, pp. 427 ff., esp. pp. 440 ff.; H. Mannheim, *Group Problems in Crime and Punishment*, 1955, p. 271 and esp. p. 273; cf. R. C. Donnelly, J. Goldstein, and L. B. Schwartz, *Criminal Law (Problems for Decision in the Promulgation, Invocation, and Administration of a Law of Crime)*, New York, 1962, 'Crime and the American Penal System', in *Annals of the American Academy of Political and Social Science*, January 1962, particularly L. B. Schwartz ('Spirit and Technique', pp. 1 ff.), and Thorsten Sellin ('An Over-All View', pp. 11 ff.). This point of view also finds expression in Japan (see Makino in *Keisei*, June 1960, especially p. 221) and in the northern countries (see *Nordisk Kriminalistik Årsbok*, 1957, Summary in English, p. xvi; cf. esp. p. L11).

[51] See the arguments developed by R. Merle, in an article, already cited, in *Annales de la Faculté de droit de Toulouse*, 1958, especially pp. 143 ff. Merle, however, prudently qualifies the presentation of his thesis on a number of points.

movement necessarily faces the following dilemma: either it intends to get rid of general prevention and the rule of law by a series of measures which would gradually result in the destruction of these principles, or it amounts to no more than humanitarianism applied—with negligible practical results—in the penal and above all the penitentiary spheres.[52]

The fundamental relation between the penal policy of social defence and the rule of law has been illustrated in earlier chapters and need not be repeated: we will merely note that the point of view which has just been outlined is based on a twofold misapprehension.

First of all, such a view stems from a misunderstanding of legislative facts and sociological evidence. If certain reforms have been accomplished during the last seventy-five years or so, this is specifically due to the gradually deepening influence of social defence ideas. In order that these reforms should be brought about, the neo-classicists had to be convinced on a number of points: first, against the views of Carrara, of the lawful character of conditional sentences; secondly, following Saleilles, that a large place should be given to individualized punishment; thirdly, against the views of Émile Garçon in France, of the value of the probation system; fourthly, in accordance with the trend ascertainable from the Gladstone Committee to the 1958 rules for the minimum treatment of inmates, of the utility of prison reform, and finally, following Donnedieu de Vabres, and in the teeth of the sarcastic opposition of certain 'pure lawyers', of the essential need for collaboration between criminal lawyers and criminologists. It was thanks to this movement of ideas that reforms could be enacted such as those which—to mention only the French example—span the period from the introduction of *relégation* in 1885 to the *mise à l'épreuve* (probation) of 1958. An honest, scientific account of the modern development of penal institutions cannot

[52] It would seem that this is more or less the attitude of Reinhart Maurach (*Deutsches Strafrecht-Allgemeiner Teil*, 1958, pp. 45 ff.). The author tries to bring the new doctrines closer to the Ferri draft of 1921, and looks beyond the moderate theory of social readaptation in order to pin-point the 'disquieting' aspect of the 'radical wing'. He also declares that social defence doctrine has not yet succeeded in producing a clear 'image' of itself. In truth, a few hastily written lines and manifestly inadequate sources are not enough to evoke the true profile of the social defence movement. On the gaps in German academic writings concerning social defence, see the comments of Dünnebier in *Juristische Rundschau*, 1956, p. 215.

afford to neglect these factors.[53] Whether we like it or not, these reforms are explicable in terms of a general trend which goes further than a humanitarian empiricism or a merely neo-classical reformism, and are evidence of 'a number of thoroughly new conceptions in penal policy'.[54]

In the second place, as the foregoing remark helps us to realize, the reforms that have been accomplished may be of great interest but do not constitute a fully-worked-out system of penal policy. Of course it would be absurd to treat them as a kind of bridgehead in enemy territory, for the true vocation of social defence is not to fight or surprise its opponents, but to convince them through frank and honest discussion. As regards the rational organization of the reaction against crime, however, the ultimate purpose of the social defence movement is precisely to coordinate these scattered ideas, heterogeneous measures, and sporadic experiments. In a most interesting book, a leading American criminal lawyer who is acutely aware of the social defence movement points out that the new ideas and reforms are introduced by successive stages into an already existing system, without an adequate effort being made to harmonize the new and the old, or to ensure their mutual assimilation. It is therefore no wonder that recent innovations do not immediately produce the expected results.[55]

In this second half of the twentieth century, the problem facing criminal lawyers and legislators is not to tone down the acknow-

[53] In this connexion, Stefani and Levasseur make pertinent reference to the influence of social defence ideas on the modern development of criminal law and of penitentiary methods: *Droit pénal général et criminologie*, 2nd ed., Paris, 1961, esp. Nos. 306, 498, 565, 676.

[54] The formula is that of Professor Andenaes in the course of a speech at a meeting of the Finnish Association of Criminalists on 5 April 1957, replying to the reservations made by Brynolf Honkasalo (Helsinki); see *Nordisk Kriminalistik Årsbok*, 1957, summary in English, pp. xvii-xx. In particular Professor Andenaes hails the programme of social defence as 'an attractive collection of points of view on criminal policy, against which few objections could be raised'. Compare the remarks of V. Soine, Director of Prisons in Finland, in the course of the same meeting; he asserted that 'even if we should detect certain defects in the new conceptual structure, it will repay us to be grateful to the originators of the idea, and not to regard them merely as persons who do harm'.

[55] Paul W. Tappan, *Crime, Justice and Correction*, New York, 1960, at the beginning of chapter 10: 'Objectives of Sentencing and Correction', pp. 237-38. Cf. L. Lundell Higgins and E. A. Fitzpatrick, *Criminology and Crime Prevention*, Milwaukee, 1958, esp. chaps. XVI, XVII and XXVI.

ledged shortcomings of the existing system by minor amendments, while being careful to avoid upsetting the traditional principles as a whole. It is not a case of *submitting* to essential reforms, since these are inevitable, but of accepting them as beneficial and of carrying them into effect with full knowledge of their novelty and their usefulness: such honest acceptance, will ensure the fullest scope to these necessary reforms.[56] This new awareness, this deliberately dynamic policy, this general intellectual trend, orientated towards a humane and social goal, are both the characteristic feature of the penal policy advocated by the doctrines of social defence and their justification, from the methodological as from the ethical or political standpoint.

One final observation still needs to be made. It may be rather surprising to note the violence of certain reactions and the persistence of certain attitudes. The virulence of some of the criticism is of course encouraging, for it indicates the disarray of those who stubbornly remain within the confines of a conformist traditionalism that is incapable of renovation: examples are to be found both among the doctrinaire theorists of Eastern Europe and among some Latin American writers who remain behind the times. In one case as in the other, anger replaces argument, some becoming obsessed in their reaction to the progress of social defence ideas.

A more curious attitude is that of criminal lawyers who, though fully aware of modern trends, still proclaim that social defence threatens the freedom of the individual by dispensing, as they allege, with the rule of law or in calling for preventive measures of a discretionary nature to be taken *ante delictum*, before any offence

[56] L. B. Schwartz points out in this connexion the influence of social defence doctrine on the American Law Institute when it drew up a Model Penal Code, capable of providing guidance to the legislations of all the States of the Union. On some points at any rate, the draft Model Penal Code derives its inspiration from the penal policy of social defence, and its approach is similar. See the same author's 'Le Projet de code pénal de *l'American Law Institute* (Progrès et temps d'arrêt en matière de politique criminelle)', *Rev. de Science crim.*, 1957, pp. 37 ff. (esp. p. 41). This movement of ideas is noticeable even in Germany, and the attention of those concerned with law reform is drawn to the humanist doctrines of the penal policy of social defence, with their emphasis on the protection of the human person: see Hellmuth Mayer, *Strafrechtsreform für Heute und Morgen*, 1926, esp. p. 38. Since 1954, Fritz Bauer has stressed the penetrating influence of social defence ideas from Scandinavia to Latin America (*Lindenfelser Hochschulwochen*, 1954, p. 72).

has been committed.[57] What must be realized is that these authors, in refusing to understand the true significance of the new movement, are in their turn simply defending the neo-classical approach even though they are aware of its vulnerability. In fact, they are hostile to all radical reform, to the introduction of a new system of sanctions, to the treatment of offenders, and also, whatever they may say, to the humanist element in social defence doctrine, which encourages the development of a new individualism of a 'personalist' kind, as this latter expression was understood, for instance, by Mounier. Above all, these authors are opposed to the kind of critical investigation of facts and institutions as they really are, that is called for by social defence. They fear all independence of mind towards an established system and a legal order which they are blindly determined to preserve. Blindly also, they cling to the classical metaphysical system, which they declare to be permanent. They may be answered in the words of Charles Péguy: 'a great philosophy is not that which introduces a final truth, but that which creates anxiety or causes perturbation'.[58] Conscious of the relative nature of human truth, the philosophy of social defence—as it must be called—indeed has such an effect.

[57] It is curious to find these allegations in the works of Eberhard Schmidt (*op. cit.*) and Nicolas Jacob (see in particular *La Vie judiciaire*, 7-12 January 1963, in an article entitled 'La Justice et les hommes'). Frey, for his part, still writes of the 'utopian assumptions' of social defence (see H. Schröder and E. R. Frey, *Die kriminalpolitischen Aufgaben der Strafrechtsreform*, Tübingen, 1960).

[58] *Œuvres en prose* (1908-1914), La Pléiade ed., p. 182.

CONCLUSIONS

WE ARE NOW in a position to conclude with a clear and complete statement of the true nature of the new doctrine of social defence. As already observed, it is not so much a single autonomous doctrine as a group of doctrines which emerge from a comprehensive intellectual trend. It is precisely this trend which in our view seems characteristic of the new social defence movement. The present author once wrote that social defence, all things considered, is no more than criminal law that is committed (*engagé*).[1] This formula would still be perfectly appropriate, were it not for the fact that the parallel with the contemporary notion of 'engaged literature' (*littérature engagée*) suggests a political flavour likely to distort one's impression of a doctrine which steadfastly stands aside from all partisan views. It is none the less true, as was stressed from chapter I onwards, that adherence to the doctrines of social defence implies a commitment, that is to say a carefully-thought-out allegiance to a certain intellectual approach which serves henceforth to guide, in a particular field, the action of those by whom it is accepted. Eminent writers such as Pisapia, Nuvolone, Strahl, and especially Graven[2] have taken pains to emphasize this particular aspect of social defence doctrine.

Social defence implies acceptance of an action of prevention and social therapy deriving its inspiration from the ideal which we have previously defined. The movement implies an effort to explain this ideal and to make the action which is based thereon understood by those who are not yet prepared to accept it. The movement involves a sort of proselytism (the word should not be understood in a pejorative sense) which may even be said to

[1] 'Les Doctrines nouvelles de la Défense sociale', *Rev. de droit pénal et de criminologie* October 1951, p. 46.

[2] See the remarks by Pisapia and Graven on the occasion of the colloquium held at Buenos Aires in 1960, *Jornadas de derecho penal*, Buenos Aires, 1962; cf. the comments by Graven, already cited, concerning the Geneva colloquium on criminal responsibility, *Rev. de Science crim.*, 1961, pp. 325-36.

take on an apostolic character. With its intermediate position and the balance which it achieves, not merely between abstract theories but also between different forms of positive action, the new social defence movement thus finds itself at a cross-roads in modern penal thought. The movement is convinced that many who are seriously concerned about problems of criminal law, criminology, or criminal sociology will necessarily come round to the same way of thinking. All that is involved is a readiness to think out these problems anew, together with a refusal to be intimidated by a renovating approach which is alone capable of pointing out new paths to follow or of throwing fresh light on well-tried methods.

The basic ideas of social defence are already accepted to a very considerable extent by numerous writers, and the extension of these ideas from year to year is indeed remarkable. Former objections are transformed into cautious reserve or qualified acceptance. Eminent specialist authors are increasingly careful to underline the importance and the success of the doctrines of new social defence. The same point of view is supported, often brilliantly, in treatises on the one hand and gatherings of specialists on the other.[3] Certain statements, sometimes violently hostile,

[3] Reference has already been made to the recognition of social defence doctrines by the Congresses at Antwerp, 1954, Milan, 1956, Stockholm, 1958, and Belgrade, 1961, and to the attention given to social defence at the meetings of the Northern Associations of Criminalists (see the annual series appearing in *Nordisk Kriminalistik Årsbok*, especially since 1955). Professor Nuvolone, for his part, on the occasion of the centenary celebration of the birth of Enrico Ferri at Mantua, while carefully pointing out the difference between positivism and social defence, had no hesitation in declaring that the latter movement is a dominant trend both nationally and internationally (see 'Le sanzioni criminali nel pensiéro di Enrico Ferri e nel momento stórico attuale', *Rev. pénale suisse*, 1956, pp. 345 ff.). The same formula is used in France by Dean P. Bouzat, 'Le Centenaire d'Enrico Ferri', *Rev. de Science crim.*, 1957, p. 18. A similar approach is to be found in particular in the *Manuale di diritto penale* by Santoro, vol. I, Turin, 1956. In Belgium, Legros writes that criminal lawyers today no longer deny the double rôle of social defence in the fields of social protection and of respect for the individual, nor the synthesis achieved by the movement between the ideal of Christian charity and the democratic notion of fraternity among all men ('Pour une Défense sociale élargie', *Revue de l'Université de Bruxelles*, July 1960). It is to be noted that these statements relate explicitly to the concept of *new* social defence; cf. the same author's 'Conscience sociale et défense sociale', *Rev. int. de défense sociale*, 1955, p. 96, and also J. Constant in *Manuel de droit pénal*, 7th ed., Liège, 1959, pp. 45 ff.). In Spain, Father Beristain sees in new social defence an endeavour to breathe into criminal law, while safeguarding the human person, 'a community and social spirit in harmony with present trends'. ('Análisis crítico de la nueva defensa social', in *Revista de estudios penitenciarios*, April-June 1962). See also the same author's

merely serve to highlight the place of social defence ideas in modern penal thought. These very criticisms, especially when formulated in an intolerant spirit, enhance the value of the new doctrine.

Finally and above all, many of those who through mental or linguistic habit still consider themselves outside the social defence movement properly so-called, nevertheless share, to a great extent, the basic doctrines of social defence and help to propagate their demands. This is quite plain in the case of Anglo-American criminologists and penologists who, instinctively mistrustful of all general theories and still barely accustomed to using the expression 'social defence', are engaged in this movement, if we may say so, just as Molière's Monsieur Jourdain expressed himself in prose, or, as Montesquieu 'did' comparative law. So it is that the Anglo-American specialists come to give implicit approval to the new doctrines and often even explicitly to support them.[4] Increasingly numerous, again, are those, such as Radzinowicz for example, who want to develop the notion of criminal science and are fully aware of what is meant by the modern approach to criminal

'Fines de la pena (importancia, dificultad y actualidad del tema)', in *Revista general de legislación y jurisprudencia*, November 1961. Cf. among German writers, T. Würtenberger, *Die geistige Situation der deutschen Strafrechtswissenschaft*, 1959, pp. 7 ff.; R. Lange, *Die Bedeutung des Strafrechts für die Sicherung des Menschen im Strassenverkehr*, 1961, p. 175. See in Japan the comments of Professor Makino, 'Interrelation of a Code of Criminal Procedure and Criminal Policy', in *Keisei*, June 1960.

[4] See in particular the book by Margery Fry already cited, *Arms of the Law*; cf. the remarks by Cicely M. Craven on the Prison Commissioners' Report for 1950, *Howard Journal*, vol. VIII, No. 3, 1952, pp. 149 ff., and the note by G. Benson, 'Punishments in Prisons and Borstals', *ibid.*, p. 198. On this point Klare has taken up and continued the humane and social tradition of the Howard League. And we may mention once again the well-known work, in the United States of America, of S. and E. Glueck, Thorsten Sellin, H. E. Barnes, Negley K. Teeters, P. W. Tappan, and many others to whom reference has often been made in these pages. J. M. Canals points out that these names are a sufficient indication of the widespread influence of social defence in specialist circles in the U.S.A. (*Op. cit.* in *Journ. of Criminal Law, Criminology and Police Science*, vol. 50, No. 4, March-April 1960, p. 549 and note 51). Moreover, we may note that at its meeting in October 1962, the Law Society paid particular attention to the problem of law reform envisaged in terms of 'the improvement of the law' (see the inaugural speech by the president under the title 'Law as a Vocation', in the *Law Society Gazette*, vol. CX, No. 12, December 1963, pp. 80 ff., in a passage which comes very close to the spirit of the penal policy of social defence). And for an even clearer expression of the same approach, see the discussion which took place at the same meeting of the Law Society on the general theme of the sentence of the Court, published under the significant title 'Punishment, Reformation and Deterrence', in the same *Review*, pp. 832-33.

law.[5] On the European continent the number of these tacit or potential disciples of social defence grows day by day, and it would take too long to list here even the principal names among them in France, Italy, Switzerland, Portugal, Belgium, or even West Germany, where this tendency has to contend with older, entrenched attitudes. However, as it is in Belgium that there emerged not only the first theory of social defence but also the first important statute to be described by that name, we may note in passing how very encouraging it is to see a criminal lawyer of such acknowledged authority as M. Cornil, the *Procureur Général* at the *Cour de Cassation* in Brussels,[6] giving his adherence to several of the essential arguments of the social defence movement even while he declared his allegiance to the neo-classical school.[7]

The problem above all is to react against a static attitude in the legislative, judicial, or even academic fields. Thus there develops a broad renovating trend, apart from adherence to the explicit doctrines of social defence understood *stricto sensu*.

Modern criminal lawyers and criminal scientists will gradually come to adopt this approach all the more surely in so far as the social defence movement does not merely open up fresh horizons in the control of crime by non-repressive methods, but also succeeds in getting rid of a certain number of obsolete elements that still encumber penal theory or are assigned an importance

[5] A noteworthy contribution of the new-found interest in scientific approach to criminal law is provided by the work of L. Radzinowicz and J. W. C. Turner in creating the Department of Criminal Science in the Faculty of Law of the University of Cambridge and in producing the *English Studies in Criminal Science*; cf. in particular vol. I, *Penal Reform in England*, 1944, and vol. IV, *The Modern Approach to Criminal Law*, 1948; cf. *Cambridge Studies in Criminology*, of which L. Radzinowicz is the editor, and the same author's *In Search of Criminology*, 1961. See also the no less remarkable work of E. Glover, H. Mannheim and E. Miller in the *British Journal of Delinquency*, appropriately renamed in 1962, *The British Journal of Criminology*.

[6] L. Cornil, Speech at the ceremonial commencement of the legal year before the *Cour de Cassation* of Belgium, 1951. See the comments by Marc Ancel in *Rev. de Science crim.*, 1952, pp. 336 ff. Cf. in France the attitude adopted by the *Procureur Général* Besson, *Rev. de Science crim.*, 1953, p. 531; 1954, p. 181; cf. *Rev. internationale de droit pénal*, 1954, p. 321.

[7] This is the case with certain eminent German criminal lawyers who are visibly influenced by social defence ideas even while they do not fully discern this (see F. Bauer, *Das Verbrechen und die Gesellschaft*, Munich, 1957), or while they ostensibly take up a very reserved attitude with regard to this trend: see the aforecited study by Eberhard Schmidt, in *Zeitschrift für die gesamte Strafrechtswissenschaft*, 1957, p. 359, and compare the first and third parts of this article in which the author implicitly comes to accept a large number of the arguments of the penal policy of social defence.

disproportionate to their intrinsic value or their genuine usefulness. The movement likewise provides a lesson both of realism and of morality for all criminal lawyers: just as it rejects a metaphysical or abstractly juridical approach, so it frees criminal science from an element of hypocrisy which is all too frequent. For it is indeed hypocritical to assert that only retributive punishment can ensure the protection of public morality, or to claim that such a penalty, written into the law and imposed by the sentence, is a theoretical one and may not be applied in actual fact: the result is that the radical transformation of the *punishment of criminals* into a process of *treatment of offenders* is relegated to the post-trial phase (in which the sentence is carried out) and hence is concealed. There is a further hypocrisy in the attribution to the administration of wide discretionary powers which the traditional 'legalist' view refused to attribute to the judge. Finally, it is hypocritical to ignore the existence of penal and penitentiary practices that are justified in themselves and that lead to the complete abandonment in fact of the old system.[8]

The aim of the movement of new social defence is precisely to incorporate these methods of individual treatment into a comprehensive penal policy which will render them fully effective, so as finally to achieve a thoroughgoing protection of society through the protection of the individual himself. The movement does not hide the fact that there is a long way to go, nor does it seek to dissimulate that much remains to be done to educate not only the legislator, the criminal lawyer, the judge, the prison administrator, who has to apply the sanctions imposed, but also, as we have seen, public opinion itself.[9] And this must be accomplished, not through a violent break with the past, but through a continuous process of evolution and reform. This process will be fully effective, however, only to the extent that the reforms in question are consciously

[8] Reference should be made to all that has already been said concerning the penal policy of prevention of crime and treatment of offenders, as this has been understood by the social defence section of the United Nations and as it has been promoted, first by the former International Penal and Penitentiary Commission (IPPC), and subsequently by the International Penal and Penitentiary Foundation (IPPF). On these problems and on the influence of social defence ideas in this connexion in Latin America, see J. J. Gonzales Bustamente, 'El problema de las prisiones', in the Mexican review *Criminalia*, February 1957, pp. 132 ff., especially pp. 147 ff.

[9] With particular reference to the magistracy, see the interesting article by Lopez Rey, 'La Justice criminelle et la formation des juges, des magistrats, du ministère public et des avocats', *Rev. de droit pénal et de criminologie*, Brussels, March, 1963

desired and are not confined to limited and, as it were, shamefaced experiments.

We live in a period of rapid change, which sometimes tends to lack confidence in its destiny but for that very reason can find the strength to accomplish a vast renewal. If we suppose that the existing system of criminal law was designed for man as envisaged in rational Cartesian terms, then the social defence movement seeks to replace this system by another, better suited to our anguished and introspective epoch, when man seems closer to Pascal than to Descartes. But the movement is aware, following the same train of thought as Pascal, that in the field of fundamental truths we in fact seek what we have already found. The movement knows that these necessary reforms have to be emphatically called for, in a humanist spirit, and that this reformist ideal should be fully known and clearly understood. The movement is aware that it will come into conflict with acquired habits and in particular with the almost instinctive resistance of some lawyers who want to remain immovably within their own familiar system and practice. This is precisely the sort of immobilism against which the social defence movement is above all directed.

In the later eighteenth century, when a great hope had been aroused by the work of Beccaria, the *Avocat-Général* Servan appealed to all the progressive intellectual forces of his time in favour of a penal reform firmly based on the notion of the rights of man. Beccaria and Servan aroused the hostility of the official attitude of their time and were also, unfortunately, opposed by some of the leading judicial figures of the day. Muyart de Vouglans, for instance, devoted himself to a purely academic criticism of Beccaria, whereas Séguier seems to have epitomized all the conservatism of the magistracy of the *ancien régime*. In the long run, however, it was the views of Beccaria and Servan that prevailed: history was to prove them right. Let us hope that the new social defence movement will not require the equivalent of the doctrinal revolt of Beccaria or the anguished protest of Servan. We may be sure that whatever difficulties and whatever antagonisms have to be faced,[10] the new doctrine will find enough devoted adherents

[10] The opposition to new ideas in the second half of the eighteenth century, a period which failed to be a period of transition—thus making inevitable the violent cataclysms of 1789—is significant, and a parallel may be drawn between that opposition and some contemporary objections to social defence. The first seven volumes

to ensure its gradual extension. Above all, we may rest assured that in any case it is the new voices which will finally obtain an attentive hearing.

---

of the *Encyclopédie* were published between 1751 and 1757. Taking as their pretext the attempt by Damiens against the life of Louis XV, in January 1757, the traditionalist party led by Fréron (answered by Voltaire in a celebrated pamphlet entitled *Le Pauvre Diable*, 1758) violently attacked the philosophical movement, alleging that it sought to undermine religion, morals, the State, and public order, and would lead to crime. Subversive books, it was claimed, had armed Damiens. And in 1766, when the Chevalier de la Barre was executed, for mutilating a crucifix, his corpse was burnt together with a copy of the *Philosophical Dictionary* of Voltaire. We may indeed ask whether some of the violent antagonists of social defence, who seek to impute to the new doctrine the very faults against which it is aimed, are not secretly dreaming of similar *autos-da-fé*. Intolerance is still at war with humanism. It is enough to recall that in the face of History—of events as also of ideas—it was not Fréron who prevailed against Diderot and d'Alembert.

INDEX

For Product Safety Concerns and Information please contact our EU representative GPSR@taylorandfrancis.com
Taylor & Francis Verlag GmbH, Kaufingerstraße 24, 80331 München, Germany

www.ingramcontent.com/pod-product-compliance
Ingram Content Group UK Ltd.
Pitfield, Milton Keynes, MK11 3LW, UK
UKHW022156190926
475702UK00003B/53

* 9 7 8 0 4 1 5 1 7 7 4 5 0 *